MW01124636

The 1988 Dodgers

The 1988 Dodgers

Reliving the Championship Season

K. P. Wee

Rowman & Littlefield
Lanham • Boulder • New York • London

Published by Rowman & Littlefield
An imprint of The Rowman & Littlefield Publishing Group, Inc.
4501 Forbes Boulevard, Suite 200, Lanham, Maryland 20706
www.rowman.com

Unit A, Whitacre Mews, 26-34 Stannary Street, London SE11 4AB

Copyright © 2018 by The Rowman & Littlefield Publishing Group, Inc.

All rights reserved. No part of this book may be reproduced in any form or by any
electronic or mechanical means, including information storage and retrieval systems,
without written permission from the publisher, except by a reviewer who may quote
passages in a review.

British Library Cataloguing in Publication Information Available

Library of Congress Cataloging-in-Publication Data

Names: Wee, K. P.
Title: The 1988 Dodgers : reliving the championship season / K. P. Wee.
Description: Lanham, Maryland : Rowman & Littlefield, [2018] | Includes
    bibliographical references and index.
Identifiers: LCCN 2017060831 (print) | LCCN 2018001001 (ebook) | ISBN
    9781538113097 (electronic) | ISBN 9781538113080 (hardback : alk. paper)
Subjects: LCSH: Los Angeles Dodgers (Baseball team)—History. | World Series
    (Baseball) (1988)
Classification: LCC GV875.L6 (ebook) | LCC GV875.L6 .W35 2018 (print) | DDC
    796.357/640979494—dc23
LC record available at https://lccn.loc.gov/2017060831

∞™ The paper used in this publication meets the minimum requirements of
American National Standard for Information Sciences—Permanence of Paper
for Printed Library Materials, ANSI/NISO Z39.48-1992.

Printed in the United States of America

To Adrian Brijbassi, Rick Ambrozic,
Rick Tanton, Nahyun L., and Roger Chong

CONTENTS

CONTENTS

ACKNOWLEDGMENTS

This book would never have happened had I not written *Tom Candiotti: A Life of Knuckleballs*, a biography about knuckleball pitcher Tom Candiotti. It was during the writing of that book in 2010 when I first came into contact with Fred Claire, the executive vice president and general manager of the Los Angeles Dodgers from 1987 to 1998.

Mr. Claire and I spoke very briefly—and exchanged a couple of emails—for Candiotti's book, but we somehow managed to keep in touch by email over the years. It was in December 2016 when Mr. Claire, while receiving treatments for cancer, reached out and suggested I do a book on the 1988 Dodgers.

Without Mr. Claire's help, along with his great passion, in getting this project started and providing contact information for various interview subjects—not to mention plenty of valuable advice at the beginning of this journey—this book would have never happened. So, really, I owe a special debt of gratitude to Fred Claire, who conceived the idea of this book and encouraged me to carry through with it.

Special thanks also go to Mike Hanafin for alerting me to important articles that helped with the writing of this book and to Jordy Cunningham for pushing me to get this book completed every time he ran into me in the press box at Vancouver's Nat Bailey Stadium (as I work for the Single-A Canadians every summer). Also, thank you to Rob Fai, my boss in baseball.

ACKNOWLEDGMENTS

Numerous former players and baseball people also were generous with their time, and I especially want to thank Joey Amalfitano, Mel Antonen, Charlie Blaney, Rick Dempsey, Mel Didier, Mariano Duncan, Chris Gwynn, Mickey Hatcher, Danny Heep, Ben Hines, Jay Howell, Tim Leary, Ramon Martinez, Bob Nightengale, Ross Porter, Phil Regan, Jerry Reuss, Gilberto Reyes, Bob Ryan, Steve Sax, John Shelby, Franklin Stubbs, Herm Winningham, and Tracy Woodson. I'd like to express extra gratitude to Dempsey, Howell, Leary, Reuss, Reyes, and Woodson for being available multiple times when I needed clarification on various topics. Howell, for instance, graciously spoke for several hours over the course of five phone interviews to make sure I had all the information needed. Leary, meanwhile, made himself available to answer a whole bunch of questions via email despite his busy schedule.

I'd also like to thank Randy Wehofer, director of media relations for the Iowa Cubs, for arranging the phone interview with Duncan; Rich Burk, director of broadcasting for the Hillsboro Hops, for arranging the interview with Stubbs at Vancouver's Nat Bailey Stadium; and Jeremy Shelby, for connecting me with John Shelby. Thank you, too, to Michael McCormick, Blue Jays baseball media coordinator Sue Mallabon, Brewers publications assistant Robbin Barnes, and National Baseball Hall of Fame library rights and reproductions coordinator John Horne for providing images from their respective organizations' photo libraries. Thank you also to Rowman & Littlefield editor Christen Karniski.

Finally, I would like to dedicate this book to Rick Ambrozic, Adrian Brijbassi, Roger Chong, Nahyun L., and Rick Tanton. You have no idea how much your words—of encouragement, support, and so on—no matter how brief, truly mean to me.

INTRODUCTION

The year 2018 marks the 30-year anniversary of one of the biggest upsets in World Series history, when the Los Angeles Dodgers stunned the heavily favored Oakland Athletics in five games. That series featured one of the most iconic home runs in baseball history and also the end of one of the most dominant pitching performances the game has ever witnessed.

Up until 2017, it also marked the last time the Dodgers had been to a World Series. They would lose the '17 classic in seven games to Houston, meaning the 1988 team remains the Dodgers' last world champion. From 1958 to 1988—the Dodgers' first 31 years in Los Angeles—the club made the postseason 11 times, winning nine pennants and five World Championships. From 1989 to 2017—the next 29 years—the numbers were 11, 1, and zero.

Being a huge baseball fan, one who considers himself very knowledgeable about the history of the sport, I'd always known about the Dodgers' title drought, but I hadn't thought much about it until December of 2016—10 months before Los Angeles would win the 2017 National League pennant—when former Dodgers executive vice president and general manager Fred Claire emailed me to wish me a Merry Christmas. I mean, I've always known that the Cleveland Indians' last title had come in 1948, the Toronto Maple Leafs' last Stanley Cup victory had come in 1967, and the Arizona Cardinals' championship drought dates back to 1947—but it doesn't mean I think enough about those teams to want to write a book about their last championship years.

The Dodgers' 1988 championship, though, is special given the way that team, with an unimposing roster, came together and beat two of the most powerful teams in baseball over the past 50 years. The Mets, seeking their second title in three years, were looking to establish a dynasty before falling to the Dodgers. The Athletics, meanwhile, were in the first year of their three-year run as American League champions—but their star-studded lineup somehow wasn't enough against the Dodgers.

In our email correspondence in December of 2016, Mr. Claire also asked what projects I'd been working on. After I briefly discussed my teaching career, which keeps me busy, Mr. Claire opined that I should probably write another book—since he'd enjoyed my 2014 book *Tom Candiotti: A Life of Knuckleballs*. I explained that for my next biography, I'd possibly write about former Red Sox pitchers Danny Darwin or Jeff Reardon—neither of whom played for the Dodgers—and Mr. Claire's response was that I could reach out to him if I thought he could help out. "Well, neither of those guys played for you," I told him, "and the only thing where I might need your help is if I'm writing a book about the '88 Dodgers—but that's been done already."

And *that* was the start of a brilliant idea. "Well, look at the calendar," Mr. Claire responded. "It's 2017 in a matter of days and if a book is written about the '88 Dodgers, it could potentially be published in 2018, in time for the 30th anniversary of the last Los Angeles Dodgers World Championship. And do you know how many titles the Dodgers have won in the last 50 years? Just two: 1981 and 1988. It'd be really interesting to do a book about that 1988 team and see what's happened to some of the lesser-known players since that time."

I did nothing for three months—as I was dealing with a death in my immediate family (and Mr. Claire himself was receiving daily treatments for cancer)—before deciding to go for it. Through Mr. Claire's help, I managed to get contact information for players such as Tim Leary, Gilberto Reyes, and Mickey Hatcher, and coaches Ben Hines and Joey Amalfitano. These individuals were more than willing to share their stories about 1988 because they still view this championship as one of the most amazing moments of their careers—and their lives. From there, more former players—and even scouts—were interviewed. Those contacted were interested in sharing their views on how 1988 has impacted their lives 30 years later.

Now, the catch is that the majority of those interviewed were the lesser-known members of that 1988 ballclub. The reason is that plenty has been said by the higher-profile guys such as Tommy Lasorda, Orel Hershiser, Kirk Gibson, broadcaster Vin Scully, and even Mr. Claire himself, who had his own autobiography—*Fred Claire: My 30 Years in Dodgers Blue*—published in 2004. To many, the '88 Dodgers were simply Hershiser's pitching and Gibson's World Series homer. The rest was a blur. These sentiments were shared with me by Mel Antonen and Bob Nightengale, a pair of well-respected sportswriters who have covered Major League Baseball since the 1980s. I think they're right. Casual baseball fans probably do think about those Dodgers as Hershiser and Gibson's team—and also Lasorda and Scully.

And that's where this book comes in. The intent of *The 1988 Dodgers: Reliving the Championship Season* is to look back at the road that has been traveled by the members of that team, with particular attention given to so many voices who were a part of the ballclub but haven't had the opportunity to reflect on a memorable season. Their voices help baseball fans remember how '88 was indeed a special year, and it was more than just Hershiser and Gibson.

LINEUP

Joey Amalfitano: Dodgers third-base coach (1983–1998)
Mel Antonen: MLB reporter; writer for *SI.com*
Charlie Blaney: Dodgers farm director (1988–1998)
Fred Claire: Dodgers general manager (1987–1998)
Rick Dempsey: Dodgers catcher (1988–1990)
Mel Didier: Dodgers scout (1983–1996)
Mariano Duncan: Dodgers shortstop (1985–1987, 1989)
Chris Gwynn: Dodgers outfielder (1987–1991, 1994–1995)
Mickey Hatcher: Dodgers utility man (1979–1980, 1987–1990)
Danny Heep: Dodgers outfielder (1987–1988)
Ben Hines: Dodgers hitting coach (1985–1986, 1988–1993)
Jay Howell: Dodgers pitcher (1988–1992)
Tim Leary: Dodgers pitcher (1987–1989)
Ramon Martinez: Dodgers pitcher (1988–1998)
Bob Nightengale: MLB columnist; writer for *USA Today Sports*
Ross Porter: Dodgers play-by-play announcer (1977–2004)
Phil Regan: Dodgers scout (1987–1993)
Jerry Reuss: Dodgers pitcher (1979–1987)
Gilberto Reyes: Dodgers catcher (1983–1985, 1987–1988)
Bob Ryan: *Boston Globe* sports columnist
Steve Sax: Dodgers second baseman (1981–1988)
John Shelby: Dodgers center fielder (1987–1990)

Franklin Stubbs: Dodgers first baseman/outfielder (1984–1989)
Herm Winningham: MLB outfielder (1984–1992); childhood friend
    of the late Dodgers infielder Mike Sharperson
Tracy Woodson: Dodgers third baseman (1987–1989)

PART ONE

THE 1988 SEASON

Fred [Claire] brought some guys in that could lead in different areas of the clubhouse. The main one, of course, was [Kirk] Gibson. . . . But there were some key guys that were on the outer edge of this team, and [manager Tommy] Lasorda gave them an identity of the "Stuntmen." And the Stuntmen happened to play an integral part of us winning [in 1988], because we were injured so badly. He gave them that nickname and that purpose, and it ultimately came back to being one of the reasons why we won. Without them, we don't win. Without [Mickey] Hatcher, we don't win. There were a couple of guys there that played key roles that ended up starting in the World Series when we had injuries, [with] Dave Anderson [being another example].

—Jay Howell, Dodgers closer

SPRING TRAINING '88
The Gibson-Orosco Incident

The eye black was a seminal moment, for sure. That was big. I mean, that was like an earthquake that happened in spring training. That was huge.

—Jay Howell, Dodgers closer

That [eye-black incident] was huge. It kind of changed how we went about preparing for every game.

—Franklin Stubbs, Dodgers first baseman

Prior to the 1988 season, the Los Angeles Dodgers had had a successful decade, winning a World Series championship in 1981 and capturing a pair of Western Division titles in 1983 and 1985. That was no small feat, as the 1980s saw a new champion crowned every single year. Between 1979 and 1987, no team won more than one World Championship, with Pittsburgh, Philadelphia, Los Angeles, St. Louis, Baltimore, Detroit, Kansas City, the New York Mets, and Minnesota capturing titles in those seasons.

In 1985, the Dodgers probably should have advanced to the World Series, but blew a two-games-to-none lead in the National League Championship Series and lost to the Cardinals in six games. In the pivotal fifth game, Cardinals shortstop Ozzie Smith hit a rare home run in the bottom of the ninth off Tom Niedenfuer to give St. Louis a 3–2 victory and a three-games-to-two advantage. In Game 6 in Los Angeles, the Dodgers led 5–4 going into the ninth, and Niedenfuer was back on the mound, trying to force a seventh and deciding contest. But when St. Louis put runners on second and third with two outs, manager Tommy Lasorda opted to let Niedenfuer face slugger Jack Clark—instead of walking him intentionally and pitching to the less dangerous Andy Van Slyke. Clark made Lasorda and Niedenfuer pay, crushing a three-run homer to deep left field for a 7–5 Cardinals lead. The Dodgers went down quietly in the bottom of the ninth, and it was St. Louis advancing to the World Series.

Following the loss to the Cardinals, the Dodgers would trudge through a two-year run of irrelevance, and attendance at Dodger Stadium would fall below the three million mark for the first time since the strike-shortened 1981 season. In 1986, they fell to fifth place with a 73–89 record, and then finished with the same record the following year, giving them back-to-back losing seasons for the first time in 19 years.

By spring training of 1988, though, the Dodgers had several new faces, including Kirk Gibson, the scowling left fielder from Detroit and ex-college football player who brought a special blend of power, speed, and reckless intensity to a team that needed more focus, one that was sometimes described as too laid back. "I think we probably should've won in '85, but we didn't have a guy like Kirk Gibson," outfielder Mike Marshall opined years later. "In '88 it was Gibby. Gibby was the guy who taught us all how to win. That's probably what we were missing in '85."[1]

"He was a competitive guy who was outwardly competitive," NBC Sports broadcaster Bob Costas said of Gibson years later in the ESPN series *Battle Lines*. "There was a ferocity about the way he approached the game and some people may have thought that the Dodger clubhouse in that era needed that kind of jolt, from somebody who not only gave it everything he had but would get on teammates if they didn't."[2]

Gibson wasn't the only addition in 1988. Besides the fiery right fielder, Dodgers general manager Fred Claire had brought in closer Jay Howell, veteran catcher Rick Dempsey, slugging outfielder Mike Davis, and smooth-fielding shortstop Alfredo Griffin. But Gibson was the key piece of the puzzle. When he arrived at the Dodgers' spring-training camp in 1988, though, he didn't know what to expect. He'd played for the Tigers his whole career up to that point, and he only knew manager Sparky Anderson's way. "Sparky's way was very 'I'm the ruler. My way or the highway.' It was very serious, very structured," Gibson once recalled.

"When I came into the Dodger camp, it was just the opposite. . . . When we got out on the field during spring training, to practice our bunts and relays and stuff, it was just very, very loose."[3] That was when Gibson began to form the opinion that the Dodgers didn't have it right; they were screwing around too much.

And that was also when the eye-black incident happened.

Hitting coach Ben Hines, who is now retired from baseball, remembers the incident like it was yesterday. "We had some guys that came together in special ways; they really believed in each other, and the tone got set very early in spring training, when one of the guys put shoe black in Kirk Gibson's hat," Hines, the Dodgers' batting coach from 1985 to 1986 and then again from 1988 to 1993, says.

> He put it on, and he had a black ring, and everybody in the dugout was laughing. This was before a spring-training game. He took it off and saw it, and he challenged everyone there in the dugout. "Who did that?" But nobody would own up to it. He said, "I'm outta here." He told Tommy, "I'm outta here. I'm not playing today." He ran to the right-field corner where our players went out of the stadium, and he left. It kinda set the tone for the rest of the year. There wasn't gonna be a whole lot of bullshit. It was gonna be "game up." It set the tone.
>
> Kirk was a football player playing baseball, and so he approached it with a different mentality than the other people. And soon, they adjusted to that mentality and picked it up.[4]

Essentially, Gibson's message to the rest of his teammates was that he hadn't come to Los Angeles to be a clown. He'd come to win a championship—and if anyone got in the way of that team goal, they would have to answer to him. "People have to understand me," Gibson recalled years later of what he told his teammates the day after the eye-black incident. "We've got a long year here. I'm here to become a World Champion. I want them to be able to count on me. But I can't deal with their behavior right now. [My message to them was] 'Your fundamentals are bad; it says we're gonna lose again.'" He told the team he'd be the best teammate they ever had. If a pitcher wanted to hit an opposing hitter, go ahead. If there was a fight, just run out to left field because Gibson would kick the guy's ass. But everyone had to understand that they all had to get serious if they wanted to win, to become world champions.[5]

Ross Porter, a play-by-play announcer for the Dodgers for 28 years beginning in 1977, noticed most players seemed to buy in to Gibson's message. Guys seemed to have more focus during batting practice and there were fewer guys clowning around during the games. "Gibson let his new teammates know in spring training that he was there to win and did not approve of pranks," Porter opines today. "He sent the message to them they should focus on one thing—winning."

Mickey Hatcher, who'd begun his career with the Dodgers before rejoining the club in 1987, noticed the team had a different type of intensity after Gibson addressed the club. "That team really came out of spring training in '88 with a bond. Everybody played hurt," recalls Hatcher today. "Guys played hard. We all just played together as a team. That really set the tone for a magical season."

Tim Leary, who was in his second season with the Dodgers in 1988, knew right away that Gibson was their leader. "That really set the tone, because he's a commanding presence that just overwhelmed the whole team. You know, that's our team leader, period."

Jay Howell, who was in his first spring training with the Dodgers following a trade from Oakland in the off-season, credits Fred Claire for bringing Gibson in and believes Gibson and Lasorda played huge roles in the clubhouse. "First of all, you've got Fred bringing these guys in, and then you've got Tommy creating the identity of our team," Howell, who'd spent three years with the A's before joining the Dodgers, explains today.

> And then you've got Gibson, our leader. Gibson didn't take any shit. Gibson wasn't having it. If guys were happy after a loss, that shit was shut down. He was the leader, no doubt about it. Not a self-appointed leader . . . he just led by example. He was a bad ass. He didn't take shit from anybody. He'd do an interview and if he didn't like the way it was going, he just said, "Look, I gotta get ready for the game. I don't have time to talk about this right now. No offense, but we got shit to do here."

The youngsters on the Dodgers, like the veterans, bought into Gibson's way. Gilberto Reyes, a third-string catcher on the 1988 team, remembers Gibson's work ethic and, to this day, admires him for it. "Kirk Gibson was a guy who fired up the clubhouse every day, every single day. No matter how he felt, Kirk Gibson was [always] ready. Even at 2 o'clock, he was getting ready to play. . . . [Everybody] knows how hard he prepared to play, to get ready for his four at-bats and to play the game. He went through the whole season like that."

Infielder Mariano Duncan spent the entire 1988 season in Triple-A after making his major-league debut in 1985. But he was around during spring training and recalls the finger being pointed at him for the prank.

> What I remember about that is I was sure people started blaming me, that I was the one who put the black stuff in the hat. But I remember it was Jesse Orosco, the pitcher. He was the one who put the black stuff in Kirk Gibson's hat. When Jesse Orosco came to us [from the Mets], he tried to make sure that everybody [was] loose and everybody [was] relaxed in the clubhouse and all that stuff. He used to make a lot of jokes. He used to joke around so much to try to keep the team in a great mood. I remember that day, he put some kind of black stuff in Kirk Gibson's hat. And when Kirk Gibson put on his hat and saw the stuff on the forehead, he started getting really, really mad. Really upset. He said he didn't play that kind of game. For some reason, he tried to confront me, thinking I was the one who did it. I just said, "I don't play that kind of game." And he went to Tommy Lasorda and said, "Tommy, I came here to play baseball. I didn't come here to joke around. When you guys want to take everything seriously, you let me know." And he took his uniform off, put on his clothes, and he left the ballpark. He went home because of that.

Howell doesn't blame Orosco for the incident. Although the Dodgers closer was a newcomer, he noticed quickly that Lasorda himself clowned around as much as the average player—even during spring training, when things were supposed to be serious. But the Hall of Fame manager, as Howell recalls, shut the clowning down as soon as Gibson said he wouldn't have any of it. "Tommy used to keep it light during spring training," he explains. "He wanted to have fun in spring training. Tommy made it fun. It was a funny clubhouse. And then you had Gibson, who said, 'No wonder you guys finished last last year. You think this is funny?' And it put a little damper on things. The day after the shoe-black thing, Tommy said to the whole team, 'Look, I don't care if you have a good time out there. But you don't touch anybody's stuff. That's it.'" (Howell, like Rick Dempsey, erroneously states that the Dodgers finished last in 1987. In reality, they finished fourth.)

Veteran catcher and former World Series MVP Rick Dempsey, another newcomer in 1988, chuckles when asked about the incident nearly 30 years after the fact. "Well, I thought, really, that that kind of got blown out of proportion a little bit," Dempsey, who'd signed as a free agent after spending 1987 in Cleveland, says today.

> Some of the players played a trick like that on him, and Jesse Orosco was the guy who did it, who put the eye black on there. I mean, we were just having a good time. But I think he was embarrassed about that and came up with that thing, he's serious about playing baseball. And we kind of ran with that. The media made a thing about that. "Well, we've got Kirk Gibson. And he's dead serious about winning baseball. And that's the way everybody should be." And we agreed with him. It was fine.
>
> That's the way Gibby was, and we rallied behind him. We made a season out of it. So, that was a good way to get started at spring training because I think, one way or another, if it wasn't the Kirk Gibson thing, something else would've happened with that particular team that got everybody on the same page. We realized how hard we had to work. With that particular ballclub, if we were gonna win, we had to get dead serious about it. And that was the starting point right there, at spring training.
>
> The media made a big thing about that, the Jesse Orosco deal. Inside the clubhouse, we all just kinda chuckled about it. Had a good time with it. But we all really realized that, yes, we had to get serious because there were a lot of teams on paper that were better than the Los Angeles Dodgers that year. Start now.

Center fielder John Shelby, who wound up finishing third on the team with 10 home runs in 1988, doesn't feel the shoe-black incident was significant either, but points to Gibson's leadership as a major reason the Dodgers were able to compete in the National League (NL). "I can't really recall what it did for our team since it happened in spring training," Shelby says today via email. "[I can say that] we had a lot of good different personalities on the team—but Gibson's presence, attitude, and the way he played the game added more character, leadership, and stability to our team, which was crucial."

As for the idea that Los Angeles might have won it all in 1985 had Gibson been a Dodger then—when asked about it some 30 years later, second baseman Steve Sax—who played for the Dodgers from 1981 to

1988—doesn't feel the same way. "I can't really say that. I mean, you know, it's hard to say. Different place, different time. Who knows? He was a big help on our [1988] team. He provided pop in our lineup and some hustle. But as for '85, I can't say that. Who knows?"

For Dempsey, the more impactful event that happened during the spring of 1988 was how the Dodgers got their identity; the reserves, whenever they got into a game, always played to win—even though it was just spring training and the games didn't count in the standings. For those guys, every game mattered.

> That season was so crazy, the way we did things. And it started in spring training, really, because a lot of the backup players—[Danny] Heep, myself, Franklin Stubbs, Mike Sharperson, all of those guys—would always get into the second half of the spring-training games when the regulars were taken out. It didn't matter what the score was. We came back and won so many games in spring training! It was crazy how we did it! And we had so much fun doing it. I don't know how it began and how it happened. We just developed a character that was just incredible, that we knew we could come back and win baseball games. It carried over into the season.

Stubbs, one of the backup players who eventually became the team's starting first baseman, does agree that the attitude the players had about overcoming any deficit was huge. But he, like many of the other Dodgers interviewed for this book, can't overlook the eye-black incident.

> I agree [with Dempsey about how the guys knew they could always come back], to a point. But I still think what really started it was when Orosco put the black paint—or whatever it was—in Gibson's hat and Gibson decided not to play that day. [The next day] he came in and said, "That's why you don't win. You don't focus, you don't concentrate or get serious when it's time to go play." When he said that, that kinda hit home a little bit. I think our attitudes changed as far as preparation [was concerned]. Everybody from that point on kind of got on the same page. It didn't matter if it was spring training or not. Every game meant something. And we played to win every game and we kind of took that attitude into the season. That was huge—because it kind of changed how we went about preparing for every game.

While some feel that the Gibson-Orosco incident might have been blown out of proportion by the media, others insist it was a seminal moment for the Dodgers' season. The split opinion was the case in 1988, and is still the same even today—30 years after the fact—when various former players and coaches are asked to recount the matter. Nonetheless, most agree that Gibson's work ethic and hustle—along with his clutch hits—carried the team in 1988. They agree on that now, just as everybody agreed back then. So much so that he was named the NL MVP that year. "People didn't vote on numbers that year," veteran writer Jayson Stark, then with the *Philadelphia Inquirer*, once recalled in the ESPN series *Battle Lines*, referring to Gibson's energy, grit, emotion, and determination. "They voted on a feeling, and that feeling was this man was a human tow truck carrying his team to the World Series."[6] Indeed. Had the voters looked solely at numbers, Gibson would have lost out to Mets slugger Darryl Strawberry (see table 1.1).

Table 1.1. Gibson and Strawberry Batting Stats, 1988

	Batting Average	Home Runs	Runs Batted In	Stolen Bases
Gibson	.290	25	76	31
Strawberry	.269	39	101	29

Bob Ryan, a *Boston Globe* columnist, covered the American League Red Sox and wasn't a voter for the NL awards. However, he knew Gibson from the right fielder's days with the Tigers. Ryan says today:

We [in the media] knew him as the football-player-turned-baseball-player from Michigan State. An aggressive, gung-ho player. He was the MVP that year with numbers that would not impress you if you hadn't seen how the whole season played out. I believe he hit .275—in those days people actually cared about batting averages and of course now we don't—and he didn't have a high number of RBIs [runs batted in]—I think it was in the 80s or 90s—but he was the centerpiece of their offense. He was the emotional leader of the team. He was always that kind of an aggressive player, played with a great deal of heart, and he had a lot of spunk and all that. He brought it to the Dodgers and it worked out great.

Kirk Gibson's leadership and clutch hits helped the Dodgers win it all in 1988. *Michael McCormick*

Duncan agrees, even though he and Gibson didn't get off on the right foot. "As a teammate and a leader, I loved to have somebody like Kirk Gibson on my team," says Duncan, who got to play with Gibson the following year. "Anytime that the guy came to the plate, he came prepared to compete. He came prepared to be there with the team. He came prepared to play the game the right way. Anytime that you have a teammate like that, you wanna be right next to him. You wanna go to war with that guy. He used to be a really, really good baseball player. He used to be a great teammate. He'd do anything to go out there and beat the other team." Catcher Mike Scioscia, a hard-nosed player himself, was also impressed by what Gibson brought. "We all thought we were gamers and played the game hard, but Kirk brought us to a different level," recalled Scioscia in 2013. "His intensity was off the charts."[7]

Ryan makes a great point about Gibson's stats—which begs the question: Will we ever see another MVP with Gibson's numbers? Count *Sports Illustrated* writer Mel Antonen as one who feels it can happen—but don't count on it. "I think it's possible, in the day and age of sabermetrics. Right now we're on a home run binge like we've never really seen before," Antonen says, referring to MLB's first-ever 6,000-homer season in the record-setting 2017 campaign. "But it's always possible it could be a down year where somebody with 75 RBIs and 25 home runs would win an MVP. But every year the circumstances are different. With the way things have been going the last couple of years, it'll be hard to believe, given we're in such a stage where there are so many home runs being hit right now."

THE STUNTMEN OF LA

We just developed a character that was just incredible, that we knew we could come back and win baseball games. It carried over into the season. I can't remember but I'm thinking that we never lost [more than] three games in a row all season long! I mean, it was amazing because we had so many come-from-behind victories. And we just played an incredible brand of baseball [where] we never gave up. It didn't matter what team we were playing, how big their stars were. We found a way to win baseball games, and we just had the most fun, ever, in a total season. We were just a bunch of older guys mixed with a few younger guys here and there. We had enough experience and enough know-how to put it all together. I don't think any team in the history of baseball will ever do what we did, with the type of players that we had. You've got to give a lot of credit to Fred Claire for finding all of those personalities. He stuck to his principles when he signed everybody. John Shelby was on that team also. It was just incredible how he put it all together.

—Rick Dempsey, Dodgers catcher

World Championship and pennant-winning teams throughout the history of baseball are remembered for their great nicknames. Say "Murderers' Row," and fans know you're talking about the 1927 Yankees. The "Big Red Machine"? That's the 1975–1976 Cincinnati Reds. Even those not around then have heard of the "Gashouse Gang"—a nickname given to the 1934 St. Louis Cardinals—if they've read up on baseball history. In a more recent era, there were "Harvey's Wallbangers," a potent Milwaukee Brewers club under manager Harvey Kuenn that simply hit the cover off the baseball during its 1982 pennant-winning season. There were the "Amazin's," the 1969 Miracle Mets. There were also the 1979 "We Are Family" Pirates, the last Pittsburgh team to be crowned champions in baseball in the 20th century. Even the Dodgers had their own moniker, "Boys of Summer," in their Brooklyn days in the 1950s, when they were the National League's most talented team.

Fast forward to 1988, and Oakland won 104 regular-season games thanks in part to the "Bash Brothers," the mashing duo of Jose Canseco and Mark McGwire. In the National League, Cincinnati was two years away from becoming world champions, with an unhittable bullpen trio of Norm Charlton, Rob Dibble, and Randy Myers known as "the Nasty Boys." In Los Angeles, meanwhile, there were the "Stuntmen of LA," a nickname coined by Dodgers utility man Mickey Hatcher during spring training, referring to group of reserve players who were nameless and faceless but necessary if the show were to go on. The Stuntmen, a group of blue-collar bench players who seamlessly stepped in whenever called upon to pinch-hit or fill in for injured regulars, were not household names by any means like Canseco or McGwire. Made up of nonstarters such as Hatcher, Rick Dempsey, and Danny Heep, these Stuntmen somehow had an uncanny knack for making the right play and getting a big hit at key moments. Because of their contributions off the bench during the course of the season and the postseason, the Stuntmen were integral members of the 1988 Dodgers.

We don't hear that nickname being mentioned at all today. And *Stuntmen* doesn't sound very intimidating or imposing either—and lacks the sexiness of the other better-known monikers. Murderers' Row? A Babe Ruth–led ball club that crushed the ball and terrorized opposing pitchers. Big Red Machine? Some of the greatest players of their era, players that you'd expect to deliver on the October stage. Even the 1934 Gashouse Gang Cardinals—who played the game with an aggressive attitude that always seemed to give them dirty uniforms, making their wardrobe resemble the grease-stained clothing worn by car mechanics—featured prominent Hall of Famers Frankie Frisch, Joe Medwick, Leo Durocher, and 30-game winner Dizzy Dean. The Stuntmen? Who the heck were these guys? "The Stuntmen were an integral part of that '88 team," Dodgers closer Jay Howell says emphatically today. "Without them, we don't win."

Catcher Rick Dempsey can only smile when the Stuntmen are mentioned all these years later. "We went through that season as a team of platoon players, the way Fred [Claire] put it together," Dempsey, now a Baltimore Orioles broadcaster, says today. "We had a lot of backup players, guys that didn't play every day. We had only three regulars, and that was Kirk Gibson, Mike Marshall, and Steve Sax. I can't think of anyone else that was a regular player! The rest of us were Franklin Stubbs and myself, Dave Anderson, Danny Heep. . . . We called ourselves the Stuntmen. That started in spring training. And it was just a bunch of guys who knew how to play. We weren't big names by any stretch of the imagination."

Dempsey, says Howell, was a huge part of the ball club. Howell remembers the pivotal fourth game of the World Series against Oakland vividly, when Tommy Lasorda gave him the ball in the seventh inning of a one-run game—just one night after he'd surrendered a game-winning homer to McGwire. With the bases loaded and two outs—and Los Angeles ahead 4–3—McGwire came up again looking to inflict more damage. But just before the A's masher stepped into the batter's box, Dempsey ran out to the mound for a quick word. "We're going with the fastball—the exact same pitch as the one from the night before," was Dempsey's message. "He goes, 'Just go with me. We're gonna shake off a bit, and we're gonna go right back to it,'" recalls Howell.

Dempsey guaranteed McGwire would be looking for a breaking ball—and Howell trusted the catcher's instincts. So, when Dempsey got back behind the plate, catcher and pitcher shook each other off. Howell then threw a first-pitch fastball—"pretty much the same pitch," he says today—and jammed McGwire, who popped the ball up to first base. The threat was over, neither team scored again, and the Dodgers hung on for a three-games-to-one lead.

"I'm curious if Rick remembers this," Howell continues.

Rick was a great addition. Those kinds of things, I don't even know if he'd even think anything of it. That's his wisdom. It comes natural. I think it's just what he does. But for me, it was huge. And the confidence he had in it. I mean, that's like, you sell it. "No, this is what we're gonna do. You're fine. Trust me." When you have a catcher like that—I mean, [starting catcher Mike] Scioscia was like that too—it's huge. "We got it. This is what we're gonna do. Don't worry about it. You're fine. We're

15

gonna shake off to a fastball, and he for sure is gonna think you're throwing something else." That was huge.

Howell pauses for a moment to reflect. He wants to make sure everybody realizes how important that one at-bat was; the momentum of the series could have swung right there.

Let me tell you, it was absolutely huge. The bases were loaded. You got a one-run lead, and the guy who hit the [walk-off homer] the night before was at the plate. What are you gonna throw? And you've got a catcher who says, "I know exactly what we're gonna do. Let me just tell you what we're gonna do." As a pitcher, I mean, to have somebody say, "Look, I got it. This is what we're gonna do. Trust me." Hell, I mean, if he feels that good about it . . . he's been around for a long time. Been around a hundred years, maybe? He thinks it's not a bad idea. Okay, I'll do it. You can't take them back. It's sorta like the pitch to Gibson [from Dennis Eckersley in Game One that went for a walk-off homer]. It could've been me. It could've been a grand slam. It could've changed everything.

Absolutely. Had he faltered there—and Oakland rallied to win the World Series—Howell might be remembered today the way Mitch Williams, Calvin Schiraldi, and Bob Stanley are remembered, namely, for their postseason failures. "So, I give him a lot of credit. I do. I give him a lot of credit for that. It was a good call," says Howell.

Dempsey apparently had made another good call prior to the 1988 season, one that's also been forgotten. It was a guarantee he made in Fred Claire's office—before he was even on the team. Obviously, we've all heard of and remember Joe Namath's guarantee before Super Bowl III that his AFL New York Jets were going to upset the NFL Baltimore Colts in the January 1969 championship game. Namath's Jets did indeed pull off a stunner in the third AFL–NFL Championship Game, shocking the heavily favored Colts 16–7. We remember New York Rangers captain Mark Messier guaranteeing a win over the New Jersey Devils in the 1994 Stanley Cup semifinals—and delivering a hat trick and an eventual title to end the franchise's 54-year championship drought. Then there was goaltender Patrick Roy guaranteeing to his teammates in between periods in the locker room he wouldn't surrender another goal—and he wouldn't, as his 1993 Montreal Canadiens (and later, 1996 Colorado Avalanche) went on to score and capture the Stanley Cup.

Dempsey's guarantee to Claire, meanwhile, happened the way he pictured it, and yet it isn't talked about anymore. As Dempsey recalls now, he'd had a bad year with the hapless Cleveland Indians—the worst team in baseball in 1987—and was looking for a change of scenery. "I came to a point in my career," the former backstop says from his home in Baltimore,

> where I just said, "I know I can still play. I've got a couple of years left. I'd like to play one time on the West Coast and stay at home and play at home."
>
> So, it became interesting to see whether or not I could get an invitation from the Dodgers to spring training. I ran into Tommy Lasorda at a banquet function and I asked him about the catching situation, and he said that it could be a possibility—that they may be looking for a backup guy to help out. So, I asked him if he'd say something to Fred Claire about it.

Lasorda agreed to talk to Claire, but Dempsey never heard back for two weeks. "I was at home in Agoura, California, and working in the yard, and I just said, 'You know what? I'm gonna go down this afternoon and find out for myself. I'm not gonna wait to hear back.' I left at about two o'clock in the afternoon. I got to Fred Claire's office. I asked to meet with Fred. The secretary told me he was in a meeting and that I'd have to wait to talk to him, so I did. About an hour later, I asked if he was still available, and she said, 'Well, he's in another meeting.'"

By seven that night, the secretary had gone home, but Dempsey refused to leave because he'd never quit at anything in his life. Knowing Claire was still in his office, Dempsey continued waiting. Shortly after seven, Claire peeked out the door.

> Fred said, "You're still here."
>
> And I said, "Yup. I'll wait as long as I have to!"
>
> So, he said, "I guess I'd better bring you in to talk to you!"
>
> We spoke for about an hour. I said to him, "Fred, I know you were in last place last year [actually, fourth place]. I'll hit a home run every 24 at-bats. I'll drive in a run every five at-bats. I'll change the pitching staff around a little bit. We'll win our division. We'll win the World Series. I'll catch the last pitch, and I'll give you the ball!"
>
> Fred said, "Well, I'd better invite you to spring training!"

I said, "Well, that'd be a good idea!"

So, he did. I went down to spring training. I had a decent spring, had a pretty good offensive run there for a while, and so on the last day of spring training, when everyone was getting ready to go in their directions, they still hadn't told me yet whether or not I'd made the ball club. I was staying in the bungalows there at Dodgertown. Fred walked in and said, "Rick, can you go to Triple-A ball for a while until we figure out what we're gonna do with Alex Trevino?"

I said, "Fred, there's no way I'm going to Triple-A ball. I appreciate you giving me an opportunity and a chance to make this ball club. But if I don't make it, I'm totally prepared to retire. And that'd be fine. You promised me a chance, and if I don't make the team, that's all right, no hard feelings. I'll just go on about my business. But I can't go to Triple-A ball after 20-some odd years in the big leagues"—at that point, it was 21 years, I think—"and take up some young kid's spot, waiting to see if I'm gonna make the ball club."

So, I just thanked him, no hard feelings, and started to pack up to go home. He went back to his office. He talked to Roy Campanella and a few other people. They said, "What do you think about Dempsey?" Roy Campanella spoke up for me and said, "I think that guy really knows what he's doing. I think he'd be great for the ball club. I think you should sign him, Fred." So, Fred thought about it for a while. He came back to my room, and he said, "Rick, you've made the team."

Trevino, a 30-year-old backup catcher who'd been with the Dodgers for the previous two years—having come over from San Francisco in a trade for outfielder Candy Maldonado—and who'd been in the majors for parts of 10 seasons, was released to make room for the 38-year-old Dempsey. "So, that's where it all began," continues Dempsey. "I had a little over 150 at-bats. I hit seven home runs. I drove in exactly 30 runs. We won the division. We won the World Series, and I caught the last pitch."

As it turned out, 1988 ended the way Dempsey had guaranteed. The Dodgers, whose longest losing streak all season was three games (which happened a total of 10 times), won the National League West by seven games over second-place Cincinnati. They went on to win the World Series, with Dempsey, filling in for injured Mike Scioscia behind the plate, catching the final pitch when Orel Hershiser struck out Oakland's Tony Phillips swinging. Dempsey, as promised, gave that baseball to Claire as the team was celebrating in the visitors' clubhouse in Oakland. "I caught the last pitch of the World Series, and I was dumb enough to give him the ball. That ball is worth a lot of money right now!" Dempsey chuckles. "I gave him the ball because I'd promised it to him when we met during the off-season." For years, Claire had that baseball in the office of his Pasadena home. But when he later found out that the National Baseball Hall of Fame, surprisingly, didn't have too many World Series final-out baseballs—only two, to be exact—Claire donated the valuable keepsake to Cooperstown. "Fred ended up donating the ball to the Hall of Fame later on, which was fine with me," adds Dempsey.

Incredibly, this story is no longer being talked about—but Rick Dempsey certainly delivered on his promise. Franklin Stubbs, as Dempsey says, was one of the LA Stuntmen. But wait—wasn't Stubbs the Dodgers' starting first baseman in the 1988 World Series? Yes, and he batted second in the lineup in every series game against Oakland, hitting .294 with a pair of doubles and three runs scored. Not bad for a guy who wasn't even a starter when the season began.

With the Dodgers acquiring free agents Kirk Gibson and Mike Davis to play the corner outfield positions, right fielder Mike Marshall and left fielder Pedro Guerrero had to give up their regular positions and move back to the infield—and the two players most affected by the changes were Stubbs and shortstop Mariano Duncan, who was sent to Triple-A. Marshall now took over first base, which was Stubbs's position. Guerrero, meanwhile, played third base, with newcomer Alfredo Griffin at shortstop and Steve Sax at second. John Shelby patrolled center field, with Mike Scioscia doing the catching.

Stubbs, therefore, would begin the season on the bench. A regular who'd smacked 23 homers in 1986 while playing primarily left field and the team's everyday first baseman in 1987, the 27-year-old Stubbs would now be a backup like the other reserves who called themselves the Stuntmen—guys such as Dempsey and Mickey Hatcher. "He had a good 10-year major-league career and is working in baseball now," Fred Claire says today about Stubbs. "He's a very good guy. He just kind of got caught in a wave of first basemen with Greg Brock [who was traded after the 1986 season to Milwaukee] and Sid Bream, who was going to be the best player. And as it turned out, Bream [who was dealt to Pittsburgh in

September 1985] turned out not only to be the best but [also] the most successful of those three first basemen."

Even with Marshall now occupying first base to begin the 1988 season, Claire refused to trade Stubbs. Through the first 53 games, Stubbs had started only four times, twice at first base and the other two in the outfield—but at least the Dodgers were in first place at 30–23. "I thought we got off to a great start," Stubbs recalls when asked what he remembered about the regular season.

> Our stars showed up early. When they did get hurt, our role players played well. I think we lost our shortstop, Griffin, for about a month. And Dave Anderson played outstanding ball at shortstop. When our starters didn't play, I thought our role players played very well. We didn't miss our starters. I thought that was a key. Our starting pitching was outstanding; our bullpen was solid. And one of the biggest things was that we never lost more than three games in a row all season—if I recall correctly. Not having long losing streaks kinda sustained us.
>
> But I think the biggest thing was 30 minutes before every ball game, everything in the clubhouse [was turned off], and we focused on what we needed to focus on to go out there to win. And everybody was always on the same page. You never got somebody off the page whenever it was time to go play.

The Dodgers were glad they didn't trade Stubbs, as Davis began slumping at the plate and was eventually benched. Through June 7, Stubbs had rarely started, though he did come off the bench in 23 other contests. But with Davis struggling, the Dodgers inserted Stubbs at first base and moved Marshall back to right field.

For Stubbs, the other big move was the trade of Guerrero, who also played first base after returning to the lineup from an injury, to St. Louis in August. "We traded Pedro Guerrero for John Tudor just before the deadline. He was a big part of our team at the time and one of our main hitters," Stubbs says today when asked to reflect on his move from being a Stuntman to becoming an everyday player in 1988. "When he left, it basically came down to me playing first base against righties, and Tracy Woodson would play against the lefties. So, that was kinda what we did. We changed it up a little bit. It was no problem. You just go out there and do what you needed to do to get the win. So, we didn't worry about who was playing; our most important thing was whoever was playing was gonna get the job done."

Although he hit only .223 during the season, Stubbs did step up on the October stage. With Oakland trotting out all right-handed starting pitchers in the World Series and Kirk Gibson sidelined with injuries, Stubbs started all five games at first base, collecting key hits in Games 2 and 5.

The regulars on the ball club respected the Stuntmen and appreciated their contributions off the bench. "Hatcher, Dempsey, Mike Davis—all those guys, they were incredible. [The 1988 championship was] a total team win. That's what it all [came] down to," Mike Scioscia said that October, referring to how that group of reserves kept delivering seemingly every time they were called upon in key situations throughout that entire year.[1] Added Kirk Gibson, who referred to Hatcher as the leader of the Stuntmen: "I think Mickey Hatcher exemplifies what this team is all about. This team has always believed in itself. I got hurt [during the playoffs], and the team accepted that I would be out. And Mickey steps in [against Oakland] and fills my role [in left field and as the number 3 hitter in the batting order]."[2] Steve Sax, reflecting back on 1988 today, also remembers those reserves fondly. "The Stuntmen were great," Sax says now. "Mickey Hatcher was a leader of the Stuntmen. That was a bunch of the guys who were the reserves. Mickey was great for the team because he added a lot of spunk to the team. The Stuntmen were really good. They provided a lot of fun for the team. They provided a lot of excitement for the guys that weren't playing. It was a way of keeping everybody loose— and that's what Mickey Hatcher did very well."

Hitting coach Ben Hines credits Scioscia, Gibson, and Orel Hershiser as being leaders of the 1988 club, but he also remembers the reserve players fondly. "Hershiser and Gibson—even though they were totally different players—really encouraged each other. They encouraged each other and really in a sense, I think, fed off each other," says Hines. "And we had a group of guys that were the benchwarmers, and they had a little title for themselves, the Stuntmen. Dempsey, Anderson, Hatcher . . . they were very good coming off the bench. And Hatcher got so good coming off the bench that Tommy started using him in our lineup sometimes against right-hand pitchers and he really helped us. They did a great job.

And when they came through, it gave our 25-man roster a real feeling of being a whole team, because of how good they were at coming off the bench."

Likewise, Jay Howell remembers those reserve players played huge roles when the starters were injured or out of the lineup. "Tommy Lasorda called the bench players the Stuntmen. Without these guys, we don't win. Hatcher had a huge [World Series]; he drove in three runs. There were several, [like] Dave Anderson coming in to play shortstop [when] Alfredo Griffin dislocated his thumb and hitting over .300 for about a month," Howell says now from his home just outside of Atlanta. "And a very key ingredient down the stretch was Dempsey. Scioscia had gotten beat up. There were some guys that had been going after Scioscia. At the end of the year, Mike was really struggling. His arm was killing him. He'd been hammered. And Dempsey—another acquisition before the season—had to catch some of those games. I don't know his numbers toward the end of the year, but I mean, here was a guy who was 40-something, and did a dynamite job back there. He was fantastic. Didn't miss a beat. Filled in for Scioscia."

Many of the Dodgers remember Hatcher, who'd bat .280 in his 12 major-league seasons, as the leader of the Stuntmen. When asked to reflect on what was a memorable year for him, particularly with his World Series performance—and talk about whether 1988 has changed him—Hatcher shrugs. "I dunno. I don't think somebody can look back and say, 'Hey, you know, this changed my life,' because I am who I am—and I always have been. I enjoy life. I take it one day at a time." However, he does appreciate the fact he was given a second chance with the Dodgers. Selected by the club in the fifth round of the 1977 amateur draft, Hatcher debuted in 1979 and played a total of 90 games for Los Angeles—splitting his time between right field and third base—before being traded (with two minor-leaguers) to the Minnesota Twins on March 30, 1981, for All-Star center fielder Ken Landreaux. That year, the Dodgers won the World Series, beating the New York Yankees in six games—with Landreaux catching the series' final out in center field. Hatcher, meanwhile, batted .255 for a Twins team that played .376 baseball and didn't come close to winning anything in the special split season caused by the players' strike.

After six solid seasons with the Twins—where he hit over .300 twice and batted .284 overall—Hatcher was released on March 31, 1987. He was signed by general manager Fred Claire and returned to the Dodgers, but Los Angeles struggled in 1987 while Minnesota stunned the baseball world by winning the World Series in a seven-game upset victory over St. Louis. So, Hatcher missed out on two championships—and he does appreciate the fact he was brought back to Los Angeles and was thus able to enjoy being a world champion in 1988. "So, no, I don't think anybody can say, 'Hey, this changed my life.' But in the Dodgers organization as a ballplayer, it's something to be recognized more for my accomplishments that I happened to have in the World Series that year," Hatcher continues. "Of course, that was all because of Fred Claire, who believed in me. At that time, I was out of baseball. Fred took a chance on bringing me in. He got me a World Series ring that I missed with the Dodgers in ['81] and the Twins in '87." (Landreaux, by the way, would spend 1988 in Rochester, the Orioles' Triple-A farm team, after playing seven seasons with Los Angeles.)

Hatcher, when reflecting back all these years later, realizes he did catch a break. The Dodgers fired general manager Al Campanis because of controversial comments made on April 6, 1987, during an interview on *Nightline* about racial equality in baseball—where he told Ted Koppel on national television that African Americans might lack the "necessities" to be a general manager or field manager. Suddenly, Claire took over Campanis's role and was in charge of player personnel. With Dodgers third baseman Bill Madlock hurt two games into the season, Hatcher's agent, Willie Sanchez, made a call to the club, and Claire signed Hatcher his second day on the job.

Had Campanis still been in charge, would Los Angeles have signed him? We'll never know. But we do know that two weeks prior to Campanis's firing, Sanchez had called regarding Hatcher but the Dodgers weren't interested. Now, things had changed. Madlock was hurt, Campanis was out, and Claire was in charge. "We had 11 pitchers and we had used Fernando Valenzuela to pinch-hit [twice in the first five games]," Claire recalled in 1988. "I knew we needed another hitter, so I asked [owner] Peter O'Malley, 'What would you think if I released [veteran pitcher] Jerry Reuss and signed Mickey Hatcher?' That night Mickey flew in from Arizona during the game and we sent him up as a pinch-hitter, down by

Mickey Hatcher, the first player Fred Claire acquired as general manager, poses with Fred and Sheryl Claire in 2017. *Fred Claire*

a run. Mickey hit a grounder that somebody [Giants All-Star third baseman Chris Brown] fumbled, and the score was tied. My phone rang and it was Peter. He said, 'Fred, are you having a good time right now?'"[3]

Hatcher is amazed that Dodgers fans who followed the team then still appreciate him for his efforts that magical season. Every time he attends an event representing the Dodgers, people want to talk about 1988. "It was special," he says. "The fans were always good with me, and it was great that I gave them something. They all still talk about it now. Even when I go do these events, they always come up and thank me for having a good series. And I'm like, 'Whoa. That was definitely a team effort, with a bunch of guys.' At that time, we were kind of old, mixed in with a few young guys, with everybody just coming together at the right time."

While Lasorda, Gibson, and Hershiser received most of the media accolades, the Stuntmen—the group of reserves led by Hatcher, Dempsey, Danny Heep, and Dave Anderson—routinely contributed off the bench. "Everything just came together in spring training," Hatcher says today. "We had a group of guys who knew they weren't starters. We formed a great bond. There were about five of us who told the starters in spring, 'Yeah, you play your three innings, we'll come in and win the games.' We took pride in it. We wanted to come in and do something for the team."

CHAPTER THREE
THE FORGOTTEN GUYS

We brought in John Tudor that year, didn't we? Tudor was a good acquisition from St. Louis; we got him for Pedro Guerrero.

—Steve Sax, Dodgers second baseman

Tracy Woodson was a total blue-collar type of guy. He was a really good, nice player. I don't know what his numbers were. Woodson, as I recall, had some big hits for us in 1988.

—Jay Howell, Dodgers closer

In 1986, I finally got my first whole year of being in the major leagues, with the Brewers. It was a great place for me at the time as they were transitioning from a veteran team to a younger team. I had a very good second half, going 6–3 after taking my lumps adjusting to the majors . . . as the major leagues is about three to five levels above Triple-A! My confidence grew and I finished the season as the number 2 starting pitcher behind 20-game winner Teddy Higuera. So, it was a shock to find out that I'd been traded in late December 1986! But, going to the Dodgers was an unexpected piece of good news.

—Tim Leary, Dodgers pitcher

Along with the stars—such as Hershiser, Gibson, and Scioscia—as well as manager Tommy Lasorda, the pitching staff, and the group of reserve players known as the Stuntmen, there were other contributors to the 1988 team that may have been forgotten all these years later. "I couldn't tell you who was on that '88 team other than Gibson," says veteran sportswriter Mel Antonen. "That makes it an incredible story. Oh yeah, Hershiser was the leader of that pitching staff. But who else was on that team?"

That's likely the consensus these days. When fans go through the list of championship teams over the years, they could probably rattle off more than just a name or two. The 1986 Mets? Strawberry, Dykstra, Hernandez, Gooden, Fernandez, and Darling, just to name a few. And oh, Mookie, Carter, and Ojeda. The '89 Athletics? Canseco and McGwire. Eckersley, Stewart, Welch, Honeycutt, Rickey Henderson, Dave Henderson, Carney Lansford, Terry Steinbach. The '95 Braves? Maddux, Glavine, Smoltz. McGriff, Justice, Chipper Jones, Mark Lemke, Mark Wohlers. The '70s Big Red Machine? Bench, Rose, Morgan, Griffey, Perez, Concepcion, Foster. The A's dynasty teams in that same decade? Reggie, Catfish, Sal Bando, Rollie Fingers, Bert Campaneris, Joe Rudi, Vida Blue. The late '70s Yankees? Reggie, Guidry, Catfish, Gossage, Munson, Piniella. The Joe Torre–led Yankees? Jeter, Williams, Rivera, Pettitte, Posada, O'Neill. And over those years they had the likes of Fielder, Boggs, Tino Martinez, Cone, Wells, Clemens, Orlando Hernandez, and of course, Jim Leyritz, whose dramatic three-run homer against Atlanta changed the momentum of the 1996 World Series.

The 1988 Dodgers? It might be fair to say they were a team with Gibson and Hershiser, and a bunch of forgotten guys. But each of them certainly contributed. For a team that didn't lose more than three games in a row all season, every player contributed in some way throughout the year. "So many of our guys stepped it up. Even some of the younger guys got some of the biggest hits of their careers that got us one step closer to even getting a chance to be in the playoffs," Mickey Hatcher says, praising the rookies when he reflects back to that season. "Everybody on that team contributed. I mean, it wasn't a 24-man roster. I think if you looked back at all the guys that Tommy [Lasorda] and Fred Claire had to find to get us through the season, I mean there probably were over 60 guys with all the pitching and all the moves we had to make to just try and survive and get there. That's what makes it even more special."

One of the young guys was outfielder Mike Devereaux, known more for his stint in Baltimore in the 1990s as well as his NLCS (National League Championship Series) MVP award won with the 1995 Braves.

But Devereaux did have 43 at-bats as a 25-year-old rookie with the '88 Dodgers. In fact, he made four starts in center field—and was used regularly as a pinch hitter—during the three weeks John Shelby was on the disabled list in April and May. On September 21, against the Padres in the second game of a doubleheader, Devereaux delivered a walk-off tenth-inning single off Mark Davis (who'd capture the NL Cy Young Award in 1989) to bring Los Angeles closer to the NL West title. Five nights later, the Dodgers were officially Western Division champions.

For Claire, the general manager, the Dodgers' third-string catcher was a forgotten guy he remembers. "Gilberto Reyes is an interesting story," Claire reflects.

> When we got to the World Series, Gilberto was with the team for the first two games in Los Angeles. But when the rest of the team flew to Oakland to continue the series, he returned to the Dominican Republic to begin play in the winter league. Of course, he was watching Game 4 on television and he saw Mike Scioscia injure his knee on a slide into second base.
>
> After the game, I phoned Gilberto to see if he could rejoin the team for Game 5. We'd gotten permission from [Commissioner] Peter Ueberroth to add Gilberto to the roster for that fifth game in Oakland. We had to explain to Ueberroth, "Look, Peter, we don't want to have another position player who hasn't caught before to be out there—in the event of an injury to our other catcher, Rick Dempsey—to make a farce of the game." So, I had Gilberto fly in from the Dominican, and he arrived just as the ninth inning had ended . . . just as we were celebrating! He walked into the clubhouse about the time they started popping champagne bottles. So, here's a guy who's flown in all the way from the Dominican Republic to get soaked in champagne.

Reyes is OK with being an anonymous member of that team. At least he was given a nickname by Lasorda. As Hershiser recalled years later, Lasorda only gave you a nickname if he felt you were good enough to be wearing Dodger Blue. "I don't know if Lasorda will ever tell you this," Hershiser—nicknamed the "Bulldog" by Lasorda—once said, "but he didn't give you a nickname until he thought you were a big leaguer. . . . He didn't call you by that nickname until he wanted you on the team. When Tommy thought you had big-league ability and he wanted you on the team, he gave you a nickname."[1]

As Reyes remembers, Lasorda gave him one way back in 1983. "Tommy gave me the nickname 'Onion Head' in my first year," Reyes recalls fondly, and goes on to explain the origin of that moniker.

> I was yelling at somebody in Spanish, "Cabeza de cebolla." It means "Onion Head." It was a pitcher. I was playing first base and I was yelling, "Hey, Cabeza de cebolla! Come on!"
>
> The pitcher said, "What? What do you mean?"
>
> I said, "It means Onion Head!"
>
> "What? No, you're the Onion Head!"
>
> "I'm not! Oh my God, you're the Onion Head!"
>
> And Tommy started calling me "Onion Head," and I got stuck with that. If someone said, "That kid looked like a real onion head," [it meant] he got a skinny body and a big, old head. That name "Cabeza de cebolla" was meant for [the pitcher] but I got stuck with that name. When Tommy [gave you a nickname], you were stuck with it. But I didn't mind. I didn't mind. I thought one day they would announce me as, "Now hitting, Gilberto Reyes, better known as an onion head." Oh, come on! That's OK. At least they remember me for something.

Although he'd debuted for the Dodgers at the age of 19 in 1983 and appeared in 19 games, Reyes was still a rookie in '88 as he had played in a total of just 11 games with the big-league club, from 1984 to 1987. On June 22, 1983, he got his first major-league hit, a double off the Padres' Eric Show. In 1988, Reyes again saw very little playing time with the Dodgers, receiving only nine at-bats and collecting one hit. That one hit, a single on September 27 in San Diego, fittingly came off Eric Show also. It turned out to be Reyes's final hit in Dodger Blue.

"That year was fun, completely fun. We got one of those teams that . . . I don't think they have anymore," Reyes, who never drove in a run for the Dodgers, says today from his home in Riverview, Florida.

> Nobody was a star. Kirk Gibson was a star but wasn't like a real star, you know what I mean? It was one of those teams. We developed star players that year, to be honest. Orel Hershiser became Orel Hershiser. Kirk Gibson became known as Kirk Gibson after that home run. A bunch of people that have jobs [today are in those positions] because of that season also. We came out of nowhere, a bunch of players that people don't

even remember their names, to be honest. They played key [roles]. Their timing was perfect for that team. We didn't have speed, but we could throw. We had pitching, but we didn't have star pitchers. You know what I mean? We had Orel Hershiser going, but that was it. Then we had Tim Belcher and Tim Leary, but people don't even remember their names right now. But we knew how to pitch. We studied those hitters like you won't believe.

Although Reyes never played much, it didn't mean he didn't study the game when he was on the bench. "I was not allowed to be sitting anywhere else [except] beside Orel Hershiser and Mike Scioscia when I wasn't playing," recalls Reyes. "You had to be on the same [page] with them. We had to be on the same kind of mind, just in case I got into the game late. Most of the time, I was getting into the game late. I had to know what [pitches] I was calling. We didn't take chances with anybody, even the [opposing] pitchers. We were tough on pitchers, sometimes, tougher than the eighth hitter [of the opposing lineup]! We didn't want to be surprised by anything. We wanted to take care of business."

As Reyes recalls, the 1988 Dodgers were like a family; they got along, yes, but they also weren't afraid to get in each other's faces when it was necessary. The big thing, though, they normally took care of business in-house without the media hovering around. "We fought with each other," explains Reyes.

We argued with each other. We did a bunch of stuff that other teams maybe are still doing, but the way we did it, there was no media [that] knew about it. When we fought [and] we argued after we lost a game that we weren't supposed to lose, we jumped all over that person. "What the—excuse my language—were you doing out there?" We just dropped the [f-bombs] on them. "What [were] you doing? What [were] you thinking?" But we did it the right way, not the bad way. We didn't want to lose any games. We didn't want that.

We knew we had [our] limits. We knew that we didn't have a power hitter; we didn't have [any] number 3, number 4, number 5 power hitters. We knew all that. But we competed harder. We didn't make errors. We didn't make dumb errors. So if you wanted to beat us, you had to beat us by the book. We bunted the ball. We did this. We did that. We pitched. We played defense like nobody else did. And we pitched, and we pitched, and we pitched. It was fun. It was a family.

As it turned out, because Los Angeles defeated Oakland in only five games in the 1988 World Series, Reyes wasn't needed for a sixth game and ultimately didn't play an inning in the postseason.

Another rookie who was with the team during the postseason—but wasn't on the postseason rosters—was right-handed reliever Tim Crews. Known affectionately by his teammates as "the Dirt Farmer," Crews stayed in Los Angeles until the end of the 1992 season. Sadly, after having just signed with Cleveland, he died in a tragic boating accident during spring training in 1993—an accident that also killed teammate Steve Olin and seriously injured fellow Indians pitcher Bobby Ojeda.

Mariano Duncan, who played with Crews in the minors, tears up when asked to talk about him. "I can remember right now the day that Tim Crews passed away," Duncan says, choking up. "I remember I was in Miami because this happened in 1993. It was the same day that my oldest boy, Mariano, was born. I remember I was in spring training and I went to Miami because my wife was supposed to deliver our baby. It was the same day Mariano was born, on March 23, 1993. I got the news from my agent, Tony Attanasio, that Tim Crews passed away in a boat accident. It was just a really sad and bad moment for me that day."

Jay Howell, Crews's best friend on the Dodgers, honors the Dirt Farmer in a special way. The Dodgers closer has Crews's number, 52, in his email address, listed right behind his own number, 50, linking the two men forever. "Tim Crews was just outstanding in 1988. He worked hard," Howell says today. "He pitched with no fear. He had good stuff— not great stuff—but he just went out there and did an outstanding job. He was a guy who didn't get a lot of credit—he never drew attention to himself—but he was one reason we won the number of games we did. I'll never forget how he was always willing to sacrifice for that team."

Unfortunately, Fred Claire acquired left-hander Ricky Horton from the White Sox on August 30th and included him instead of Crews on the postseason rosters. At the time, Los Angeles had only one left-hander— Jesse Orosco—in the bullpen, and Claire felt he needed a second south-paw in the mix. But Crews, 4–0 with a 3.14 ERA in 42 games in 1988, took the news like a man and never had any ill will toward the organization. "Tim was crushed not being on the postseason roster but he never said a word. He was the ultimate team player," Howell recalls. "He was all about winning. And during the playoffs and World Series, he was with the team, in uniform, and he was our biggest cheerleader."

Infielder Tracy Woodson also remembers Crews was all about winning. "Yeah, he was," Woodson says now. "He was. I wasn't very close to Tim, but I played a lot with him in Triple-A and in LA. He didn't have the greatest stuff, but he was ready to go whenever they called his name. He was ready to go. And he helped a lot. It's very unfortunate what happened to him."

Howell can't say enough about the contributions of Crews and Brian Holton, another forgotten member of the 1988 bullpen. A game from June 25 in Cincinnati exemplifies the type of effort they gave that year. The Reds scored four runs off Fernando Valenzuela in the bottom of the first to take a 4–0 lead and chase the former ace. Holton came in, threw one pitch, and got the final out of the frame. The Dodgers then erupted for five runs in the top of the second off Jose Rijo, and Crews came on to start the bottom of the second and proceeded to throw four shutout innings, facing just one batter over the minimum. Alejandro Peña then took over and worked the next three and two-thirds innings, and was one out away from picking up the save. Tommy Lasorda, however, went with left-hander Jesse Orosco to face left-handed hitting Jeff Treadway. Orosco got that final out on just one pitch, and was credited with the save. Holton, who got one out on just one pitch, was the pitcher of record and was correctly credited with the win.

Crews and Peña, who combined to work seven and two-thirds innings of shutout ball, didn't get any decision or the save—but that was the type of team the Dodgers were. Everybody came in and did his job. "The role I'm in is to keep us in the game," Crews later told the *Los Angeles Times*. "I'm not one to get a lot of wins and losses."[2]

"I had an opportunity to play with Tim Crews in the minor leagues and in the major leagues," Duncan says today. "That guy was a helluva guy. Nice guy, good family man, good father, good husband. And when I found out he'd passed away, I took that one really hard. And Mike Sharperson. I had the opportunity to play with him too in the major-league level."

Duncan alludes to infielder Mike Sharperson, best known for his All-Star appearance with the Dodgers in 1992. Unfortunately, Crews wasn't the only member of the 1988 Dodgers to lose his life during his playing career. Sharperson, who batted .271 in 59 at-bats in 1988, died tragically in 1996 at the age of 34. "When he had that car accident, he was in Las Vegas playing for the San Diego Padres' Triple-A team there," Duncan recalls.

> And he got promoted to the big leagues by the Padres that night. On the way home, he tried to go home and pack his suitcase to go to the airport the next day. And I heard he just got killed in a car accident that night. It was another sad moment for me because I can't believe something like that happened to the nicest guy. I got the opportunity to spend some time with Mike Sharperson. He used to be a great teammate, a good friend. I can say he was a good father, a good husband, a good friend. When you hear about something like this, when somebody like that lost his life . . . I took that one hard, very hard.

Woodson was closer to Sharperson than he was to Crews for the simple fact that Sharperson and he both played on the infield. It's no secret that pitchers are each other's best friends while hitters spend more time with other hitters. "I was very good friends with Sharperson," recalls Woodson.

> We'd played winter ball together, we'd played a number of years in Albuquerque, and back and forth. So, I was very close to him. I actually cried when I got the news that he'd been in the car accident. I think he was being re-called to the big leagues. I was in Columbus, in Triple-A, and heard the story. I think I was on the bench, actually, when somebody came and said that, and I started crying right there in the dugout. He was just kind of a happy-go-lucky guy. The one year they weren't doing very well, he was their best player at the time, and [because of the rule that] each team had to have a player, he was elected to the All-Star team. It was too bad with what happened to him. It's hard when that happens, especially during the season.

As for Holton, 1988 was by far the best season of his six-year major-league career. Although he'd gone 16–6 with a 3.44 ERA in Triple-A as a 21-year-old in 1981, the right-hander didn't get promoted to the Dodgers until 1985. After appearing in a total of just 15 games for Los Angeles in 1985–1986, Holton worked 83 1/3 innings in 1987 with a 3.89 ERA while averaging 3.5 walks per nine innings. But in 1988, Holton was tremendous, lowering his ERA to 1.70 in essentially the same number of innings (84 2/3). He allowed only one home run, and also lowered his walks rate to 2.8 per nine innings.

Jay Howell, who'd lead the Dodgers in saves from 1988 to 1991, says the bullpen was one of the major strengths of the ball club, even if those relievers are forgotten today. "There were a couple of notable guys in the bullpen, and Brian Holton was huge for the whole year," recalls Howell, who himself is probably forgotten today despite having a successful five-year run as the stopper in Los Angeles, where he notched a 2.07 ERA (including a pair of sub-1.60 ERA seasons).

> Tim Crews had a very good year. If you looked at the statistics, along with Alejandro Peña, nobody had an off year. Each one of those guys had really good numbers for leaving people on base. They all almost had their career year in '88. I know Holton did. Crews had a really fine year as a long guy. Holton was amazing—fantastic year he had. If you looked at the numbers of the bullpen, all the way through, almost each one of them had amazingly solid years. You couple that with a guy like Hershiser eating up innings, and then we could fill in. That bullpen was strong, and I wanna give kudos to those guys.

Catcher Rick Dempsey remembers being impressed with how some of the relievers, in particular Holton, simply came in and did their job. "[Holton] just had a year that was amazing," Dempsey says now. "If you looked at the record books to see how good he really was that year—and everybody else, really—you'd say, 'Wow, those are big numbers.'"

In the NLCS, Tommy Lasorda relied on Holton for three straight games—in Games 4 to 6—while Howell was serving a two-game suspension. Holton recorded a five-out save in Game 5 against the Mets—while facing the minimum five batters—and five nights later worked two shutout innings in Game 1 of the World Series. While that was his only series appearance, Holton's role was crucial. He pitched the sixth and seventh innings, allowing only one Oakland baserunner. The Dodgers were behind 4–2 when he entered and down just 4–3 when he left—keeping the game close enough for Kirk Gibson's ninth-inning heroics. The postseason proved to be his last hurrah. In the off-season, Fred Claire traded the right-hander, along with minor-league infielder Juan Bell and pitcher Ken

Howell, to Baltimore for future Hall of Fame first baseman Eddie Murray. After that trade, Holton pitched only two more years in the majors—logging ERAs of 4.02 and 4.50 in 1989 and 1990, respectively, for the Orioles—before playing the final two years of his professional career for the Dodgers' Triple-A club in Albuquerque. At the age of 33, Holton's professional career was over.

Pitcher Ken Howell—no relation to Jay Howell—pitched in only four games with the 1988 Dodgers and wasn't included on the postseason rosters for the NLCS or World Series. He did, however, contribute in June when the Dodgers ran out of arms. Recovering from off-season surgery at the beginning of that year, Ken Howell logged a 6.39 ERA in his one start and three September mop-up appearances. On June 16, the Dodgers faced Atlanta in a night game in the finale of a road trip, which was immediately followed (with no travel day) by an eight-game, six-day homestand, beginning with five games in three days (two doubleheaders) with San Diego. With a lot of innings to come in the Padres series, the Dodgers planned ahead and recalled Ken Howell from Triple-A to make that start in Atlanta.

The Dodgers needed Howell to go as long as he could against the Braves—and he went six full innings while allowing nine runs on 15 hits in taking the loss. Unfortunately, he also hurt his left knee in a home-plate collision with Dale Murphy when the Atlanta right fielder tried to score on a passed ball. Howell threw 100 pitches, and only one other pitcher (Crews) was used that night, allowing the rest of the pitching staff to be well rested for the following series. Who knows; perhaps without Ken Howell's innings in that spot start, the starting rotation might have been juggled and there might have been other injuries to the staff that could have altered the course of the rest of the season and playoffs.

Tim Leary, who was 17–11 that season, remembers the entire pitching staff being tough, 1 through 10. Everybody, he recalls, had outstanding numbers. Going into the postseason, Leary knew the Dodgers had a shot if they pitched the way they'd done all season long—even if Hershiser was the only marquee name on the team. "That's the stuff that we had in our memory banks going into the postseason: 10 to 11 pitchers all with sub-3.00 ERAs [actually, eight]," says Leary. "And every pitcher pitched out of the bullpen at some point, except [maybe] John Tudor."

Tim Leary won 17 games with six shutouts for the Dodgers in 1988. He also led the team in strikeouts that season. *National Baseball Hall of Fame and Museum, Cooperstown, New York*

Actually, of the nine Dodgers pitchers who saw action in the 1988 postseason, only left-handed reliever Ricky Horton—acquired on August 30 from the White Sox for Shawn Hillegas—had a regular-season ERA over 3.00. Horton notched a 5.00 ERA in 12 appearances for the Dodgers following the trade (and 4.87 overall for the year), and allowed 10 of 17 inherited runners to score. In the postseason, however, Horton turned things around by working four and one-third scoreless innings over four appearances against the Mets. He did allow a pair of inherited runners to score in the eighth inning of Game 3, the final two tallies of a five-run frame that turned a 4–3 lead into an 8–4 loss.

Dempsey remembers Horton for another reason (or so he thinks). "Rick Horton, our left-hander, was the most superstitious guy you ever want to meet in your life!" says Dempsey with a laugh.

> He had a routine. You've gotta watch this guy on film somewhere. It was amazing. He'd never hand me the baseball. I could never hand him a baseball coming into a game. Sometimes I just reach out to give him the ball when he would come in to pitch, and he would not take the ball from me. When I went to give it to him, it'd drop on the ground. He had to walk around to the back of the mound and walk up; he'd scrape with his left foot three times and his right foot. He did all sorts of superstitious things that I swear was the same every single game all season long! It got to the point where it was almost hilarious to watch him go through this routine. To warm up, he'd throw, like, four breaking balls and four fastballs and two sliders—whatever he had—in the same sequence. And, man, don't walk up on the mound on him because it was taboo! It was funny! It was just hilarious! You gotta watch him sometime and see how superstitious he was!
>
> [Third baseman] Jeff Hamilton was incredibly superstitious also. Every inning he came in, he would put his batting glove, or glove, inside his other regular fielding glove. It'd be turned at a certain angle. He went over and took three sips of water, spit them out, and then took three regular sips of water. And I'm telling you, it was not a phony. This thing went on for the entire season. Of all the things that these guys did that were so superstitious, it was crazy. And everybody watched it, and everybody respected that he was gonna be that way. But you'd better not touch his glove or move it anyplace else—because he couldn't play if everything wasn't in order.

Leary, however, remembers Brian Holton, not Ricky Horton, as the guy who was superstitious in the bullpen. "[Holton] was, by far, the most superstitious baseball player I ever played with. In the fourth inning he would 'lasso' his left thumb with a shoelace! He jumped over foul lines, and all that stuff. And he called people 'Bub.'"

When told that Dempsey had remembered the superstitious reliever as Horton, Leary shrugs. "Horton might have been [as well]? As I was a reliever and spot starter in 1987, I was in the bullpen a lot. In '88 when Horton was on the team, I wasn't in the bullpen until the postseason [and wouldn't know]! [But] to me, superstitions are the end zone of 'routine.' And 'Confidence' equals 'Routine' plus 'Preparation' plus 'Game Plan.' Dr. Bob Rotella, PhD Sports Psychologist for the PGA Tour, wrote that formula in one of his books. It simplifies coaching, the mental game, as routine is usually the trouble area for high-end athletes."

Leary does agree with Dempsey that it was best to leave the superstitious guys alone and let them do their routines. "Having a good routine triggers confidence in the mind and crowds out negativity. So, superstitions *act* like a routine as they are part of the routine in preparing to compete. Just like starting to play catch at 7:07 p.m. for a 7:37 p.m. start—as back in '88 we started games at 7:37 p.m. Failing to prepare is preparing to fail. Routine, preparation, and game plan are *all* part of preparing. A golfer going through a pre-putt routine on a two-foot putt is a prime example. You have to be a machine. The mind can be a hindrance without proper mental techniques!"

A quick Google search revealed that Brian Holton was the one who was superstitious. According to Holton himself in 1990, he buttoned only three buttons of his warm-up jacket. He had a towel and wrapped it around his neck, with the tag always being on the right side. In his left pocket he had a lasso. He always sat in the same seat in the bullpen and in the dugout. He came up on the mound from the first-base side. He wiped the pitching rubber four times with each leg and spun around clockwise. He caught the ball with one foot on the dirt and the other foot on the grass. He never changed catchers; if the catcher wasn't ready after batting in the last half-inning, Holton would wait for him. He didn't throw to anyone else. And he sang, "You take the high road, I'll take the low road" on the mound to himself.[3]

But hey, whatever he did, it all worked out for the Dodgers in 1988.

Leary brings up an interesting name: John Tudor. The ace of the mid-1980s Cardinals, Tudor was 21–8 with a 1.93 ERA in 1985 but pitched poorly in Game 7 of that year's World Series against Kansas City. Two years later, Tudor's Redbirds again lost the seventh game of the World Series, this time to Minnesota. He finally got that elusive championship ring in 1988 after being traded to Los Angeles in August for Pedro Guerrero. "I was disappointed and surprised," Tudor said of the trade when asked to reflect upon it years later. "But it gave me a chance to go over there and win a world championship, which didn't happen in St. Louis. The Dodgers were a good team with a good group of guys. Then I got a chance to come back and play my last season in St. Louis [in 1990], so it was kind of the best of both worlds."[4]

Mariano Duncan, Los Angeles's primary shortstop in 1985–1986, was disappointed the club traded Guerrero, his best friend on the Dodgers. "I remember in 1985 when I came up to the major leagues, Pedro Guerrero really took care of me," reflects Duncan now.

> He took the opportunity to take me [under] his wing, like his son. He told me, "Mariano, I know we're from the same hometown. I know how great you are. I want to help with your family. I just want you to come with me." I was so glad that he did. I lived in Pedro's house until he found me a place to live. He found me a car to drive. He took care of me in every way. When any major-league player does that kind of stuff to a rookie, to a player who just came up to the major leagues for the first time, you have to thank that player and you have to thank God to meet somebody like him. And Pedro became my best friend on the Dodgers.

Horton, like Tudor, was with the Cardinals in 1985 and 1987, and won a ring with the '88 Dodgers. While he pitched effectively in the 1988 NLCS, he struggled the following year—logging a 5.06 ERA in 23 relief appearances—and was released in July 1989. And, like Tudor, the left-handed Horton returned to the Cardinals to finish his major-league career. Following a midseason release by St. Louis in 1990, Horton ended his professional career with minor-league stops in the Milwaukee and Cleveland organizations.

Because he didn't pitch in the 1988 postseason, it's easy to forget that Dodgers ace-to-be Ramon Martinez was a member of that championship ball club. But Martinez, who was called up in August, actually got in a handful of starts over the final weeks of the season. In fact, before the acquisition of John Tudor, the Dodgers had planned to, at least temporarily, go with a four-man rotation of Hershiser, Leary, Belcher, and Martinez.

Now a special assignment pitching instructor with Baltimore, Martinez is happy to reflect on 1988 today. "That year helped establish my career," Martinez recalls. "When I got called up in mid-August in 1988, I had the opportunity to spend time with the team, with a championship team, that year. I didn't participate in the World Series but I helped the team, especially that moment when I [made] my debut."

While most baseball fans might remember Martinez as the older brother of Hall of Famer Pedro Martinez, that's not how he's remembered by Dodgers supporters. Ramon Martinez—best known by Dodgers fans as the ace of the talented, yet underachieving, 1990s LA teams—was one of the NL's best pitchers during his prime. A four-time 15-game winner with the Dodgers, Martinez went 20–6 in 1990 at age 22 to finish second in the NL Cy Young Award balloting behind Pittsburgh's Doug Drabek.

A 20-year-old at the time of his 1988 call-up, Martinez had gone a combined 13–6 with a 2.58 ERA in 24 starts with Double-A San Antonio and Triple-A Albuquerque. In his first two weeks in the majors, Martinez picked up where he left off, logging a 1.73 ERA in his first four big-league starts. In three of them, he allowed just one run while working at least seven full innings. "I remember we had a one-game lead in the Western Division [actually, it was a two-and-a-half-game lead] and we were gonna to face the San Francisco Giants," Martinez says now. "They were [three and a half games] behind and in second place [actually, third place]. I got the opportunity, in my debut, to pitch against San Francisco. I went seven and two-thirds innings—and didn't give up any runs [in the Dodgers' extra-inning victory]—and [two days] after that we [started] a seven-game [winning] streak. That [helped to] establish my career. At that time, the Giants had a great team and I had to face them in my debut. The Dodgers and Giants play a lot of times. It's a big rivalry."

After a second straight no-decision in his second start against Philadelphia and then a 5–1 loss on August 23 to David Cone and the Mets, Martinez finally collected his first major-league victory on August 29 when he defeated Dennis Martinez (no relation) and the Montreal Expos, 2–1. Martinez would split time between the rotation and the bullpen in

September—pitching more effectively as a reliever—and was on the post-season roster for neither the NLCS nor the World Series.

Both Martinez and Tudor filled in admirably down the stretch—but do you remember the guys whom they replaced in August? Well, Shawn Hillegas, whose 10th and final start came on August 8, was demoted to Triple-A—and would be traded to the White Sox before the end of the month—and Fernando Valenzuela, sidelined by shoulder woes for much of the second half of 1988, was injured at that point. There was also Hall-of-Famer-to-be Don Sutton, who'd returned to Los Angeles at age 43 for his final season. Signed by general manager Fred Claire on January 5th, Sutton missed 37 games with a sore elbow and won only 3 of his 16 starts with a 3.92 ERA—going winless in his last nine outings—before being released on August 10. He never pitched again, finishing his career with a 324–256 lifetime record.

The day Sutton was released, Claire had nothing but praise for him. Wanting the insurance of a veteran arm since Bob Welch had been dealt to Oakland, Claire didn't regret signing Sutton in the off-season. "I knew the person I was dealing with," said Claire, "and liked all the parts of that person and the personality. . . . You look at Don's record last year [with the Angels]—190 innings and 34 starts—and I thought it was a good move, that he could help us. I felt initially that Don would contribute even if it was only our young pitchers watching how he went through spring training. I have no reservations about it."[5]

"I would have liked this year and this relationship to end on a more successful note," Sutton said then. "I would not have wanted the injury, would have wanted more wins." Knowing the Dodgers were in a tight divisional race at the time—following his latest loss, a 6–0 debacle in Cincinnati, Los Angeles's lead in the NL West had shrunk to a half game—Sutton said he wasn't surprised the club made the move. "I've always known it was a possibility, but it was not always in the forefront in my mind."[6]

Sutton's final victory may have come on May 14, but his contributions to the 1988 club were significant, according to closer Jay Howell. "Don Sutton was very influential for me," recalls Howell now.

> I played with him over in Oakland [in 1985]—and he was traded to Anaheim [that September]—and then he had come back to the Dodg-

ers. It was sad to see him go [when he left Oakland] but he really enjoyed Anaheim. I think he really liked it there. So, I was happy that he could thrive with the Angels. He was with us in '88 and he did some yeoman's work for us. He'd been with LA before, obviously, the bulk of his career, and he had come back. And Lasorda was going to the bullpen early with him. That wasn't fun for him. Don was still putting up some decent numbers and doing a good job and taking the ball. We needed it. It was too bad. But maybe Tommy just felt like he had the bullpen and he could use it and he could have Hershiser eat innings and take them away from Don. Not everything was perfect on our team, but Don would take the ball every fifth day. You knew what you got [out of him]. I kind of felt sad to see him go. He was a wealth of knowledge.

Don had a really great way of going through an opposing lineup and categorizing them and it was really interesting the way he'd do it. Most of the time you'd go through the lineup, and you look at it and you go, "This guy, I don't want him on the bases." You look at "Who's gonna steal a base? I'll make sure I pitch to this guy. I'll give him a pitch to hit; I just don't want to walk him." But Don was more "I want to know who the first-ball hitters are. I want to know who's hacking." He'd go down through the lineup. That was his first thing. He'd circle the first-ball hitters, and it was down the line for him. You know, the stolen-base guys. Then he'd look at walks. Who takes walks? Who's taking? He'd start with first-ball hitters. Who were your hackers? Then who's walking; who's got an eye? He would know. "This guy's taking the first pitch. I'm throwing him a cockshot first pitch [a pitch right down the middle]." Don had a really good way of going through the lineup and setting it up for you, and as a relief pitcher I would go to him. I would say, "Hey. You mind if we go through this?"

"Yeah, no problem!" He'd walk you right on through it. I'd never done that that way, the way that Don would do it. A wealth of knowledge.

Dempsey, who was 38 years old in 1988, smiles when Sutton's name is brought up and then says,

Don just was a veteran guy that was just so typical for that ball club. Those were the kind of people that knew the game of baseball, we were all on our last legs, the last couple years of our careers, we still had a little fight left in us, and a lot of knowledge about the game. Don Sutton had pitched some amazing games over the course of his career. And he'd done so much. To have him back for that brief period, some of the games that he pitched for us, he pitched his heart out. That's what it was. He wasn't the Don Sutton of the earlier, younger days. He didn't have that capability. But he was so typical for that team because he had a great baseball knowledge in how to get hitters out. He still had a lot of tricks up his sleeve and he used every single one of them. The box was empty when he pitched his last game for the Dodgers. It was over with. And he moved on, but he left that little bit. He left everything on the table when he pitched those last few games with the Dodgers. I can remember that about him.

I watched him as he pulled his little tricks and he could throw that knuckle-curveball, and the things that he did in order to make it all happen. And I just smiled at him. It was amazing. He had a great, great career for the Dodgers—but man, when we all got together at the end, we just did everything we had to do, to win baseball games, and that just made it so much fun.

Since Kirk Gibson was the National League MVP in 1988, people might assume he led the Dodgers in RBIs that season. Wrong. And while Gibson and Mickey Hatcher each had eight RBIs in the postseason to lead the club, they weren't the only Dodgers with that total.

Well, people have forgotten. They've forgotten that right fielder Mike Marshall, despite his reputation for being a player who wouldn't play hurt, was the Dodgers' leading RBI man with 82 while clubbing 20 homers. He then added eight postseason RBIs, including a three-run homer in Game 2 of the World Series against Oakland. But as far as memorable postseason moments are concerned, fans remember homers by Gibson and Mike Scioscia—but they've mostly forgotten about Marshall's three-run blast, one that gave Los Angeles a two-games-to-none lead, meaning Oakland had little margin for error the rest of the way as the A's had to win four of the next five games.

Marshall, now the associate head baseball coach at New Mexico Highlands University, spoke in 2013 to *Los Angeles Times* writer Bill Plaschke, who noted the following of the much-maligned right fielder during his playing days: "Marshall was ripped by the media and public for not playing hurt. He was attacked by his teammates for not being tough." When LA fans thought of Marshall, they thought of his whining and his inability to start Game 4 in Oakland. He was perceived to be, as Plaschke noted, "an enigma, the anti-Gibby, a star dressed in a shrug," and a player who simply didn't have the passion for the game.[7]

"I know I was not very well liked," Marshall told Plaschke in the 2013 piece in the *Times*. "I wish I had been tougher. I wish I had played. . . . Some of my injuries, did I handle them perfectly? No, that was something I always regretted. I always wanted to be 100 percent. I always thought the team was better with someone else if I wasn't 100 percent. But, in hindsight, there are times I should have just rolled myself out there."[8]

While fans might have forgotten Marshall's contributions in 1988, members of that team haven't. Steve Sax, teammates with him in Los Angeles from 1981 to 1988, calls Marshall a terrific player. "Mike Marshall was a big threat in our lineup. He had tremendous power," Sax says. "He was an outstanding teammate, and we couldn't have accomplished what we did that year without him. Mike Marshall had incredible power. I mean, when he connected with the ball in the right way, it was a no-doubter. He hit some of the furthest home runs I've ever seen. His power would play in any era, big-time. He just had big-time power."

Fred Claire, who traded Marshall (along with Alejandro Peña) to the Mets following the 1989 season for second baseman/center fielder Juan Samuel, has nothing but praise for his right fielder. "Mike Marshall was definitely a big part of our team in '88. He had a good major-league career for 11 years. And like many of the players from '88, he's remained in the game. He's now a college coach and it's great to see him have that passion for the game and continue to contribute to it. Mike was tremendous for our ball club during his years in the organization and shouldn't be forgotten for his contributions to the Los Angeles Dodgers."

REGULAR-SEASON MEMORIES

Whenever you think of the '88 Dodgers, you don't necessarily think about the regular season as much as you think about the Kirk Gibson home run and the upset victory in the World Series.

—Mel Antonen, *Sports Illustrated* writer

The 1988 baseball season is probably remembered today for the beginning of the Oakland A's dominance in the American League. Led by the pitching of Dennis Eckersley and Dave Stewart, as well as the power and speed of Jose Canseco—baseball's first 40–40 man as the A's masher smacked 42 home runs and stole 40 bases—and a fearsome lineup, Oakland won the first of its three consecutive AL pennants. In Boston, 1988 is remembered for "Morgan Magic," as third-base coach Joe Morgan took over as manager at the All-Star break and the Red Sox won his first 12 games—and 19 of his first 20. A month later, Boston set a major-league record with its 24th straight home victory en route to its second AL East title in three years.

Around the majors, there were other noteworthy feats. The Baltimore Orioles began the season with a major-league record of 21 consecutive losses. Toronto's George Bell became the first player ever to hit three homers on Opening Day. Future Hall of Famer Roberto Alomar collected his first hit. Left-hander Frank Viola, the Minnesota Twins ace, notched 24 wins to capture the AL Cy Young Award, one year after earning World Series MVP honors against the Cardinals. Teammate Jeff Reardon became the first pitcher to save 40 games in both leagues after registering 42 saves for Montreal three years earlier. The New York Mets, led by Darryl Strawberry and Kevin McReynolds, won 100 games and captured the NL East for the second time in three years. In August, the Chicago Cubs finally had their first game under the lights at Wrigley Field, the last major-league ballpark to have lights installed for play after dark. Cincinnati's Tom Browning, who'd won 20 games as a rookie in 1985, threw a 1–0 perfect game on September 16 against the Dodgers to become only the second left-hander in the 20th century to toss a perfecto, joining Hall of Famer Sandy Koufax (1965).

Of course, the final month of the season saw Orel Hershiser pitch shutout after shutout after shutout to, in his final start of the year, break Don Drysdale's major-league record with 59 consecutive scoreless innings pitched. Hershiser followed that performance up by throwing two more shutouts in the postseason, as Los Angeles upset both the Mets and Oakland to win the World Series.

And there was also Kirk Gibson's memorable World Series home run off Eckersley to win Game 1, setting the tone for the Dodgers' five-game victory.

Now, as for the Dodgers' regular season—other than Hershiser's streak? Those in the media—including veteran sportswriters Bob Ryan, Mel Antonen, and Bob Nightengale—say today that nothing really stands out. If you were to ask any casual baseball fan, you might expect the same answer.

Yes, Los Angeles might have been the champions, but perhaps the main takeaway from 1988 for some relates to steroids, as the so-called steroids era is generally considered to have begun in the late 1980s. On September 28, 1988, *Washington Post* sports columnist Thomas Boswell put the notion of steroids in baseball into the air, saying on national television that the A's Canseco was "the most conspicuous example of a player who has made himself great with steroids."[1] (The day before on September 27, Jamaican-born Canadian sprinter Ben Johnson was stripped of his gold medal in the 100-meter sprint at the 1988 Summer Olympics in Seoul after he was tested positive for stanozolol, a steroid that is commonly used as a performance enhancer and is banned from use in international sports competition.) That October, when Oakland went to Fenway Park to play Boston in the ALCS (American League Championship Series), Red Sox rooters in right field chanted "STER-oids! STER-oids!" at Canseco, who at the time denied taking any performance-enhancing drugs. Of course, today we know better—thanks to Canseco's 2005 tell-all book in which he admitted using anabolic steroids during his playing career—and in 2010 Boswell would say on Ken Burns's *Baseball* documentary that the problem of steroids in baseball "was already spreading by 1988."[2]

For others, the takeaway from 1988 might be how managers, with Oakland's Tony La Russa leading the way, began to change the way bullpens were being utilized. The way that La Russa used Eckersley, his bullpen ace, for almost exclusively ninth-inning situations, would become a model that other teams followed, and the modern closer had been invented. The concept of a multi-inning closer, or stopper, died a quick death. For instance, when Dan Quisenberry saved 45 games in 1983 and Bruce Sutter saved 45 in 1984, they worked 139 and 122 2/3 innings, respectively. In 1988, Eckersley needed only 72 2/3 innings to save 45 games, and only 23 of his 60 appearances lasted longer than one inning. Two years later, Bobby Thigpen would set a record with 57 saves, but he did it while working only 88 2/3 innings. Lee Smith, who'd become baseball's all-time saves leader in 1993, wouldn't pitch more than 75 innings in a season in the 1990s. In 1991 Smith, who finished second in the NL Cy Young balloting, would save 47 games while logging 73 innings. By the 1990s, teams across baseball had adopted La Russa's model of employing a single closer and using him for strictly one inning. By contrast, Jay Howell, the Dodgers' primary closer in 1988, notched 21 saves with 8 of them being two-inning efforts and 6 others lasting more than one inning. But he wasn't the only one Tommy Lasorda employed to close out ball games; Alejandro Peña was called upon to notch 12 saves, Jesse Orosco had 9, and even rookie starter Tim Belcher was moved to the bullpen—and collected 4 saves—when Howell went on the disabled list in June.

The modern closer concept became so widespread overnight that only one major-leaguer recorded 30-plus saves with 100-plus innings in the same season during the 1990s: Doug Jones in 1992 with Houston. Jones, who debuted with Milwaukee in 1982, has his own theory about the birth of the modern closer, which again has been traced to 1988. It's about having a hard thrower come in for one inning to throw heat and bring the crowd to its feet—and at the same time making sure he doesn't blow out his arm due to overwork. "Baseball has changed over the years to all the different things that basically cable TV brought on," Jones, who notched 36 saves and 111 2/3 innings with the 1992 Astros, said in 2015.

> The excitement of the strikeout and a long home run . . . really sells tickets. So, velocity and the ability to hit lots of home runs seems to be what ownership wants. They want the excitement of the game and the thrill of that. When I pitched, it was all about getting outs. They didn't care what you did. No matter what it looked like, get them out. It was all about making the hitters swing and get outs. . . . We didn't have pitch counts. We didn't have the restrictions they put on kids today for their health. You were either healthy enough to do it, or you didn't play very often—or at all. That was the case when I was coming up. . . . [But] today's crop of pitchers in the last generation have been all about the radar gun. . . . Now they've got everybody monitored by two or three health professionals on a daily basis."[3]

Really, the main takeaway from 1988, depending on who you talk to, could be the beginning of widespread steroid use or the birth of the modern closer. It was the start of an Oakland dynasty that never was. It was the year the Cubs finally played home games under the lights. But don't tell those Dodgers that nothing stands out when thinking back to Chavez Ravine in 1988. For them, the regular season was actually filled with many memorable moments and comebacks.

For second baseman Steve Sax, one that stands out came on Opening Day, April 4, against San Francisco at Dodger Stadium. Although the Dodgers lost 5–1, Sax thought the way the first at-bat of the season went was an omen that this was going to be a very special year. "My first at-bat that year was against Dave Dravecky—I was the leadoff hitter—and I remember during Double-A ball, my brother [Dave Sax] was on the team with me," Sax recalls today.

> Dave Dravecky broke five bats from our family. He broke three of mine and two of my brother's in one game with that really good cut fastball he was throwing. I remember getting up against him, facing him, Opening Day of 1988. And I thought, he might just start me off with a fastball—and then put me away with that really good, that really devastating cutter that he had. So, I was just sitting on a fastball, looking for a fastball, and sure enough, he threw a fastball and I hit a home run on the first pitch of the season. And that was like an omen for our

year—because I didn't hit very many home runs. I swung one time, I hit a home run on the first pitch of the season, and that was kinda the way the season went for us.

Sax had two of the Dodgers' three hits that afternoon, and would finish the year with five home runs, one off his career high accomplished in each of the previous two seasons. Two of those 1988 homers came in Philadelphia on May 26—a wild, 10–8 victory where he again homered on the first pitch leading off the game—but Sax thinks the one he hit on Opening Day was the biggest.

Sax had a strong season at the plate—batting .277 with 175 hits in an NL-leading 632 at-bats—but Rick Dempsey praises the second baseman's defense that year. In fact, Dempsey believes his advice to Sax before the season made a difference with his throwing. "I gotta take a little credit for Steve Sax," the veteran catcher says with a laugh. "Remember how much trouble he had throwing the ball to first base when he had that phobia?"

As the story goes, in a game against Montreal in 1983, Sax went out to be the relay man on a ball hit into the alley. The throw came in to Sax, and he didn't need to throw it hard but did. The ball scooted away, allowing a run to score. The play got in Sax's head, and he began to lose confidence. Soon after, balls hit to him would become an adventure; seemingly every other throw he made from second base landed in the stands.

Sax's habit of throwing away balls soon became part of baseball lore. Pedro Guerrero, whom the Dodgers had moved from the outfield to start at third base as a replacement for the departed Ron Cey, had a reputation for being a defensive liability at third. As the story goes, Guerrero would tell Tommy Lasorda he first prayed the ball would never be hit to him—and then prayed it was not hit to Sax.

Dempsey knew he could help the Dodgers' second baseman. "I was just kinda laughing about that one day in spring training," Dempsey recalls.

And I said, "You know, I can correct that phobia." Saxie goes, "Why? How are you gonna do it?" He couldn't throw the ball to first base! And we knew how important he was to the ball club.

So, I went out there to him one day and said, "Have you ever been on a rowboat where you had a rudder and you moved the rudder to the right and the boat went left, and you moved the rudder to the left and the boat went right. Have you ever seen that?"

"I've seen that before!"

I said, "That's what your problem is! You've got your rudder all fucked up!"

Sax was puzzled by the analogy, so Dempsey elaborated:

"When you field the ball, Saxie, and you go to throw the ball to first base, do not let your rudder go to the left. Because then you're gonna throw it to the right!"

"What do you mean by that?"

"As soon as you catch the ball, and you're looking at the first baseman, when you go to throw it, take your back leg and as soon as you let the ball go, follow your throw to the bag instead of letting your leg go back around behind you in a different direction."

He goes, "Okay." So, he fielded a few groundballs, and as he threw the ball nice and easy to first base, he kinda followed his throw with his right leg to first base.

Overnight, he was so excited about the fact that he could throw the ball where he wanted to throw. Everything fell back in place again for him! We all laughed about it, and we moved on. But he never made a throwing error again from second base. It was amazing!

Dempsey, because of his ties with the Orioles and his broadcasting work in Baltimore, hasn't talked much about his Dodger days for years. But he clearly enjoys taking a look back some 30 years later. "You know, that was pretty cool. That was a nice little thing," Dempsey pauses for a moment before chuckling about the Sax story.

That was another thing that came together for the Dodgers—Saxie not having any trouble throwing the ball to first base! It was so funny just how lightly everybody got criticized—but how easily everybody took it. Nobody got upset! Guys just overcame a lot of that kinda shit, because this team was a loose team. But once we got on a roll, man, we just went with it. That's all I can say. We just went with it, and we had the best time ever. For the older guys, we just had a great time. There were characters everywhere you looked. There was somebody who could just make you laugh every day.

You know, I haven't talked much about the Dodgers since then—so, it's fun to reflect back 30 years later.

First baseman Franklin Stubbs began the season on the bench, but when right fielder Mike Davis struggled for the first two months, some changes were made. Mike Marshall, who'd been playing first base, returned to right field, and Stubbs began to receive more playing time at first base. Although he batted only .223 on the year, Stubbs did have some key hits and moments, including doubling and scoring the winning run on a balk in an extra-inning game in San Francisco in late July. His first-pitch, three-run pinch-hit homer won a game for Tim Belcher at Wrigley Field in mid-July. And on July 6, Stubbs had another memorable hit against the defending NL champion Cardinals, as his eighth-inning grand slam off closer Todd Worrell broke up a tie game and helped the Dodgers sweep St. Louis out of town.

Franklin Stubbs, shown here in a Brewers uniform, began the 1988 season as a Stuntman for the Dodgers before becoming the team's everyday first baseman. *Milwaukee Brewers*

"I remember that one," Stubbs says with a smile. "Worrell was a tough pitcher. I knew he didn't walk many people and he didn't want to walk in the winning run. In that at-bat I fouled off his high fastball and I felt like I had a pretty good chance to get a pitch to hit. If he couldn't throw that pitch by me, I could pretty much hit anything else he threw. I remember he did throw me a nasty slider in that at-bat and I was able to foul it off. Then he threw me a 3-and-2 fastball, and I hit it over the right-field wall at Dodger Stadium."

There was one game Stubbs never got into, one in which Tommy Lasorda originally wanted him in as a pinch hitter. It was July 16 at Wrigley Field, a game that was eventually called in the ninth with the score tied 2–2 due to darkness. "I'd started that game at first base and we were trailing by a run but the tying run was at third base with one out," recalls infielder Tracy Woodson. "I was up to hit, but they brought in a right-hander to face me."

The season hadn't begun well for Woodson, who'd battled with Jeff Hamilton for the third-base job during spring training. Hamilton had won the job, which meant Woodson had opened the year in Triple-A. Eager to return to the majors, Woodson batted .319 with 17 homers and 73 RBIs in 85 games with Albuquerque, and was eventually rewarded with a call-up in early July. On July 26, Hamilton would go down with an injury, and Woodson would receive the opportunity to start at third base. From the time he was recalled, Woodson would start 46 of the next 81 games. While he struggled initially—on August 7 his batting average had dipped to .191 with just three extra-base hits in 24 games—he would go on a roll in down the stretch. From August 8 to September 9, Woodson would hit .297 in 25 games, including an 11-game hitting streak. He'd return to the bench when Hamilton returned to action—but still found at-bats in September and ended his second year in the big leagues batting .249.

But on July 16 in Chicago, Woodson didn't know Hamilton would soon be sidelined with an injury. He had to prove to the Dodgers right away that he could contribute. It was the sixth inning and the Dodgers were trailing 2–1. The Cubs removed Jamie Moyer, a lefty, and brought in right-handed reliever Les Lancaster to face Woodson. Lasorda was ready to make a counter move, with the left-handed-hitting Stubbs coming in to pinch-hit. It was an obvious move to make with the game on the line; after all, the right-handed-hitting Woodson, called up in early July from Triple-A, was batting only .083 (1 for 12) for the Dodgers up to that point.

"Tommy goes, 'Hey Stubby, get ready.' But I told Tommy, 'No, no, Tommy, I'm gonna get this guy in. I'm gonna drive him in.' So Tommy let me hit—he was surprised that I said that, but I think he didn't have a choice because I backed him into a corner a little bit—and I hit a sacrifice fly to center to score the run," Woodson says. "Later, Kirk Gibson came up to me and goes, 'I'm glad you got that guy in, because you would've been sent back to Triple-A if you hadn't!' But in that situation, I didn't want to get pinch-hit for. They brought me up for a reason."

Stubbs might have lost an at-bat that day, but he looks at Lasorda's decision to stick with Woodson as one of the reasons the players loved their manager. "Whoever his players were, he was behind them 100 percent. He let you go out and play the game," Stubbs says. "Didn't hold you back. If you saw something or thought something or noticed something, and you could take advantage of it, he would let you do it. He gave you freedom to do that. You know, just don't make a mistake—which we didn't."

Center fielder John Shelby, who batted .263 with 10 homers and 16 stolen bases in 1988, had his ups and downs offensively. He had a 24-game hitting streak from May 14 to June 9 but then went through a 40-game stretch from mid-July to late August where he hit just .187. He also smacked a solo home run off Danny Darwin for the only run in Orel Hershiser's fourth consecutive shutout in September, a 1–0 victory over Houston on September 20. But Shelby, known as being a quiet player during his career and never one to bring attention to himself, focuses on the team's success when asked to pick out his most vivid regular-season moment from 1988. "No one particular thing stands out," Shelby says. "I just remember it being a fun season especially when we won games."

When pressed again, Shelby deflects and praises the other members of the Dodgers. "The Stuntmen were awesome and we couldn't have [done] what we did without them. Every part of our team played an important role. Orel was consistent and dominant. Fred Claire is an awesome human being and did an outstanding job as the GM putting our team together. He deserves a lot of recognition and praise for that. Tommy was one of my all-time favorite managers. He was great to play for, always energetic, enthusiastic, and no one cared about the Dodgers more than him."

Closer Jay Howell, who for seven consecutive seasons from 1985 to 1991 led his club in saves (or was tied for the lead), also prefers to focus on the contributions of his teammates. He recalls how utility men Dave Anderson and Jeff Hamilton were able to fill in when starting shortstop Alfredo Griffin was sidelined with a broken hand in May and third baseman Pedro Guerrero was out of the lineup with recurring neck problems in June. Griffin, who suffered a broken bone in his right hand when he was hit by a Dwight Gooden fastball on May 21, would be out of action for a total of 59 games before returning in late July. Guerrero, meanwhile, would miss 51 games after being sidelined on June 5. The Dodgers, one of baseball's most surprising teams in 1988 after two disastrous seasons, would remain in first place throughout the first half of the season despite having the unheralded Anderson and Hamilton in the lineup. But over a 45-game stretch from May 21 to July 8, Anderson—a .242 hitter over a 10-year career—would bat .304. He started 60 of 61 games from May 21 through July 24, and Los Angeles went 35–26 in that span.

"On that bench, there were big contributors," Howell, who notched 142 saves between 1985 and 1991, says now. "There were several guys like that, [for example,] Dave Anderson coming in to play shortstop for Alfredo Griffin. Here's a guy not known for his bat, but when he came in—I think Griffin dislocated his thumb or something like that—Anderson hit over .300 for about a month. He'd never done that before, yet there he was. He was integral. Another guy who was fantastic: Jeff Hamilton, [in his first full season], playing third base. And I don't know if Jeff ever had a year comparable to what he did that year."

For some players, 1988 marked their best season in the majors, period. For right-hander Tim Leary, it was definitely the case. A 17-game winner that season, Leary never again had the same level of success. Interestingly, at the time, he actually wasn't even sure he'd make the big-league club in 1988. And Leary, who fulfilled his childhood dream of playing for his hometown Dodgers, actually didn't start out in the organization. Before becoming a world champion in Los Angeles, he'd been given up by two different clubs.

Selected by the Mets second overall in the 1979 draft out of UCLA, Leary made his major-league debut in 1981 but faced only seven batters before leaving with a strained elbow. When he strained his elbow a second time during spring training the following year, Leary was shut down for the entire season. Between 1981 and 1984, he made a total of 23 appearances (including 10 starts) for the Mets while also spending time in Triple-A before being sent to Milwaukee in January 1985 as part of a four-team trade also involving Texas and Kansas City. Although it was a change of scenery for the former first-round pick, Leary was still headed for Triple-A. "I remember I had a great season in Vancouver, the Triple-A club for the Brewers, in 1985 that set me up for eight straight years in the majors starting mid-September that year," Leary reflects today from his home in Santa Monica, California. "I remember Tom Candiotti was on that team in 1985—and at one point he was a Dodger—[where] he really mastered his knuckleball to go along with his curveball, slider, and 82 to 83 m.p.h. fastball. We played at Nat Bailey Stadium in Vancouver and won the Pacific Coast League championship that year. It was good memories."

In 1986, Leary was promoted to the Brewers, winning 12 of his 30 starts. But that December, he was traded, along with right-handed reliever Tim Crews, to the Dodgers for first baseman Greg Brock. "I was surprised that the Brewers would trade away their number 2 starting pitcher; at the end of 1986, I went 6–3 to end up 12–12 and was clearly number 2 behind Ted Higuera! And I really liked it there," Leary says today.

> However, going to the winter workouts at Dodger Stadium in January '87 and for two weeks in February was awesome! But it didn't really hit me that I was a Dodger until Vero Beach and Sandy Koufax is in uniform as a spring coach! And then to watch Fernando [Valenzuela], Orel [Hershiser], Bob Welch, and others throw bullpens with precision. . . . For some unknown reason, I'd lost three to five miles per hour off my fastball from the previous seven of nine years [as I was hurt in '81 and '82]. I did everything normal in the off-season. So, I had a very poor spring, barely made the team, spot started, and relieved. Terrible year! But at least I was in the majors getting major-league experience—as nothing can prepare you for the majors except the majors [because] the level of play is five times above Triple-A or the best winter ball!

Leary isn't exaggerating about having a "terrible" 1987, a year in which he went 3–11 with a 4.76 ERA in 39 appearances, including 12 starts.

Tim Leary went 12–12 in 1986 and was the Brewers' number 2 starter, but Milwaukee still traded the right-hander to the Dodgers in the off-season. *Milwaukee Brewers*

I didn't pitch well in spring or during the season, and I knew I needed winter ball. My wife was pregnant and Mike Brito, the scout who signed Fernando [Valenzuela], helped me get with the Tijuana team in the Mexican Winter League. That was perfect, as I could drive 163 miles, pitch nine innings, put ice on my shoulder, and drive home! Then I go to class the next day at UCLA as I needed just one final quarter to graduate! The owner of Los Potros de Tijuana let me skip the games that I didn't pitch in. Over the course of the season and postseason I trained with small weights for my shoulder muscles and did everything else a pitcher needs to do between starts.

After leading the Potros de Tijuana to the 1987–1988 winter league championship, Leary didn't have much time to rest.

I took a break from mid-January to mid-February and went to spring training with the best stuff that I'd ever had. As I'd gotten my fastball velocity back, my arm was super strong, and most important was I'd improved my split-finger pitch so as to throw it in any count. That set me up for a great spring—which I desperately needed for fear of being released—and in my third start of the season I pitched a shutout against the Padres with 11 strikeouts. My confidence kept growing and by the second half of the season I won 10 games after the All-Star break.

Indeed. Leary was 10–5 with a 2.96 ERA in his 17 second-half starts, finishing 3 victories shy of 20. When he reflects back, Leary remembers a run he had in July, when the Dodgers went on a roll despite the fact that they were expected to fall out of first place. "I pitched four games on one road trip," he recalls. "All on three days' rest, except the first one, which was the first game after the All-Star break. I went seven innings, nine innings, nine innings, [and finally] nine-[plus] innings [before getting pulled after a single leading off the 10th]."

Actually, the starts were on July 14 in Chicago, July 18 in St. Louis, July 23 in Pittsburgh, and July 27 in San Francisco, meaning two of those starts came on three days' rest. Leary had the standard four days' rest when he made that start against the Pirates. Nonetheless, he was outstanding in all of those outings, recording three victories. "[I had a] game-winning RBI against Rick Sutcliffe in a 1–0 win at Wrigley; a [6–2] win in Pittsburgh; a 1–0 win in St. Louis with [Mike] Marshall hitting a homer in the top of the ninth and I completed the game; then [I was pulled] with [none] out and a runner on first base in the 10th inning in San Francisco . . . and we lost."

Another one of Leary's victories came on August 2 at Dodger Stadium, where the right-hander tossed his fifth shutout to defeat Jose Rijo and the Reds, 2–0. He didn't pitch when the teams met again at Riverfront Stadium a week later, but third-base coach Joey Amalfitano remembers an incident in Cincinnati where a frantic Fred Claire made a panicky comment—and pitching coach Ron Perranoski had an amusing response to the general manager.

Dodgers fans will remember Amalfitano as a longtime fixture in the coach's box for the ball club as he spent 16 seasons as Tommy Lasorda's third-base coach, from 1983 to 1998. A rookie infielder on the 1954 World Series champion New York Giants—and six decades later a special assistant in player development for the 2010s San Francisco Giants—Amalfitano has the rare distinction of being a member of World Championship teams on both the Dodgers and Giants. Now working in player development in the minor leagues within the Giants organization, Amalfitano has seen three World Championship teams in San Francisco in recent years, in 2010, 2012, and 2014. But of course, 1988 will always have a place in his heart. "I have a lot of very fond moments of that year," Amalfitano recalls with a smile. "I remember [something] Fred [said] in Cincinnati. We'd gone from a seven-game lead to a half-game lead, and Perranoski, the pitching coach, was standing there. I remember Fred saying, 'Oh my God, we're down to half a game.' We had, like, about 28 more games to go at that point."

Actually, on that date, Wednesday, August 10, the Dodgers had exactly 50 games remaining going into that night's action. The night before, they'd lost 6–0 to Reds left-hander Danny Jackson, allowing second-place Houston to move to within a half game. Los Angeles, despite leading the division, was also starting to have some question marks on its pitching staff. Left-hander Fernando Valenzuela had been placed on the disabled list with a left shoulder strain earlier in the month, and veteran right-hander Don Sutton, who'd been ineffective, was about to be released.

"Perranoski made a classic statement," says Amalfitano, continuing his story. "He said, 'Oh, Fred, look at it this way. We've got a half-game lead with only 28 to go. If we had a half-game lead with 150 to go, that wouldn't be too good!' So, we ended up winning by [seven] games. I'll always remember that. He said, 'Well, look at it this way. We have a half-game lead with 28 to go versus a half-game lead with 150 to go! You know?'"

Of course, during that era, it was first place or nothing. No other option was available. The divisions hadn't yet been realigned to place Houston—and Cincinnati—outside of the NL West. There was no wild card in 1988, no NL Central, and no postseason for second-place teams. Naturally, Claire became nervous as the lead had shrunk from eight games three short weeks earlier—after Leary, on a five-hitter, had blanked the Cardinals 1–0 in St. Louis on July 18—to now a measly half game.

"I don't know what it did for us, [if it helped motivate the team] . . . but I'll never forget that," adds Amalfitano. "I thought it was a great line, and it was true! It's true! You never wanna get ahead of yourself. I was with the Cubs [as a coach] in 1969 and we had a helluva nice lead in August [being ahead of both the Cardinals and Mets by nine games as late as August 16], but we didn't make it. We didn't make it. [The 2016] team [which won the World Series for the Cubs' first championship since 1908] obviously has helped to make everyone forget that year!"

On that August 10 night in Cincinnati, Hershiser worked eight-plus strong innings to outpitch Jose Rijo, and the Dodgers won 8–5—while the Astros lost ground by losing to San Francisco. Yet, Cincinnati manager Pete Rose, whose fourth-place Reds were seven games back, boldly told reporters afterward that LA wouldn't win the NL West. "I personally don't think the Dodgers are going to win it," Rose proclaimed, citing the injury to Valenzuela as a crippling blow to Los Angeles's chances. "I said a couple of weeks ago that I want to catch the two teams in front of us, which are Houston and San Francisco. I think the Dodgers are going to miss Fernando Valenzuela. It's going to put a lot of pressure on their young pitchers. And they've got a tough schedule to go."[4]

As it turned out, the Reds manager was wrong. From that point, Los Angeles never looked back; the Dodgers went on to win 9 of their next 11 games, and their lead was never seriously challenged again. "I didn't mean it disrespectfully," Rose would reflect later that season about his August comments. "All I was saying was that when you take a Fernando Valenzuela off a pitching staff, it puts more pressure on a Tim Leary and Ramon Martinez and Tim Belcher. . . . They've withstood the challenges and I give them credit."[5]

Rick Dempsey recalls Belcher getting yanked early in a game during that series in Cincinnati.

I remember Tim had gone a couple of innings and kinda ran out of gas. Fred came in and said right in front of Tim, "Hey, what do you think of this guy?" I said, "You know, he's a darn good five-inning pitcher." And boy, did Tim ever get mad! I said, "Tim, the way you pitch, you don't have a good off-speed pitch, and after five innings, they figure you out." The next thing you know, he has an off-speed pitch overnight—a split-finger fastball—and the guy goes 12–6 and he learned something about pitching. When he won his 100th big-league game [in 1996 with Kansas City], he sent me the ball.

Tim Belcher, a rookie in 1988, won three games in the postseason for the Dodgers. *Michael McCormick*

One of the wins during the Dodgers' hot streak following Hershiser's victory over Rijo came on Saturday, August 13, at home against San Francisco. The game marked the major-league debut of future ace Ramon Martinez, who started and pitched into the eighth inning while throwing 123 pitches. "We were in a pennant race at the time when I made my major-league debut. I got the opportunity, in my debut, to pitch against San Francisco," Martinez recalls. "I went seven and two-thirds innings, and didn't give up any runs." Martinez, just four outs away from a shutout, wouldn't be around for what turned out to be a wild finish. He was pulled after putting two men on with two outs in the eighth. In came Jesse Orosco, who promptly gave up a game-tying single to Will Clark (with the run charged to Martinez).

With the score 1–1 in the 11th, Pedro Guerrero led off with a fly to right that fell in for a single. As Guerrero took his lead at first base, he thought that Giants pitcher Joe Price had balked and let the umpires know what he thought. No balk was called. But the fun was about to begin. Moments later, Guerrero advanced to second on a passed ball, and he started talking to second-base umpire Joe West about the non-balk call. The discussion became heated, and Guerrero began yelling at West, who ejected Pedro. Lasorda came out to argue, and he got tossed too.

Once order was restored, Franklin Stubbs pinch ran for Guerrero. A walk put runners on first and second, and John Shelby tried to lay down a sacrifice bunt. The ball rolled foul, ruled the umpires—but the Dodgers thought Price touched the ball, which would make it fair and load the bases. Mike Davis, the Dodgers' last available position player on the bench, stood on the top step of the dugout and argued vehemently about the call. Home-plate umpire Paul Runge told him to sit down, but when Davis didn't, Runge ejected him. Two outs later, with runners now on second and third, the Giants walked Alfredo Griffin to load the bases. The pitcher's spot was due up, and the Dodgers, with Davis having been ejected, were out of position players.

With nobody else left, they turned to pitcher Tim Leary, who'd just beaten the Giants with his arm—and bat—the day before, to pinch-hit for reliever Alejandro Peña. The day before, he'd worked eight and a third innings for the win, gotten a single off Rick Reuschel, and delivered a sacrifice fly. Now, against Price, Leary worked the count full and, with the count at 3 and 2, knew the Giants reliever had to throw a fastball. There was no way Price was going to throw another pitcher something other than a fastball with the bases loaded and a full count, with the winning run on third. Just as everyone in the ballpark predicted, Price threw a fastball, and Leary—who'd bat .290 in his first 100 major-league at-bats—smashed a single up the middle for the game-winner.

"Bases loaded, base hit up the middle! I remember that game," says Dempsey, recalling the contest as though it'd happened just yesterday. "It was amazing. It just didn't matter . . . I don't know how it all happened. You just can't explain it, how we won a lot of those ball games. You just can't explain it. And man, oh man, we were all kinda shaking our heads, but we were running with it."

"I got to pinch-hit in the 11th inning in August against the Giants," recalls Leary with a smile. "They walked the number 8 hitter to get to me with the bases loaded and two outs. I got the count to 3 and 2, got a base hit up the middle, and we win the game! It was a special game against the Giants. The night before, I'd pitched and won."

As Leary explains, he loved the NL because he had a chance to bat every start. "Hitting was always my favorite part of sports. Other than my 'walk-off' single in the 11th inning in that August 13, 1988, game versus the Giants, I had some other memorable hits. My first home run was off [Hall of Famer] Steve Carlton in '84 at [Philadelphia's] Veterans Stadium [on April 20 while with the Mets]. No decision for either of us [as we were tied] 1–1 after nine innings [and the Mets won in 10 innings]. But I was [almost] a .300 hitter in my first 100 at-bats!"

Comeback victories on August 20 and September 11—with Kirk Gibson leading the way—were memorable too.

In the August 20th contest against Montreal in Los Angeles, Tim Belcher and the Dodgers trailed 3–0 going into the seventh. Back-to-back doubles by Gibson and Mike Marshall put the Dodgers on the scoreboard, before Tracy Woodson homered in the eighth to make it a 3–2 game. In the ninth, Gibson hit a bloop single to drive in the tying run and then proceeded to steal second base. With two outs and John Shelby at the plate, Expos pitcher Joe Hesketh threw a pitch that eluded catcher Nelson Santovenia and went all the way to the backstop screen. Gibson raced to third and then decided to try and score—and he slid in ahead of Santovenia's throw to Hesketh, who was covering the plate but failed to make the tag as the ball popped out of his glove.

Gibson then leaped in the air and waved his left arm jubilantly as his teammates all raced out of the dugout to embrace him. It was the Dodgers' sixth straight win as they'd now opened up a huge five-and-a-half-game lead in the NL West with only 40 games left.

Woodson remembers that game well. "I think I homered in, like, the seventh or eighth inning to cut it to one run," he says today.

And then we tied it up, and [Gibson] was at second base. I remember the catcher was Nelson Santovenia, and [the ball] went between his legs. And when it hit the backstop, it kinda shot up in the air. I can always remember Gibson coming around third base and just not stopping—and just flying through, sliding in, and then just pumping his fist. That's kinda how I liked it. I always wanted to pump my fist if we won it—because I got excited. I think just to see his excitement . . . I mean, that was a big win for us. It was later in the season, and we kept getting closer and closer to clinching. So, I think that just kinda showed what kind of a player he was, especially his speed. For a big guy, he could run.

"You know what, that was a great play," adds Stubbs. "You didn't see that very often. Back then, Dodger Stadium had a little more room behind home plate, so you could actually do that. And he was great instinctively at doing those things."

Jay Howell recalls that game as well, and mentions the rally cry that came after victories like that one. "What was crazy about that year was there were certain games that were big wins," Howell says.

We'd come into the clubhouse, and we'd all get together, and there was this rally. It'd simply begin with, "What a team!" Then Gibson would yell, "What . . . a . . . *fucking* . . . team!" And Tommy Lasorda would yell, "What a team!" Then it'd go, "What . . . a . . . *fucking* . . . team!" I mean, literally everybody joined in. I'd never seen anything quite like it. One of the games was where Gibson scored from second base in a tie game on a passed ball. You don't see that every day. We came in, and it was the rally cry again, and it just built.

"That was funny," laughs second baseman Steve Sax. "We'd win a game and when we were coming off the field, everybody would yell, 'What a fucking team!' Lasorda started that. And then we just sort of picked it up. It was funny."

When reminded about the rally cry, Dempsey could only smile. "Oh yeah, I remember that. That was created, I think, by Tommy Lasorda, who had to be, by far, the most fun manager I've ever been around." Stubbs, meanwhile, credits the team leader for the rally cry. "That was Kirk Gibson, man," says Stubbs. "His main thing was, 'It doesn't matter what, it doesn't matter who; the most important thing is that we win.'

That was his rally call at the end of every victory when we came into the clubhouse. He'd always say, 'What an eff-ing team,' and we kinda rallied behind that."

Three weeks later against Cincinnati on September 11th, Gibson and Belcher both homered off left-hander Tom Browning (who'd toss a 1–0 perfect game against these same Dodgers five days later at Riverfront Stadium). But Los Angeles trailed 3–2 in the bottom of the ninth with Gibson on first base and two outs, facing Reds closer John Franco. On an 0-and-2 pitch, Shelby hit a grounder down the third-base line, and rookie third baseman Chris Sabo dove to stop the ball from getting through the infield. Sabo, however, then threw away the potential game-ending out, and Gibson hustled all the way from first to score the tying run.

Jeff Hamilton, the very next batter, worked the count full against Franco, and then ended the game with a homer to left field. "This is the biggest hit I've ever had," Hamilton said that day. "I had a home run last year to win a game against San Diego, but this one happened in the middle of a pennant race. It's much bigger."[6]

As for Gibson's mad dash around the bases? With the ball rolling into foul territory after Sabo had skipped his throw past first baseman Dave Concepcion, third-base coach Joe Amalfitano frantically waved Gibson home—but he didn't have to. Gibson had already decided he was coming home, putting his head down and churning toward home. "He didn't even have to wave," Gibson said afterward. "Joe and I hook up real good and I can tell if I've got a chance. My position with Joe is this: Always give me the shot to score, let me put the pressure on them."[7]

For the other Dodgers, seeing Gibson's intensity and the way he always gave 100 percent made everybody else feel like they had to give 100 percent, too. "No doubt," agrees Woodson. "Yeah, and we just found different ways to win games. It wasn't necessarily conventional. We probably did not have the best lineup there was in baseball. We had to do different things with different guys. You know, Gibson was the MVP and he hit 20-something home runs. He didn't hit, like, 50 home runs or have 150 RBIs. I think that was a big deal, because that was how much he meant to the team. Same with Hershiser. He just went out there every day and you knew you had a chance to win every day he pitched."

Dempsey believes the whole year was magic. How else could you explain all the dramatic victories throughout that summer? "You just can't explain how we won a lot of those ball games," says Dempsey, shaking his head. "We had enough older guys around there, Mickey Hatcher and myself. We look at each other and go, 'You know what? Let's just go with it!' It was almost miraculous how many times we came back to win ball games. But Tommy Lasorda never let us get down about any loss that we had. The players themselves would never let the young guys put too much pressure on themselves. We just knew exactly what to say, exactly what to do. And it paid off every day."

As Howell recalls, the team celebrated victories with that "What . . . a . . . *fucking* . . . team!" rally cry. But when the team lost—which didn't happen too often—Gibson wouldn't allow any nonsense in the clubhouse. "And then there was the [Pedro] Guerrero story," remembers Howell.

> That one was huge; it came late in the year. That one was where we were in St. Louis, and Guerrero had a couple of the Cardinal players slip in the backside of the locker room. We'd lost the game, and Guerrero was already showered and ready to go. Gibson walked up—I think there were two guys; I don't remember who they were [but] I was standing right there—and he said to them, "Hey, if you fuckers wanna be in our locker room so bad, why don't you tell your agents to trade you here? Otherwise, get the fuck out!" Guerrero didn't like it, and had a few words. Gibson took his jersey and just snapped the buttons right off of it, [and] pulled the jersey off. "Oh really? Well, then let's just fucking go!" Then all of a sudden, there was a little bit of a mêlée there. We all separated them, and Gibson went into Lasorda's office and said, "Tomorrow when I suit up, if that guy is in this locker room, then I'm out. He's gone or I'm gone." Needless to say, he was traded that day, and we got John Tudor.

In reality, no trade was conducted immediately following the Dodgers–Cardinals series in St. Louis, which concluded on July 20. But less than a month later, on August 16, Guerrero was indeed dealt to the Cardinals for Tudor, who'd make nine starts for Los Angeles down the stretch. "It was a fun team. It was a good group of guys," Tudor acknowledged in 2016 when asked about the trade. "I wasn't quite sure about it when I first got traded over there—because I really loved playing in St. Louis. But going over there—with Mike Marshall, Gibby, Mike Scioscia, Mickey Hatcher, and Orel, and Jay Howell and the other pitchers, it was a tightly-knit group of guys and they were on a mission. It was fun to watch."[8]

With 20 games left in the season, Los Angeles had a five-game lead over second-place Houston. Three nights later, Hershiser would pitch his third consecutive shutout, beating Atlanta 1–0. The winning run came in dramatic fashion when Gibson walked to lead off the bottom of the ninth and Marshall followed with a game-ending double to left field. With 17 games remaining, the Dodgers now had a six-and-a-half-game lead. The NL West race was essentially over. They'd make it official on September 26 in San Diego, rallying for three runs and a 3–2 victory to clinch the division.

For Tracy Woodson, there was one other memorable regular-season event that stood out: Hershiser's pitching in September. Hershiser would add fourth and fifth consecutive shutouts—blanking Houston and San Francisco—before working 10 scoreless innings in his final start on September 28. That gave him 59 consecutive scoreless innings, breaking ex-Dodger Don Drysdale's major-league record of 58 2/3 set 20 years earlier. "Anytime I get asked about my most memorable moments in the big leagues, I always say there are two things," says Woodson from his home in Richmond, Virginia. "One, I homered off Nolan Ryan for my first major-league home run." The two-run shot off baseball's all-time strikeout king came on April 13, 1987, in Woodson's seventh major-league game. Woodson would hit only four more the rest of his career. "Two, winning the World Series. If there was a personal favorite moment, it's the Ryan home run. If it's a group, together where you win something, there's no question; there's not even a second choice. It's the 1988 World Series victory."

But in terms of a memorable regular-season event from 1988? For Woodson, it unequivocally was Hershiser's scoreless-innings streak. "I think Hershiser's pitching streak was the biggest," says Woodson.

I don't think that will ever be broken. I don't think it can be broken. It's just too hard now. It's gonna be hard for a pitcher to go nine innings nowadays, and he was doing that a lot. I mean, that was six full games plus. I just don't think you're gonna have six complete games in a row nowadays, especially with the bullpens the way they are and the specialty roles. If you go seven innings now, you're looking at having to go eight games now to even get close to that mark. That's gonna be a tough mark to break.

CHAPTER FIVE

HERSHISER'S CONSECUTIVE SCORELESS INNINGS STREAK

[Hershiser] just didn't give hitters a chance; he didn't give hitters hittable pitches. So when they were swinging, they were hitting the top of the baseball, primarily. Everything he threw was at the knees or below. He was more than just in a zone. It was real precision. Every hit he gave up was just a jam-shot flare, or a grounder that got through the infield somehow. He just never made a mistake.

—Tim Leary, Dodgers pitcher

Entering play on September 1, 1988, you could argue that Reds left-hander Danny Jackson was the best pitcher in the National League. Traded by Kansas City with shortstop Angel Salazar to Cincinnati for right-hander Ted Power and shortstop Kurt Stillwell during the off-season, Jackson was having a career year. He'd won 11 of 13 decisions in July and August—giving him an NL-leading 19 victories entering September. Out in Los Angeles, right-hander Orel Hershiser, in his fourth full season as a starting pitcher, was having an outstanding year, too. Not historic by any means—18–8 with a 2.84 ERA through August—but Hershiser was still in the Cy Young Award conversation with one month to go.

As former Dodgers pitcher Jerry Reuss reminds us, though, Hershiser had had a career year in 1985, when he was 19–3 with a minuscule 2.03 ERA in his first full season as a starter. A September call-up in 1983, Hershiser appeared in eight games—all in relief—and wasn't used in the Dodgers' four-game NLCS defeat against Philadelphia. He then appeared in 45 games the following season, making 20 starts. Hershiser began the year as a reliever and had a 5.96 ERA in late May of 1984, before he made his first big-league start on May 26 against the Mets, where he allowed just one run in six and a third innings. Tommy Lasorda then inserted him into the starting rotation—where Hershiser stayed throughout the second half of the year—and the right-hander put together a scoreless streak of 33 2/3 innings before Atlanta's Dale Murphy, the two-time reigning National League MVP, smacked a two-run homer on July 24th to end it.

In 1985, Hershiser began the year as Los Angeles's number 3 starter behind Fernando Valenzuela and Reuss. By season's end, he'd established himself as one of baseball's top young pitchers. In addition to his 19 victories, he also completed 9 of his 34 starts with five shutouts. However, with the Mets' Dwight Gooden (24–4, 1.53 ERA, eight shutouts) and the Cardinals' John Tudor (21–8, 1.93, 10 shutouts) both having career seasons, Hershiser had no shot at winning the Cy Young—and finished third in the voting.

"I wasn't a part of the '88 team," says Reuss, who pitched for the Dodgers from 1979 to 1987.

> I knew some of the players and some of the people involved with the '88 team, but I left in early '87. But with Orel, he had a pretty good year in 1985, probably a career year that anybody would like to have. I think he found out who he was in 1985, and because of the way he pitched, he was the top pitcher that year. It was an interesting group in that we had four guys [Valenzuela, Hershiser, myself, and Bob Welch] record double figures [in victories] and if I'm not mistaken, all four of us had over 200 innings. [Actually, the '85 Dodgers had three 200-inning pitchers, with Welch finishing 32 2/3 short.] We gave a lot of innings, and when you have four guys like that, it was a good staff. Orel had a really good year in 1985. But then he came along in 1988 and left that in the dust.

In 1988, both Hershiser and Jackson entered September on a roll. Both had pitched on August 30, with Jackson beating Pittsburgh to improve to 19–6—and coming just one out shy of his 13th complete game—and Hershiser defeating Montreal while going the distance for his 18th victory. Table 5.1 shows how Jackson and Hershiser stacked up entering September.

Table 5.1. Jackson and Hershiser Pitching Stats through August 1988

	Jackson	Hershiser
Wins	19 (1st in NL)	18 (2nd in NL)
Complete Games	12 (1st)	10 (tied for 2nd)
Starts	29 (tied for 2nd)	28
Innings	215.1 (1st)	212 (2nd)
Shutouts	5 (tied for 2nd)	3
ERA	2.59	2.84
Strikeouts	140	144
Walks	59	64
Batting Average	.210	.226

Neither was among the top four in ERA, and Hershiser wasn't even the ERA leader on his own team, as the newly acquired John Tudor was second in the NL at 2.37 and teammate Tim Leary (with an NL-best six shutouts) was fourth at 2.44. If the awards had been handed out at that time, Jackson—by virtue of being ahead in all of the above categories except for strikeouts—would likely have finished just ahead of Hershiser in the Cy Young balloting.

Then, on September 4, Jackson blanked the Cubs 17–0 at Wrigley Field (tying Leary for the NL lead in shutouts) for win number 20—while also going 4 for 5 with four runs scored—and followed that up five nights later with his 14th complete game, a 5–2 victory at Dodger Stadium (over rookie Ramon Martinez), to improve to 21–6 with a 2.43 ERA. It appeared the Cincinnati left-hander—coming off a 9–18 season in Kansas City—had clinched the Cy Young. Pete Rose, his manager, certainly thought so. "I've been around several Cy Young winners," Rose said then. "I played with [four-time winner] Steve Carlton. I played with John Denny [who won the NL award in '83]. I'm not taking anything away from Hershiser, but I think it would be a mistake not to vote for Danny Jackson."[1]

But not so fast. Beginning in September, Hershiser would go on a run never before seen in the history of the game. One night after Jackson's 20th win—and sixth shutout—Hershiser notched a shutout of his own, beating Atlanta 3–0. He would, in fact, not be scored upon the entire month (see table 5.2 for Hershiser's September stats).

Including four shutout innings to close out the Montreal game back on August 30, Hershiser had put together a streak of 59 consecutive scoreless innings, breaking the major-league record of 58 2/3 set by

Table 5.2. Orel Hershiser's September 1988 Starts

Date	Opponent (Score)	Innings Pitched	Hits Allowed	Runs Allowed	Bases on Balls	Strikeouts	
September 5	@Braves (3–0)	9	4	0	1	8	Win, shutout
September 10	Reds (5–0)	9	7	0	3	8	Win, shutout
September 14	Braves (1–0)	9	6	0	2	8	Win, shutout
September 19	@Astros (1–0)	9	4	0	0	5	Win, shutout
September 23	@Giants (3–0)	9	5	0	2	2	Win, shutout
September 28	@Padres (1–2, 16 innings)	10	4	0	1	3	No decision

Hall of Famer Don Drysdale in 1968. In all, Hershiser had thrown the equivalent of six-plus consecutive shutouts—five complete-game efforts in a row, plus 10 scoreless innings in a no-decision in his last start of the year in San Diego—establishing a record that will likely not be matched. "[The streak] got down to the last couple of games, so it really was intensifying," pitching coach Ron Perranoski recalled in 1998 when the *Los Angeles Times* did a retrospective on the 1988 Dodgers. "I remember warming him up in the bullpen in San Diego in that last game. And Orel looked at me, 'Gosh, Perry, I'm really nervous.' I looked at him and said, 'I'm real nervous, too.' And he had to go 10 innings [to break the record], and that's the way it went."[2]

With the scoreless-innings streak to end the season, Hershiser finished 23–8 with a 2.26 ERA, including 15 complete games and eight shutouts. He ranked third in the league in ERA, behind only Joe Magrane (2.18) and David Cone (2.22). In November, Hershiser was named the unanimous winner of the NL Cy Young Award, receiving all 24 first-place votes and 120 points in the balloting. "I always thought he was going to win it, anyway," Jackson reflected when asked about it one spring-training afternoon three years later.[3]

Jackson, who'd be hammered for 16 earned runs over his final four starts, finished the year at 23–8 and 2.73. In what was easily his best season in the majors, Jackson notched 15 complete games and six shut-outs—and received 15 second-place votes for the Cy Young balloting to finish second behind Hershiser. He'd pitch nine more seasons but reached double figures in victories only twice more, going 12–11 in 1993 and 14–6 in 1994. In fact, those two seasons were the only ones in which the left-hander would be over .500 for the remainder of his career.

But never mind the fact that Hershiser was better than Jackson or Cone or any other pitcher in 1988. While the MLB Network didn't include Hershiser's campaign on its top nine list of baseball's greatest pitching seasons in its "Prime Nine" feature, some observers felt the Bulldog's campaign deserved a place on the list. According to baseball historian John Thorn, Hershiser's season was so dominant that it should be compared to the seasons of some of the all-time greats. "Hershiser in '88 is a pitching season to rank up there with Bob Gibson's in 1968, with Walter Johnson's 1913," Thorn opined in the ESPN series *Battle Lines* in 2003.[4] Bob Gibson in 1968 was 22–9 with a 1.12 ERA in 304 2/3 innings while

Orel Hershiser, who did not allow a run in the entire month of September, won 23 games in 1988 and the NL Cy Young Award. He also pitched back-to-back shutouts during the 1988 postseason, leading the Dodgers to the World Series championship. *Michael McCormick*

completing 28 of 34 starts, 13 of them for shutouts. From June 2 through July 30 that year, Gibson threw 99 innings and allowed just two runs—one on a catchable wild pitch and the other on a bloop double that landed inches fair. Gibson was so dominant that season that MLB lowered the height of the mound the following year from 15 inches to 10 inches—and also reduced the size of the strike zone. Johnson, pitching in the dead-ball era, was 36–7 with a 1.14 ERA in 1913, notching 10 shutouts while pitching 346 innings.

Hershiser, pitching in a completely different era, definitely had a season to remember with all the zeroes in September. "I can't say anything more about Orel Hershiser," Tommy Lasorda remarked that October. "I saw it, but I can't believe it. I can't believe anybody can achieve his mastery for as long as he did. . . . There's no way we'd be in the Fall Classic without the Bulldog."[5]

LA closer Jay Howell, who rarely got into Hershiser's games that season, still chuckles about an interview involving the Dodgers ace that year. "I remember one funny interview we'd done," Howell says now.

> We were sitting at a table. They had the cameras on us. [Tim] Belcher might have been in there. Hershiser was there. It was the pitchers. There might have been four or five of us sitting there and talking pitching. "What do you do? How do you prepare for a game?" All the rest of us had said our little bit. "We get ready for the game, we prepare, go over the hitters . . ." We're talking general stuff like that.
>
> And then Hershiser starts talking. Orel is being somewhat humble in his discussion about how he gets his mind right and how he gets prepared for a game. He tries to keep it simple. He's talking general stuff like that. I jumped in the middle and said, "So, what you're telling us is that you throw all your shutouts in the same way?" And I'll never forget the look on his face. It was just absolutely fantastic. That's what it was like. You throw all your shutouts the same way. You prepare yourself and you go out there, and there are certain hitters you do not give in to. If you want to walk 'em, you walk 'em. You strategize your game, you pitch to the guys you know you can get out, and you throw the pitch that you know gives you the best odds. And you do that over nearly 10 games in a row? I mean, only one other guy has been close to that.

Left-hander John Tudor, who'd come over from St. Louis in August (and finished fourth in ERA at 2.32, just behind Hershiser), had a chance to witness the entire streak, including the record-breaking game where Hershiser and Padres pitcher Andy Hawkins both threw 10 shutout innings. "You don't really say anything to anybody about a streak—I mean, that's an unwritten rule; it's like telling somebody he's throwing a no-hitter in the bottom of the ninth—but Orel was incredible that year," Tudor recalled in 2016. "He was pretty amazing. I think the most amazing thing of that whole situation was that he broke Drysdale's record [in his final start] of the season—and in order for him to break that record, both pitchers [Hershiser and Hawkins] had to throw nine shutout innings in order for Orel to have a chance to throw the 10th, in order for him to break Drysdale's record. That's a really incredible little piece of information right there in itself. But he was obviously locked in. . . . He was fun to watch."[6]

Tim Leary, the 1979 number 1 June draft pick of the Mets, agrees that you never talk to a player who has a streak going. As he recalls too, Los Angeles was actually trying to score runs in regulation in Hershiser's final start, but the baseball gods simply didn't let them. "You know about the baseball superstition when no one talks to a pitcher throwing a no-hitter? No one would talk to Orel about it," Leary says. "And during that game in San Diego, we were trying to score. If we could've won that game 10–0, we would have and it would've been fine. But as things happened, it was just magical that it did go extra innings, and that was a record that was apparently made to be broken."

When asked to reflect on Hershiser's performance some 25 years later, infielder Dave Anderson told Josh Suchon, former radio cohost of the postgame *DodgerTalk*, that during the streak, the infielders had a lot of easy groundballs to catch. "The amazing thing is it was happening at the end of the season, after a lot of innings under his belt. It's not like he did it at the beginning of the season. It was right at the end," Anderson added. "I can't remember a time there was a runner on third and two outs, where there was pressure on us defensively. . . . You just knew he was going to pitch, how he wanted things to happen. It was amazing to be part of that, to see a team with big-league hitters not get a guy to second base."[7]

Steve Sax, Hershiser's teammate for the first six years of the right-hander's big-league career, recalls the Bulldog was simply unhittable in 1988. "Orel was just dead on, everything he did that year. He was just dominant," Sax says now. "He was just throwing fastball, slider. He was basically throwing two pitches. But his fastball had a lot of movement. He was always ahead of the hitters. He had just pinpoint control. He never got himself in a bind where he was in a lot of hitter's counts a lot of the time. He was mostly in the pitcher's count—so he was dictating the sequence during the at-bat."

According to Howell, Hershiser's streak actually benefited the rest of the team because it took the pressure away from everybody else because all the attention was on the ace right-hander with the season winding down. "The season that Hershiser put together was just really mind-blowing. To watch him do that was really, really something," Howell explains today. "And it took some focus off of the finish for the year, which was nice. It was always, 'Well, Hershiser's starting. Is he gonna do it? Is he gonna . . . ?' It took some eyeballs off of the rest of the team. I mean, there was a lot of pressure on him to do it, to pull it off. It's one of the best things to ever be a part of, to watch somebody have that kind of success. And really, everybody was pulling for him to do it."

Mike Scioscia was behind the plate for nearly the entire streak—with Rick Dempsey catching Hershiser in one game—but third-string catcher Gilberto Reyes believes he was Hershiser's good-luck charm. Although he never caught an official inning in a game pitched by Hershiser that year, Reyes was actually a big part of the streak. He'd often race down from the bullpen to warm up Hershiser before many of those September innings. "You know, I brought good luck to Orel Hershiser," Reyes recalls with a laugh. "To be honest, sometimes Orel wanted me to warm him up before the game when he was pitching. Then let's say Dempsey or Scioscia made the last out [of a half inning]; I always was the one who had to catch Orel between innings until [Dempsey or] Scioscia got ready [putting their catcher's gear on]. I was always there when Orel threw the first couple of [warm-up] pitches. I knew how he liked it—outside, inside. After the first pitch, I knew the second pitch was gonna be outside. I really knew his rhythm. He didn't have to say anything."

Hershiser's streak is now considered by sports historians to be among the greatest in sports history, with some ranking it just behind Joe DiMaggio's famous 56-game hitting streak in 1941. Several pitchers in the NL have put together impressive scoreless-innings streaks since 1988, but nobody has gotten to even 50. Arizona's Brandon Webb had a scoreless-innings streak in 2007 snapped at 42. In 2014, Los Angeles's Clayton Kershaw put together a 41-inning scoreless streak before giving up a solo homer to end it. The following year, teammate Zack Greinke had a streak of 45 2/3 scoreless innings before it was broken. Mets knuckleballer R. A. Dickey once had a streak of 44 2/3 consecutive innings without allowing an earned run in 2012 (where he allowed just one unearned run).

Count *Boston Globe* columnist Bob Ryan as one of those who doesn't think Hershiser's record will be broken, but he wouldn't use the word *never*.

"Well, *never* is a dangerous word," Ryan explains today.

I'm sure that when Drysdale [set his record in 1968], people said it wasn't gonna be broken. I'm sure before that, it was [Walter Johnson in 1913 with 55 2/3 consecutive scoreless innings] and people didn't think *that* was gonna be broken. It's *unlikely*. I'll go with that. The game has changed. Pitchers don't develop nine-inning rhythms any longer; it's no longer a concept that anyone could grasp. It's highly unlikely. In order to do it, you'd have to pitch in succession of sevens, most likely [meaning, go seven shutout innings every time out]; it'd take a lot of starts in a row. I think it's pretty safe to say that Orel has a very good chance of going to his grave holding that record. But two treacherous words to employ in these matters are *always* and *never*. But for that year in 1988, everything about the Dodgers was just Hershiser, Hershiser, Hershiser.

At least one person, though, *hopes* Hershiser's record gets broken one day—and that's Hershiser himself. "The legacy of the scoreless innings streak might grow with each year," he opined in 2012, "but I hope somebody breaks it. Some people might be surprised to hear that. But I truly do. Records are meant to be broken. I want another pitcher to experience what I was able to experience. It was an out-of-body experience. I'll be so happy for that pitcher."[8]

Veteran sportswriter Bob Nightengale thinks someone might come along and break the record. After all, in the 2010s, baseball fans had witnessed some magnificent prolonged pitching feats by several of the game's best pitchers. Madison Bumgarner, for instance, led San Francisco to the 2014 World Series title by logging a 1.03 ERA while throwing a postseason-record 52 2/3 innings. Bumgarner, the MVP of both the 2014 NLCS and World Series, has often been mentioned in the same breath as Giants Hall of Famer Christy Mathewson, who pitched three shutouts in the 1905 World Series. The Cubs' Jake Arrieta, in 2015, won the Cy Young Award after setting a major-league record with a second-half ERA of 0.75. Dodgers ace Clayton Kershaw, regarded as the best pitcher of his generation, had captured five ERA championships and three Cy Young Awards—not to mention a MVP Award as well—entering the 2018 season.

"I think those are comparable, particularly with what Bumgarner did in the postseason in 2014," says Nightengale today. "Obviously, Arrieta had an unbelievable streak. [It's remarkable] what Kershaw does [every season]. I think [a scoreless-innings streak as long as Hershiser's] will be done again. I do. I think because guys have come so close."

Franklin Stubbs thinks the record will fall someday—for the simple reason that records are made to be broken. But he says it's still a record to be appreciated. "You know what? All streaks are made to be broken," Stubbs explains.

> You've gotta set something to have somebody break it. You know, Don Drysdale set it before [Hershiser did]. And then he set it. Those things go on for a while. They don't just happen overnight. It takes a special season for a special pitcher to be able to do it. I'm sure eventually somebody will come along. But I don't know if it's gonna be in the near future or not. But eventually it will get broken—like [how] every record falls. It's a very special record, and I tell you what, he had a tremendous season and I was very proud to be a part of it.

Ben Hines, the Dodgers' hitting coach, probably sums things up the best. It really doesn't matter if his streak is broken down the road. What's important was that Hershiser led the Dodgers to a World Championship. "We had a group of guys that were leaders, guys like Mike Scioscia and Kirk Gibson," Hines recalls today from his home in Los Angeles County, where he's retired after being a member of major-league coaching staffs in Seattle (1984), Los Angeles (1985–1986, 1988–1993), and Houston (1994). "But the guy that really won the season and the National League Championship and World Series was Orel Hershiser. He pitched excellent all year long. I don't know how many [losing streaks] he stopped during the season. I think he had to have [done] it at least six or seven times after we had lost consecutive games, and he flipped the momentum several times during the season."

Hines is right. Without Hershiser's pitching, the Dodgers might not have gotten to the postseason. They might not have won it all.

And we may never again see a pitcher dominate the way Hershiser did in the final seven weeks of 1988.

PART TWO
THE METS SERIES

I remember the NLCS with the Mets most of all. New York had won 10 of 11 regular-season meetings with the Dodgers with one rainout not made up. To me, the most important hit of the 1988 season was Mike Scioscia's two-run homer off Dwight Gooden in the ninth inning of Game 4 in New York that tied the contest, 4–4. The Mets were that close to taking a 3–1 edge in the series. Without Scioscia's home run, the Dodgers probably don't win the National League pennant and the World Series.

—Ross Porter, Dodgers play-by-play announcer

METS SERIES MOMENTS
More Mets Magic

I remember the Jay Howell incident with the pine tar. I remember writing about that and defending him. I know I did. As I recall, it was terrible weather. I remember it being wet. It had to do with inclement weather, as I recall. I remember I defended him in the papers back then. Would I defend him today? I dunno! But I'm pretty sure I defended him. I did then.

—Bob Ryan, *Boston Globe* columnist

The summer of 1988 was a great one for sports fans in Los Angeles. In June, the LA Lakers overcame a three-games-to-two NBA Finals deficit to defeat the Detroit Pistons for their 11th World Championship. They were the NBA's first repeat champions since the Boston Celtics in 1968–1969, fulfilling coach Pat Riley's promise to repeat as champions. While the LA Kings had had another typical bad season—they finished below .500 for the sixth time in seven seasons and hadn't won a playoff series since 1982—the organization made a huge splash in August by acquiring superstar Wayne Gretzky, an eight-time National Hockey League MVP, in a blockbuster trade with Edmonton. And in April, the LA Raiders drafted Heisman Trophy winner Tim Brown, making the star wide receiver the third player on the Raiders roster to have won the Heisman (with the others being Marcus Allen and two-sport star Bo Jackson, who was also playing for the Kansas City Royals). While the Raiders wouldn't make the playoffs in 1988, Brown would spend 16 productive seasons with the organization and be inducted into the Pro Football Hall of Fame in 2015.

And yes, the Dodgers surprised the baseball world by capturing the NL West with 94 wins in 1988—despite many pundits predicting them to finish fourth in the division. It was a good run by a team that suffered numerous injuries—with shortstop Alfredo Griffin, slugger Pedro Guerrero (who was eventually traded in August), left-hander Fernando Valenzuela, and even closer Jay Howell, among others, sidelined at various points during the summer—and it was a treat witnessing Orel Hershiser's record scoreless-innings streak to close out the year.

But now in October, the Dodgers were expected to be brushed aside by the New York Mets in the NLCS. And even if they somehow survived that series, there was also Oakland, another dominant club, to contend with. Yes, it had been a good run, but this was not going to be the Dodgers' year. While the Dodgers would have home-field advantage in both the playoffs and World Series—thanks to an old rule that had the NL West and AL East receiving home-field in the league championship series in even-numbered years and the NL champion having it in the World Series—they weren't going to be favored in either series. (The AL West and NL East, meanwhile, would have home-field in odd-numbered years and the AL champ having it in the Fall Classic, regardless of regular-season records.)

Ramon Martinez, a rookie in 1988, recalls how all the experts counted Los Angeles out right from the beginning. "That year when we won, I enjoyed being part of that team. I was a reserve because they didn't use four starters that year," Martinez says today. "They used three starters, pretty much, and then you get a day off, and then Orel Hershiser took over everything. It was unbelievable the way the team was built. It was one group of guys that wanted to play and wanted to get the job done. It was an unbelievable experience."

Because the Dodgers already had Hershiser, Tim Leary, and Tim Belcher—and general manager Fred Claire then acquired John Tudor, the NL's ERA leader at the time of the trade in August—there was no need for Martinez in the postseason. There was no need for that fifth starter and, as it turned out, there wasn't much of a need for Tudor, the fourth starter who ultimately was lost to an injury in the World Series, either. Still, Martinez was with the team and learned a great deal being on the bench in September and during the postseason.

I remember that year when we played the Mets—who were one of the best teams in baseball—we beat the Mets. But nobody gave us a chance. People said, "Well, you beat the Mets; they're a good team. But you're never gonna beat Oakland." Oakland was an unbelievable team that year. They got [Jose] Canseco, [Mark] McGwire, and a bunch of those guys. "OK, you've got no chance." But when we played Oakland, we beat them, and we beat them easier than the Mets. Like I said, it was unbelievable. I didn't participate, but I remember that time I was practicing and keeping [in shape]. I was like an emergency guy just in case they needed somebody. That was a great experience. It was one of the best experiences I had, playing for that '88 team."

The Dodgers had lost 10 of 11 to New York during the season, and the star-studded Mets—who'd already won the World Series in 1986—were expected to establish a dynasty. With the likes of Darryl Strawberry in the lineup and Dwight Gooden on the mound, the Mets had won 100 games and were poised to make it two championships in three years.

And the Mets didn't just dominate on the scoreboard; in the first regular-season series between the two clubs they managed to put a Dodger on the disabled list and get another suspended. In May, the Dodgers lost Griffin for a month when one of Gooden's fastballs fractured the shortstop's finger, and they then lost Guerrero for four days after he hurled his bat at Mets pitcher David Cone after being hit by a pitch and got suspended. Guerrero, who at the time was the Dodgers' leader in batting average (.326) and tied with Mike Marshall for the club lead in RBIs (26), acknowledged Griffin's injury was a major part of his motivation for throwing his bat at Cone, who'd hit Griffin with a curveball. "The only thing I'm concerned about is, these things happen and pitchers don't get anything. I mean, I'm being suspended for four days, and [Cone] is still going to be pitching," Guerrero told reporters when informed of his suspension. "We now got a guy [Griffin] who was hit the other night, and he's out 21 days. [The Mets] still have their whole team."[1]

To make matters worse, the Mets even pounded former ace Fernando Valenzuela, who surrendered five runs while recording only five outs before he was pulled. In their next series less than two weeks later, Mets lefty Sid Fernandez threw a pitch that nearly got leadoff man Steve Sax on the head. While nothing happened to Fernandez, Tim Belcher and Tommy Lasorda were both thrown out of the same game when Belcher hit rookie

Kevin Elster with a pitch in the back. "We've got no vendetta against the Mets," Rick Dempsey said the night Sax was nearly hit. "But they throw at our No. 1 hitter, and they put our No. 2 hitter out of the lineup. And it could cost us the pennant."[2]

The only time the Dodgers had beaten the Mets? It happened on June 1 at Shea Stadium, and the Mets very well could have won that one too,

Pedro Guerrero, traded to the Cardinals in August 1988, went on to bat .311 with 42 doubles and 117 RBIs the following year, finishing third in NL MVP voting. *Michael McCormick*

as they battered both Jesse Orosco and Jay Howell for two runs before the latter got a line-drive double play off the bat of Lee Mazzilli with two men on to end the game 4–3. (In case you're wondering about the answer to this trivia question, reliever Brian Holton was the winning pitcher that night at Shea. The only Dodgers pitcher to record a win against the Mets during the 1988 regular season, Holton went four innings of one-hit ball in relief of Belcher, who had been ejected for throwing at Elster.) And even the one time Hershiser faced the Mets, Los Angeles lost. It came on August 24 at Dodger Stadium, where Hershiser nursed a 1–0 lead through seven innings only to see some Mets magic in the eighth. Mookie Wilson tripled. Keith Hernandez singled him home. Kevin McReynolds, with a runner on third, drove a ball to center field, deep enough for a sacrifice fly. Mets won, 2–1. That, by the way, was the last time Hershiser lost a ball game, as he then went the entire month of September without allowing a run. That's 59 consecutive scoreless innings—and counting, going into the 1988 postseason.

But surely the Mets weren't intimidated. They'd overcome a pair of dominant Mike Scott starts in the 1986 NLCS against Houston en route to their World Series victory. Scott, the 1986 NL Cy Young Award winner, had led the majors in ERA (2.22), innings (275 1/3), strikeouts (306), strikeouts per nine innings (10.0), and strikeouts-to-walks ratio (4.3). The Houston right-hander, 18–10 during the year, had also led the majors with his 5.95 hits allowed per nine innings and 0.92 WHIP (combined walks and hits per inning). Yet, the Mets took that series anyway, winning all of the non-Scott starts (including two games started by future Hall of Famer Nolan Ryan).

So, they'd been through it before. And remember the August 24 victory against Hershiser when they'd been shut out through the first seven innings? It was more of the same in Game 1 of the 1988 NLCS.

Through the first eight innings at Dodger Stadium in the series opener, Hershiser blanked New York on five hits—all singles. But the Mets struck for three runs in the ninth—on a single, a walk, and doubles by Darryl Strawberry and Gary Carter—to stun the Dodgers, 3–2. The ninth-inning outburst was nothing new for the Mets, known as the "Miracle Mets" for their 1969 World Championship run and again in 1986 when they shocked both Houston and Boston in a postseason filled with such dramatic comebacks. The Mets' three-run ninth—with the final two runs coming after they were one strike away from defeat—must have evoked memories of their three-run 10th inning in Game 6 of the 1986 World Series, when New York rallied with two outs and two strikes in a game that ended with Mookie Wilson's groundball going through Red Sox first baseman Bill Buckner's legs.

Jay Howell, who'd quietly ended the 1988 season with an 18-inning scoreless streak heading into the postseason, remembers being surprised at getting the call in that ninth inning. "We started the playoffs against the Mets, and [Hershiser] went eight innings and left a runner on, out at second base," says Howell, who during his own scoreless-innings streak had allowed only three walks and three hits with 25 strikeouts. "Lasorda goes to me, and I come in there, and I'm facing Gary Carter. I didn't wanna throw him any fastballs. I got ahead of him 0-and-2 and I threw a curveball out of the zone, and he went and fished it. He hit a little pop-up. Nobody could get it. It was in no man's land. We ended up losing that game to the Mets, but Hershiser's [consecutive-scoreless-innings] record doesn't carry into the postseason, so I didn't have that hanging over my head."

Actually, when Howell entered the ball game, the score was already 2–1. With the Mets down 2–0, Gregg Jefferies had opened the ninth with a single and Strawberry drove him in with a one-out double, ruining Hershiser's shutout bid. Lasorda pulled Hershiser at that juncture and went to Howell, who walked Kevin McReynolds and fanned Howard Johnson on a curveball before surrendering the go-ahead two-run double to Carter with two strikes. "I remember when Lasorda came out to hand me the ball, I kind of looked at Tommy questioning, 'What are you doing? *That's* Hershiser. I don't finish his games,'" adds Howell.

Howell had a point. Hershiser had completed eight of his final nine regular-season starts—the exception being the very last outing where he worked 10 innings in San Diego to set the consecutive-scoreless-innings record—and Howell hadn't appeared in a game started by the Bulldog since August 10 in Cincinnati. Of Howell's 21 saves on the season, only three had come in games won by Hershiser. It was, as Howell recalls, a foreign experience being on the mound to close out a potential Hershiser victory. "Lasorda said, 'He's done. Finish it. You've gotta finish it.' For me, that was weird . . . because *nobody* finishes Hershiser's games."

Phil Regan, the Dodgers advance scout responsible for following the NL East teams in 1988, remembers a controversy involving his scouting report that came up in Game 1. "There was a sportswriter in New York named Red Foley," Regan recalls today.

> I was sitting up in the press box because you usually get a lot of information from them. He said, "This season, whenever Gary Carter gets two strikes, he just kind of flicks the ball out over second base. He just goes right. He shortens up and just barely hits the ball."
>
> Well, the first game that we played the Mets was at Dodger Stadium. It was the eighth inning and Gary Carter came up with two strikes [Carter's at bat actually came in the ninth]. I told them this in the meeting, that Carter, with two strikes, will shorten up and just try to hit the ball and has hit a lot of balls to right field. It came up in the eighth inning, and here he was with two strikes, and he blooped the ball in. I think the controversy was that Tim McCarver was broadcasting the game. He said, "I don't know who didn't report the things on this, but everybody knows that with two strikes this year, Gary Carter shortened up and just tried to hit the ball to the outfield." I didn't wanna talk to the press [after the game], but the players said, "Phil said that to us right at the end of the meeting!"

In reality, McCarver's specific comments on the ABC broadcast, at the beginning of Carter's at bat, were, "I can't understand why the outfield is *this* deep with Gary Carter hitting. They're playing deep because they're defending against the Gary Carter of five years ago and his reputation, not this year."[3] And according to the broadcast, the Mets were 5–9 in postseason games in which they trailed going into the eighth inning—the best record by any team in big-league history. The Dodgers, meanwhile, had come back only one time in the 61 postseason games in their long history, dating back to their days in Brooklyn. That one comeback victory, as noted on ABC, was the famous 3–2 Brooklyn victory at Ebbets Field in Game 4 of the 1947 World Series in which Cookie Lavagetto's pinch hit, opposite-field two-run double off the right-field wall in the ninth inning ruined Yankees pitcher Bill Bevens's no-hitter and potential win. (Despite issuing a World Series–record 10 walks—and allowing a fifth-inning run thanks to a pair of walks, a sacrifice bunt, and a fielder's choice—Bevens had held the Dodgers hitless for eight and two-thirds innings.) For the

Dodgers in their long postseason history—which dated back to 1916—
it'd been nothing but heartbreak for the most part.

After all, this was a franchise with a lengthy history of disasters
when the lights were shining the brightest. Sure, since the club moved
from Brooklyn to Los Angeles following the 1957 season, the Dodgers
had won four World Championships to add to the one they'd won in
Brooklyn in 1955 in a seven-game classic against the Yankees. There was
1959, when the Dodgers swept the Milwaukee Braves in a best-of-three
pennant playoff before upsetting the Chicago White Sox in the World
Series—the first-ever championship for a West Coast team. There was
1963, when the Dodgers stunned the two-time defending champion
Yankees in a four-game sweep, with Sandy Koufax (two complete-game
victories), Don Drysdale (complete-game shutout), Johnny Podres (eight
and one-third innings), and Ron Perranoski (two-thirds of an inning)
combining to allow only four runs in four games. Game 4 in 1963 also
marked the only time the Dodgers had won the deciding game of a World
Series at home, and the series itself marked the first meeting between
teams from New York City and Los Angeles for a major professional
sports championship. There was 1965, when Koufax tossed complete-
game shutouts in Games 5 and 7 to beat the Minnesota Twins. Finally,
there was 1981, when the Dodgers overcame a two-games-to-none deficit
to defeat the Yankees in the World Series.

But the franchise had a much longer list of dubious meltdowns dating
back to the time when Woodrow Wilson was the president of the United
States. There was 1916 when the club, then known as the Brooklyn Rob-
ins, lost a 14-inning World Series game to Babe Ruth, who at the time
was a pitching star with the Red Sox and went all 14 frames. In that series,
Brooklyn scored first in each of the final four contests—but still lost four
games to one, as Rube Marquard and Jeff Pfeffer (who'd combined to win
38 games during the season with sub-2.00 ERAs) couldn't shut Boston
down. Four years later in the 1920 World Series against Cleveland (in a
best-of-nine affair), the Dodgers surrendered the first grand slam in the
history of the Fall Classic—hit by the Indians' Elmer Smith in the fifth
game—and hit into the only unassisted triple play in World Series history,
turned by second baseman Bill Wambsganss in that same contest. Also in
that game, Cleveland's Jim Bagby hit the first World Series homer by a

pitcher. The shell-shocked Dodgers were then blanked in each of the next two games, 1–0 and 3–0, and lost the series while being outscored 21–8.

Following the collapse to Cleveland, the Dodgers would trudge through a two-decade run of irrelevance before finally ending a 21-year drought and winning the NL pennant in 1941. But more disaster followed in the World Series. There was Game 3, when knuckleballer Freddie Fitzsimmons took a shutout into the seventh inning before Yankees pitcher Marius Russo lined a drive off Fitzsimmons's knee that broke his kneecap. With the hard-luck Fitzsimmons forced to leave the game, reliever Hugh Casey allowed two runs in the following inning and the Dodgers lost, 2–1. Then, there was Brooklyn catcher Mickey Owen's dropped third strike in the ninth inning the following afternoon, when with nobody on and two outs, the Yankees took advantage and erupted for four runs to turn a 4–3 Dodgers victory into a crushing loss. Had Owen hung on to reliever Casey's third-strike pitch, the game would have been over and the series tied 2–2. Instead, the Dodgers catcher's gaffe allowed Tommy Henrich to reach first base, extending the game, and the rest was history. Brooklyn lost the series the next day.

In the 1947 World Series, Lavagetto's game-winning double and Al Gionfriddo's memorable catch in left field to rob Joe DiMaggio of an extra-base hit were a couple of highlights for the Dodgers, but they still lost to the Yankees in seven games. Two years later, in the series opener at Yankee Stadium, Brooklyn's Don Newcombe took a four-hit shutout into the ninth, only to give up the first game-ending homer in World Series history as Henrich led off the bottom of the ninth by taking Newcombe deep. The Dodgers, who managed only two hits, lost in five games.

In 1950, Brooklyn, a veteran club boasting seven All-Stars, needed a victory over a young Phillies team (known as the Whiz Kids) in the regular-season finale at Ebbets Field to force a tie atop the NL standings and a best-of-three playoff to decide the pennant winner. Instead, Dick Sisler hit a 10th-inning, opposite-field three-run homer off Newcombe to give Philadelphia its first NL pennant in 35 years. As Dodgers broadcaster Vin Scully recalled years later, Brooklyn could have won it in the ninth but squandered its opportunities against Robin Roberts. With runners on first and second and none out, Duke Snider lined a single to center. Cal Abrams, the runner on second, raced for home. "Instead of hitting the inside of the bag at third, Abrams, a New York kid, rounded third by the way of the coach's box and he failed to score," recalled Scully, a rookie broadcaster then. "Center fielder Richie Ashburn threw him out at the plate. Later in the inning, the Dodgers had the bases loaded with one out and Carl Furillo fouled out."[4] Gil Hodges then flied out, and an inning later Sisler would hit the pennant-winning blast. Roberts, who pitched all 10 innings, earned his 20th win. Newcombe, who also worked all 10 frames, ended the season 19–11.

In the 1952 World Series, Brooklyn took a three-games-to-two lead against the Yankees, with the final two games at Ebbets Field. The Yankees won both, 3–2 and 4–2, to deny the Dodgers yet again. In the seventh inning of Game 7, Brooklyn loaded the bases, but Duke Snider popped out, and Jackie Robinson hit a pop-up to the right of the mound. With pitcher Bob Kuzava looking to his fielders, Billy Martin charged hard from his position deep at second base and caught the ball off his shoe tops, ending the inning. Brooklyn never threatened again. The following year, it was Martin who dashed the Dodgers' hopes once again as he singled home the series-winning run—his World Series record-tying 12th hit that October—in the bottom of the ninth in Game 6.

Of course, there were the meltdowns in the 1951 best-of-three pennant playoff, necessitated after the Dodgers blew a 13 1/2 game lead—with Brooklyn losing to the New York Giants on Bobby Thomson's "Shot Heard 'Round the World" ninth-inning homer—and in the 1962 NL tie-breaker series (another best-of-three playoff) after both the Dodgers and Giants had relocated to California. As in 1951, the 1962 Dodgers had a comfortable lead after eight innings in the series finale but again allowed four ninth-inning runs—this time with the winning run scoring on a bases-loaded walk—as San Francisco took the pennant. While the 1951 and 1962 playoff games counted as regular-season contests, the Dodgers' failures nonetheless showed again how the franchise always seemed to collapse in big games.

Fresh on everyone's minds now was how Los Angeles had lost its last three postseason games—all last-inning victories by the opposing team, with the Cardinals' Ozzie Smith and Jack Clark crushing ninth-inning homers in the final two games of the 1985 NLCS and now this latest meltdown against the Mets in the 1988 NLCS opener.

As for the Mets? In the 1969 World Series, there were all kinds of miracles. There was Tommie Agee in Game 3, leading off with a homer against Jim Palmer and then saving at least five runs thanks to two outstanding catches in center field. There was pinch hitter J. C. Martin in Game 4 being hit in the wrist—by Orioles reliever Pete Richert's throw to first—after laying down a sacrifice bunt, allowing the winning run to score. There was manager Gil Hodges showing a ball with shoe polish on it to convince the umpires that Mets left fielder Cleon Jones had been hit on the foot in Game 5, another key moment in the series. For the entire 1969 postseason, the Mets outscored their opponents 10–1 from the eighth inning on, further showing their magic in late-inning situations.

Four years later, the Mets had the worst record of any team to play in a World Series—at 82–79—and yet miraculously took Oakland to seven games after knocking off the 99-win Reds in the NLCS. The '73 Mets, remarkably, had been 12 games below .500 with 44 to play in mid-August, in last place on August 30, and had finished with the ninth-best record in the 24-team major leagues. They were second to last in the NL in runs, batting average, stolen bases, doubles, and home runs—and third to last in triples—and they were still one win away from being world champions. (The NL West champion Reds had scored the NL's second-most runs and had stolen 148 bases to the Mets' measly 27.)

Then, of course, 1986, in a postseason with more miracles, capped by Boston reliever Bob Stanley's Game 6 wild pitch followed by first baseman Bill Buckner's infamous error and yet another Mets rally in Game 7. In the NLCS against Houston, the Mets even hit the first-ever postseason come-from-behind, ninth-inning game-ending home run, as Lenny Dykstra took Astros reliever Dave Smith deep with a runner aboard for a 6–5 victory and a two-games-to-one lead. Controversy followed in the pivotal fifth game, with the series tied 2–2, as Craig Reynolds appeared to clearly beat out a second-inning double-play ball with runners on the corners and one out, thanks to a slow pivot by Mets shortstop Rafael Santana. But first-base umpire Fred Brocklander called Reynolds out, negating a run. The game went 12 innings before the Mets prevailed thanks to an infield hit, an errant throw on a pick-off attempt, and a game-ending single by the slumping Gary Carter, who'd been just 1 for 21 in the series. But had Brocklander made the proper call earlier in the game, the Mets might have lost in nine innings. It was yet another example of Mets Magic in postseason competition.

And in one of the most famous games in NLCS history—Game 6 at the Astrodome—the Mets, trailing 3–0, rallied for three runs in the ninth and then prevailed 7–6 in 16 innings, capturing the NL pennant. Had the Mets lost, they would have gone to a seventh game against Mike Scott, who'd already beaten them 1–0 and 3–1 earlier in the series. But the Mets avoided having to face Scott in a winner-take-all affair, and New York went on to defeat Boston in a Fall Classic filled with more miraculous comebacks.

Now this magic had carried over into the 1988 NLCS. With the history of both franchises' fortunes in postseason play, surely the Mets were expected to dispose of the Dodgers now that they had, first, scored a run off Hershiser, and second, rallied against Howell. Who was going to stop them now?

Regan, the Dodgers advance scout from 1987 to 1993, remembers Tommy Lasorda feeling hopeless just prior to Game 2. "OK, so we lost that first game," Regan says now.

But here's the thing I remember. It was a very tough game to lose. The next day, I was in Fred's office. Tommy Lasorda was in there and we were talking. Tommy was very down. He got up to leave and said, "Well, I don't know what I'm gonna say. I gotta go down there in that clubhouse. I gotta say something to motivate these guys. I don't know what I'm gonna say." And Fred Claire said, "Tommy, you'll think of something to say."

Well, at that time when Tommy walked into the clubhouse, [he didn't need to say anything]. David Cone had written an article for the paper. One of our infielders made copies of this—Cone had made real critical comments like "the Dodgers are dead; we're gonna sweep them," something like that—and they posted it in everyone's locker. We went on to beat them and went to the World Series. So, Tommy didn't have to say a word. They were motivated when he got there. To me, that was a big thing. That was a big turning point. It motivated our team, I know that. What I remember about that is Tommy not knowing what to say to motivate them, and Fred saying, "Tommy, you'll think of something!"

Yes, and it was Cone, 20–3 during the regular season, who got the starting assignment in Game 2 for the Mets. Following Game 1, he'd written a first-person column in the *New York Daily News* (courtesy of a ghostwriter), in which he described Hershiser as being "lucky for eight innings" and was critical of Howell's curveballs. "As soon as we got Orel out of the game, we knew we'd beat the Dodgers," wrote Cone. "We saw Howell throwing curveball after curveball and we were thinking: This is the Dodgers' idea of a stopper? Our idea is Randy [Myers], a guy who can blow you away with his heat. Seeing Howell and his curveball reminded us of a high school pitcher."[5]

The infielder responsible for making copies of the column was short-stop Dave Anderson, who'd arrived early at the ballpark for Game 2. A Dodgers public relations member showed the article to Anderson, who then made copies and underlined all the key passages before plastering the clubhouse with them. He put them in the trainer's room, on the walls of the clubhouse, on the chairs of teammates, and on Lasorda's desk. "Trying to do something, you know, to motivate the boys," Anderson would recall years later with a laugh.[6]

Los Angeles made Cone eat his words, hammering him for five runs in two innings in a 6–3 victory. "Our entire bench was screaming at him," Tim Belcher recalled in the 2001 book *True Blue*. "Rick Dempsey was on the top step of the dugout. Every time Dave threw a curve, Dempsey said, 'Aw, that's high school.' And Dave heard it. It bothered him. He knew he screwed up."[7]

When reminded today that he was one of the Dodgers who heckled Cone during the 1988 playoffs, Dempsey doesn't seem to recall. "Well, I could've been. I could've been," Dempsey says now. "I can't remember what David Cone said. It's been quite a few years since I've even thought about this. But I kind of vaguely remember what you're talking about. What did David Cone say about us?" When reminded about the details of that column, the former catcher simply laughs. "Nobody ever got bothered or upset, really, about it. It was almost something that you just laughed about. You know, it's easy to see what they were trying to do. I mean, the Mets beat us, what, 10 out of 11 games during the course of the year?"

Tracy Woodson—along with several other teammates—no longer recalls the Cone heckling, but he does remember how Lasorda would use opposing players' comments as bulletin board material. "I don't remember much about that. I know [Cone] had done something. But Lasorda was big on taking advantage of what was in the paper and using it to our

According to Rick Dempsey (shown here in a Milwaukee uniform from 1991), the Dodgers never really got bothered or upset by the comments made by David Cone in the papers during the 1988 NLCS. *Milwaukee Brewers*

advantage. He'd say, 'Guys, are we gonna let him do this and say this about us?' That type of thing. Gosh, we always used that stuff."

When asked today about Cone's column, both John Shelby and Steve Sax also say they don't recall. "I don't remember much about that incident. [I just remember] the Mets series was intense because they had beaten us

[10 out of 11] during the season and we knew beating them to go to the World Series was not going to be easy," says Shelby.

"I don't really remember what that was about. I know something was said and that actually helped out team in the clubhouse," adds Sax.

Franklin Stubbs remembers something was said, but also knew Cone was going to be tough after the second game. "I don't remember what Cone wrote but I think he pitched Game 2," Stubbs says today. "I think he said something beforehand and the guys kind of took that to heart and we had a little bit more incentive to play in that game. We jumped on him pretty good in that game. But in Game 6, he came back and kinda stuck it up our butts a little bit."

Mariano Duncan, who was in the Dodgers organization from 1982 to 1989 but wasn't part of Los Angeles's 1988 major-league roster, wouldn't have been upset by Cone's comments—simply because he viewed the Mets right-hander as a big-game pitcher. Cone, in fact, would come out of the bullpen to record a save in Game 3 before winning his Game 6 start to keep the Mets' season alive. "Well, frankly, I have nothing bad to say about David Cone," says Duncan, who'd be teammates with Cone on the 1996–1997 Yankees.

> He was a good pitcher. He was like that his whole career. When he went to the mound, he tried to go out there and beat the other team. He always went out there to compete. And about all the comments he made, I used to be that kind of player when I played where I don't pay attention to that kind of detail. The players can say whatever they want, but at the same time they have to go out on the field and perform. And every time you go out there and perform the way that the man performed, I don't have anything bad to say about him. Because you know, baseball is like that. Baseball was like that before, and it's still like that now. If you wanna go out and play the game, and you believe something or worry about something that somebody says, you'll never perform the way you're supposed to on the field. And I said this about David Cone before, when he used to pitch for the Mets, "You know, that guy is a good pitcher." And I had the opportunity in 1996 to play with him as a teammate. And that guy was a very competitive guy. Like I said, whatever he said didn't bother me. Whatever David Cone said before, it didn't bother me. Like I said, whatever the player said, they can say. But if you come to the field and perform the way you're supposed to perform, that's what really mattered to me.

Veteran *USA Today* sportswriter Bob Nightengale is one person who remembers Cone's column. Nightengale, in fact, brings it up when mentioning his most vivid memories of the 1988 NLCS. The Kirk Gibson homer stands out in the World Series, according to Nightengale, and everything else is pretty much forgotten. As for the NLCS, he feels Cone's column and Mike Scioscia's fourth-game homer—which we'll get to later—stand out more than anything else. "Just that moment [the Gibson homer] stands out way above the rest. Everything else was just a blur compared to Gibson's home run. It was like the NLCS with the Mets; David Cone had told the *New York Daily News*, 'Oh, it's like we're playing a Triple-A team.' Kinda bashed the Dodgers. Lasorda used that as motivation throughout the playoffs. And Mike Scioscia's home run, when it looked like the Dodgers were dead [also stands out]."

What Dempsey really recalls is how the team regrouped when the series shifted to New York, and how his pep talk might have fired up the players.

> What I remember is that we were a very unique and a very close ball club. I remember we had a meeting in Los Angeles before we went to New York to play the Mets in the playoffs—because they'd beaten us in all but one game. We got in that meeting. We talked about our game plan, how to pitch certain guys, and blah blah blah. I know I was the oldest guy on the team, and I had the last say.
>
> I got up and I said, "Guys, in New York, the fans are gonna be very, very important for their ball club. They get so loud, they get so fanatical, they get so far behind their ball club, that it's almost hard to think about what you wanna get done out there on the field in the middle of the game. I suggest that all of us, when those crowds get so loud that you can't think, pulling for their team, for Strawberry and all the guys that were doing so well, that's when you get up from behind home plate and you go out to the mound to talk to the pitcher. But you don't say a word. You let the crowd burn out. Let them burn themselves out—because that takes a bit of the anxiety out of the inning for the Mets." And it worked perfectly. Every time they got so loud, we'd just stop the game. Mike Scioscia and myself, we'd go to the mound and we'd talk to the pitcher until the crowd calmed down. And then we went back. It took a lot of their momentum away from them because they had incredibly good fans. They were so behind their club that year that it was really hard to beat them, especially in New York.

More drama ensued when the NLCS shifted to Shea Stadium for Game 3, which was pushed back a day because of a rainout and played on a wet, muddy field. The rainout allowed Lasorda to bring back Hershiser on three days' rest, and the game featured an incredible fifth-inning sliding catch by Gibson in left field to rob Mookie Wilson of extra bases. With the game tied 3–3 in the top of the eighth, pinch hitter Mike Sharperson walked with the bases loaded to force in the go-ahead run. Lasorda, who'd gotten seven innings from Hershiser, turned to Howell, his closer, to begin the bottom of the eighth. Howell ran a 3-and-2 count to Kevin McReynolds, leading off the inning, and suddenly Mets manager Davey Johnson came out of the dugout and asked home-plate umpire Joe West to inspect Howell's glove. Harry Wendelstedt, the crew chief and left-field umpire, ran in to also take a look, and promptly ejected Howell for having pine tar on his glove. The Mets took advantage, scoring five runs off the next three relievers—Alejandro Peña, Jesse Orosco, and Ricky Horton—and won 8–4 to take a two-games-to-one lead.

Once again, the Mets had rallied to win a postseason game in which they trailed in the eighth. But interestingly, 30 years after the fact, several of the Dodgers players seem to think that Los Angeles hung on to win that particular game following Howell's ejection. (Which goes to show that many people, including the players involved, remember just Gibson's home run and Hershiser's streak—and to a lesser extent, Scioscia's homer.)

"Before we got to the World Series, I'd gotten thrown out of a game in New York for having pine tar on my glove," Howell says now.

It was cold, you couldn't really grip the ball, and I relied a good bit on my curveball. I was suspended [for two games]. I had to go to [NL president] Bart Giamatti, and I went with Gene Orza [the associate general counsel of the MLB Players Association] the day after I was thrown out of the game.

It was Harry Wendelstedt [who threw me out]. Lasorda sprinted out there and demanded that they just throw the glove out and I should stay in the game [but] it didn't [work]. I was thrown out of the game. The next day I had to go to Giamatti's office. It was almost surreal. I went in there with Gene. Those two were yucking it up, telling jokes—Polack jokes—back and forth. Gene was with Giamatti, and Giamatti just had a great sense of humor. And I said, "Hey! This isn't funny! It's the play-offs and I'm suspended. This is serious!"

Bart said, "I know. You'll be a free agent after the year. No one's gonna pay attention to this. I talked to [former pitcher] Jim Kaat. I know how it works. Two weeks after the [World] Series, there'll be a story. And you'll never be in the paper. It'll be over. It'll be a done deal."

Gene said, "Well, what is that? What are you talking about?"

He said, "I can't really talk about it."

Sure enough, after the World Series, the Pete Rose story broke. [It was the news of the allegations that Rose had bet on baseball, that he was being investigated for gambling on the sport.] He was right. Nothing happened. I signed back with the Dodgers. There was the collusion, of course. But I was happy to sign back with LA That's where I wanted to be.

Tracy Woodson remembers it was an ex-teammate of Howell's who'd squealed on him to the Mets. "That was in New York," Woodson says. "He'd come in to [try and] close the game. I think New York had somebody that had played with him previously, and knew that he had put stuff on his glove, or whatever it was." The ex-teammate was former Mets infielder Tucker Ashford, a minor-league coach in the Mets organization who'd played with Howell in 1982 with Triple-A Columbus in the Yankees organization. He watched Game 1 on television and made two observations; he didn't remember Howell throwing a curveball that broke as much as it did that night, and he noticed how dark Howell's cap was. Believing the Dodgers closer was using pine tar, Ashford called his contact with the Mets and informed them of his suspicions.

"I was actually in the game at the time," Woodson says now.

I went out to the mound and kinda listened to what was going on. Once again, we needed somebody else to come in at that point and finish it. So, it worked out for us. [As far as pitchers using pine tar for a better grip], I think some do, especially with the weather. I think some guys use it to help them pitch, period. But if they do, you try to find out if you were on the other team. I think they were trying to do it to try and affect us, and in some way make it work against us.

It's interesting to get Woodson's perspective, since he's now a head baseball coach in college. Would it be an unwritten rule in professional sports to do nothing if you knew the opponent was, in a sense, cheating? Or, would you use that knowledge to your advantage? Something similar came into play with Los Angeles's NHL team—the Kings—in the 1993 Stanley Cup Finals. The Kings were poised to take a two-games-to-none lead against the Montreal Canadiens, with a one-goal advantage in the dying seconds of Game 2. In an effort to salvage the series, Montreal asked referee Kerry Fraser to measure the curve on the blade of Kings defenseman Marty McSorley's stick—as the Canadiens had suspected he was using an illegal stick (one that had too much curve on the stick blade). The stick was ruled illegal, McSorley was assessed a penalty, Montreal scored on the ensuing power play to tie it, and the series turned. Los Angeles never won another game in the series. On the Kings' side, they said they wouldn't have done what the Canadiens did had the roles been reversed; they didn't believe in winning like that. "Games are meant to be decided between the players, the heart and soul of the players, the passion of the players, the toughness of the players," then-Kings head coach Barry Melrose, now an ESPN hockey commentator, would say years later. "I would never do that as a coach. I said that after the game and I still believe that today. [Canadiens coach] Jacques [Demers] didn't cheat or anything, it's in the rulebook, but I just don't think games should be won or lost for that."[8]

Getting back to the question, would it be an unwritten rule in professional sports to do nothing if you knew the opponent was, in a sense, cheating? "No, I don't think so," Woodson answers without hesitation.

> I mean, if you know something that's going on [you use that knowledge to your advantage]. To me, it's just like steroids now. There's a lot of guys that have gotten upset with the steroids. It's an unfair advantage. I always look back on my career and think, "Gosh, would it have helped me to make me hit more home runs, stay in the big leagues longer, and make more money?" It definitely worked. It works for some guys. There were a lot of guys that stayed in the big leagues and made a lot of money because of steroids. And I think that's where it became a disadvantage to pitchers who were facing guys who were on steroids, and vice versa.

Steve Sax only laughs when thinking back to Howell's pine-tar incident. "I remember Tommy coming out to the mound and trying to talk the umpire out of it," Sax laughs. "Jay got [ejected and later] suspended for having pine tar, and Tommy came out there to try and talk him out of it. I thought that was hilarious. It wasn't gonna work. I think it was Jesse Orosco that stepped in for Jay Howell and did a good job—did what he had to do to continue our winning ways. We always had guys that were picking everybody up, and that's, I think, kind of the mark of our team in '88. We always had somebody picking everybody else up."

Some 30 years later, several Dodgers players who participated in Game 3, when asked to recount the details of that particular contest, erroneously think they'd hung on to win. But in reality, it was their second loss in three games and the season was quickly slipping away. Surely, the Mets had gained all the momentum through three games, especially with the way they'd just exploded for five runs following Howell's ejection. Yes, Hershiser had been perfect all September and Gibson had made that incredible sliding catch to rob Mookie Wilson of extra bases—and the Dodgers still lost and the Mets were ahead in the series.

Boston Globe columnist Bob Ryan recalls that he, like everybody else in the press box, thought the Dodgers were finished. "I covered the entire thing in New York and L.A. I remember the lousy seats we had at Shea, in the auxiliary [press box] in the outfield. But I was always taken by the beauty of Dodger Stadium," Ryan says. "I remember that the Mets were heavily favored and this was year 3 [of their three-year run in the NL East]. They won in '86 and everybody thought it was gonna be [another] long run again for the Mets. The Dodgers, on paper, were a totally overmatched team. You look at some of the lineups the Dodgers had . . ."

And now, New York would have its ace, Dwight Gooden, going in Game 4. The Mets, having won both of the Hershiser games, surely would be ready for late-season acquisition John Tudor, whose last postseason start (with the Cardinals in the 1987 World Series, a six-run, four-inning affair against Minnesota) was a disaster. With a well-rested Gooden on the mound ready to go, the Mets were on the doorstep of a second World Series trip in three years.

CHAPTER SEVEN
SCIOSCIA'S FORGOTTEN
HOMER—AND THE FORGOTTEN HOLTON

John Shelby was such a big part of 1988.

—Fred Claire, Dodgers general manager

Mike Scioscia's home run that [tied] that big game [in the NL Champion-ship Series] was huge—it looked like the Dodgers were dead. And then just knocking off the Mets was such a stunning thing. Nobody really believed it. Everyone thought, "OK, it's gonna end here. It's gonna be an Oakland–Mets World Series." We were all just stunned. Nobody saw it happening.

—Bob Nightengale, sportswriter

Before Kirk Gibson ended Game 1 of the 1988 World Series with his iconic two-run homer, Mickey Hatcher had opened the scoring with a two-run blast off Athletics ace Dave Stewart to give Los Angeles a quick lead. When Hatcher is asked today about that particular long ball, the former Stuntman leader is quick to point to another home run—one that he feels has been overlooked and forgotten all these years later.

"First of all, my home run was nothing compared to the one guy that, I think, everybody keeps forgetting about—and that was Mike Scioscia's home run," Hatcher reflects today.

I think that's what got us to the World Series. My home run would never have happened. Gibson's home run would never have happened.

99

We never would've had an opportunity to do that, if Mike Scioscia didn't hit that home run against the Mets off Gooden, which took us to extra innings and we ended up winning. I think that was the biggest win of the season for us right there. Orel came into that game, didn't he? Orel came into that game in relief. So, I mean that really brought our team together right there. That tied the series up. We would've been down 3–1. So I really think that Mike Scioscia's home run is the one that's always overlooked. You know, Gooden was just throwing the ball outstanding. I mean, that was another one of those key moments for us that year. It was just magical.

Let's go back a little bit. Hatcher is referring to Game 4 of the NLCS at Shea Stadium. Dwight Gooden started for the Mets that night and was in command going into the ninth with New York ahead, 4–2. He'd thrown 118 pitches to get through eight, but starters tended to throw more pitches back then than they do today—especially an ace of Gooden's caliber—so the pitch count wasn't an issue. The Mets were about to take a three-games-to-one lead and would have a chance to finish Los Angeles off the following afternoon.

And oh, there was history against the Dodgers. As ABC had pointed out earlier in the series, the Dodgers had come back only once in their long postseason history when trailing going into the eighth inning, dating back to their days in Brooklyn. That one comeback victory was the famous Cookie Lavagetto pinch-hit, two-run, ninth-inning double in the 1947 Fall Classic that broke up Yankees pitcher Bill Bevens's no-hitter. And that was it.

John Shelby, who'd driven in the Dodgers' only two runs (with a two-out single in the first inning), led off the ninth against Gooden, who'd allowed only one hit and four baserunners since the first inning. "Gooden had us. He had us beat. He had John Shelby two strikes and no balls with two outs," third-base coach Joey Amalfitano says today, although there actually were no outs. "And it was the ninth inning. Shelby would not walk in a pedestrian zone. He walked him! That happened almost 30 years ago, but I could still see Doc Gooden's eyes when he walked Shelby, like, 'What did I just do?' And then [on the next pitch] Mike Scioscia got the barrel on the ball, and we tied the score, and then we won it."

Amalfitano had a point about Shelby. In 1988, Shelby had 545 plate appearances with 128 strikeouts and only 44 walks—which represented the highest walk total of his career. In his 11-year career, according to Baseball-Reference.com, he averaged only 28 walks per 162 games. Yet, Gooden walked him, and then proceeded to give up a two-run homer to Scioscia, who was looking for a first-pitch fastball and guessed right.

"The adrenaline was pumping, I was sure I was going to close it out," Gooden recalled 25 years later in an interview with the *New York Daily News*. "Scioscia wasn't a power guy so when he comes up, I'm thinking he's going to take a strike, knowing I just walked a guy. I was thinking completely the opposite of what he was thinking." In 2012, the two men talked about the homer when they crossed paths at a clinic for kids at Yankee Stadium. Recalled Gooden: "[I asked Scioscia], '. . . You knew I was going to lay a fastball in there for a strike with the first pitch, and you were looking to jump me, right?' And Mike smiled at me and said, 'Absolutely I was.'"[1]

The game remained tied until Gibson homered off the right-field scoreboard against Roger McDowell in the 12th inning. With Los Angeles out of relievers and the Mets threatening with the bases loaded in the bottom half, Hershiser came out of the bullpen to get the final out, and the Dodgers escaped with a series-tying 5–4 victory.

Shelby, a quiet player during his career and never one to attract attention to himself, acknowledges today that his walk was crucial. "Beating the Mets with Doc Gooden pitching was not easy," Shelby says now. "I walked to get on base and then Scioscia hit one of the biggest home runs in the series. Without his home run, who knows how things may have turned out for us?"

"And that carried us," continues Amalfitano. "That shifted the momentum, if there's such a thing as momentum—and there is in sports. It shifted it to us. And we went home. It was a classic series. That was a very, very good series. Both teams were very good. We took it to seven games, and we ended up on top."

Steve Sax remembers homering on the first pitch of the 1988 season against San Francisco and recalls thinking it was an omen for the year. When asked what his vivid memories were of the NL playoffs, Sax points to Scioscia's homer. "Like the one I hit Opening Day, nobody really expected Scioscia to hit the home run. But he put a good swing on that pitch. That allowed us to have another game going forward, to try to beat the Mets. And we went back to Los Angeles, and we won Game 7."

Rick Dempsey remembers thinking the Dodgers were going to advance to the World Series when Scioscia's fly ball went over the fence. "Once Scioscia hit that home run, we knew we were gonna shut them down from that point," Dempsey says now. Right-hander Tim Leary agrees. With the Dodgers having new life and their pitching staff healthy and ready to go (even with the absence of Jay Howell for another game), they weren't going to lose. "Our strength coach, Pat Screnar, did a fantastic job that spring and year, as we all stayed healthy and strong, and 1 through 10, we had the best and deepest pitching staff in baseball," Leary says now, referring to the confidence the entire team had in all the pitchers.

"Mike Scioscia's home run was huge," continues Dempsey. "We don't get to the World Series without that home run."

Scioscia, of course, wasn't known for his offensive power. Known primarily for his defense, Scioscia was just a .191 lifetime hitter against Gooden in 72 plate appearances and had homered only three times during the 1988 season. In fact, he averaged only five homers a season throughout his 13-year career—with a career-best of 12 in 1990.

Jay Howell recalls how tough the veteran catcher was, having opposing players try consistently to run into him—but Scioscia still wound up not missing a lot of games, appearing in the Dodgers' lineup for 130 games in 1988. Howell brings up one particular collision from June 1990 in Cincinnati to illustrate how players on other teams wanted to take their shots at him. "I remember in Cincinnati, [Reds pitcher] Norm Charlton almost took his head off coming home on a fly ball," Howell says. Actually, the play Howell is referring to came on a double to left field by Joe Oliver. Charlton, who was on first base after being hit by a pitch, had gone all the way to third on Oliver's two-out hit. But once he reached third, Charlton ignored third-base coach Sam Perlozzo's stop sign and kept on running. The Cincinnati pitcher rounded the bag, intending to race home and challenge Scioscia at the plate, with shortstop Alfredo Griffin's relay throw coming in. "[Charlton] just went out of his way to cold-cock him," Howell continues. "Both of them collided; I mean, it was a tremendous collision. I hadn't seen a collision like that in a long time; he was definitely going to take Scioscia out."

Right-hander Ramon Martinez says he learned a lot watching the veterans on the 1988 team play, in particular Scioscia, who was rarely 100

According to several Dodgers on the 1988 team, the home run hit by Mike Scioscia (shown here before a regular-season game at Dodger Stadium) in Game 4 of the NLCS in New York was one of the biggest of the whole year.
Michael McCormick

percent healthy. "In my first year when I made my debut, I saw a bunch of guys who played hard every day," says Martinez now.

> I remember Mike Scioscia. He had a problem with his right ankle. He was injured and he was still playing. They had to make a special boot—a special shoe—to [be used] on his foot. He didn't give up; he just wanted to play. [There were also guys like] Mickey Hatcher, Mike Davis, Mike Sharperson. I mean, they were a bunch of guys that just wanted to play. Kirk Gibson always played hard. He just played hard every game. That's a great group of guys. If you wanna see a group of guys that wanna play every day, guys who never gave up, it's these guys.

Jerry Reuss, a Dodger from 1979 to early 1987, speaks glowingly today about Scioscia's prowess behind the plate. "I was blessed in the eight years that I pitched for the Dodgers—because I'm convinced I had two number 1 catchers to throw to [with the tandem of Scioscia and Steve Yeager, with the latter being traded to Seattle after the 1985 season]," Reuss says now.

> And when you get that, it sure makes the job a whole lot easier, and the success reflects in the numbers.
>
> For Scioscia, what his strongest point was, as far as a hitter, he was a contact hitter and you could put him pretty much anywhere in the lineup except leadoff. And you probably wouldn't want him to bat ninth. But anywhere from number 2 to number 8, he had a pretty good bat. He could do the job. He wasn't a power kind of guy—so you keep him out of the middle of the lineup—but he could hit the ball. He could hit in situations. Offensively, that was his strong point.
>
> Defensively was where he shined in his ability to call a game. Going over hitters with Mike, you'd have a game plan and if something wasn't working, Mike had an immediate solution, and brought it out to you on the mound. "This isn't working; let's try this." He always had a solution. He identified a problem and he had a solution. And probably what's more impressive than anything, if the game plan went along and you didn't use everything, he'd remember it not only the next start you had against that team—but also he'd remember it beyond that, sometimes as much as a year. "You remember a year ago? We didn't do it then; this might be a good time to do it now."

Others remember Scioscia for his feel for the game, knowing that he'd eventually move into a managerial role following his playing days. "Mike Scioscia was definitely a leader," hitting coach Ben Hines says. "He always had a great feel for the game, during the game. Some guys have a feel for the game, but they don't have it during the game. And Scioscia had that. He had a good idea about the pace of the game, and when certain things should be done, like hit-and-run or the squeeze and the safety squeeze. He was always telling Tommy [Lasorda], 'Hey! Squeeze now, squeeze!' Or, 'Hit and run now, Tommy! Hit and run! Let him steal! Let him steal now, Tommy!' Tommy would heed a lot of his advice."

"There are certain guys that understand the game better, that can see the timing and the patterns of the game," recalls Howell.

The time to hit-and-run, pitchout, those kinds of things. And I noticed that Mike Scioscia would lean over to Tommy—and I had this feeling that he was gonna be a manager, or that he should be a manager—and say, "Not a bad time for a hit-and-run here." They had a relationship that it was OK. If it was somebody else, that wouldn't fly. But Scioscia had Lasorda's ear to do that, and he didn't really make that public. But it was one of those inside things that I knew that Scioscia has really keen insight. And I could tell by the way he called games, and the things that he did behind the plate with the play call. Like in a fastball situation, he might shake you off twice and then go back to it. And he was always on top of the defense, the defensive plays that we might have for a bunt or a pickoff play at second, and he was always thinking one step ahead. He'd make suggestions. I don't know what percentage Lasorda went with it, but I never saw it outside of that. I never encountered it. And I thought it was an interesting dynamic. And kudos to Scioscia. No wonder he's well-regarded as a good manager. And it's not by accident.

The more Howell discusses Game 4 of the 1988 NLCS, the more fond memories he recalls. "Getting back to when I was thrown out, I had to watch the game at a neutral location," Howell reflects.

I was not allowed to go to the stadium. I was watching with a friend of mine, Tom Likovich, and [actor] Marty Gottlieb. We were sitting there watching the game. I was super bummed out. Out they come for BP. They were showing the team, and I looked at our guys. They had my number written onto their helmets. Literally every player had my number written somewhere on their helmets or on their uniforms. It was just kind of an amazing feeling to think that your teammates would stand for you like that.

The game goes on. . . . Brian Holton was like a yeoman out there, pitching in a playoff game in a tie game on the road in New York, and held them down for three innings—in extra innings. [Actually, it was Alejandro Peña who did that.] Another one of our long guys [Ricky Horton] did as well [earlier in the game for two innings when the Dodgers were trailing], and then Hershiser, in between starts, came out of the bullpen and closed it out. And that feeling that I had was . . . like I'd never had a feeling like that. Like being part of a team that really had each other's back like that. It was amazing.

Scioscia—along with Gibson and Hershiser—was the hero in Game 4, but as Howell points out, little-known Brian Holton did an outstanding job that night. Except he didn't go three innings. Regardless, very few people remember the guy known by his teammates as "Bub," whose best season in his brief six-year big-league career came in 1988. But the man who wound up spending nine seasons in Triple-A ball—seven of them in the Dodgers' system in Albuquerque—certainly came up huge, including on the October stage when the lights were shining the brightest. At the age of 28 and in his second full major-league season in 1988, the right-hander won seven games in relief with a 1.70 ERA and one save in 45 appearances. That October, Holton made four relief appearances against the Mets and A's—including a combined three scoreless innings in two of the most memorable games in Dodgers history. In Holton's postseason debut, his one scoreless inning came in a contest remembered for Scioscia's ninth-inning homer—but Los Angeles might not have come back if not for his pitching out of a runner-on-third, none-out jam in the sixth. Six nights later, his two no-hit innings in the World Series opener were overshadowed by Gibson's ninth-inning dramatics, which also might not have happened if not for Holton's performance. "Brian Holton was outstanding that year," Howell says today. "Have you heard anyone mention his nickname? It's 'Bub.' Yup. Bub Holton. Don't know the origin of it. I mean, he was just Bub. I don't know why we called him Bub. I'm not exactly sure why we called him Bub. Great guy. He was a soft thrower. He threw soft." Right-hander Tim Leary also remembers Holton fondly. "Brian is a great guy. He called people 'Bub.'"

"Interesting thing about him was that when you'd bring him in after one of the starters—Hershiser, Belcher, Leary, all of whom threw pretty hard—he was a big gear change from the standpoint of his effectiveness as he had a terrific curveball," continues Howell.

> Just a great curveball. It wasn't a roundhouse. It went straight down. He really had a classic drop, and I attribute that a lot to the Dodgers [being] curveball oriented, with [Sandy] Koufax there [as a pitching instructor in the organization]. Ron Perranoski had a good one. But I mean, they taught it. He just happened to have a really good one. I think Lasorda had a good one. And I think Lasorda really appreciated that. He loved it. He thought it was a great pitch.
>
> You look at the numbers that year—and I was reading back over that—and I knew that. I knew that about him. I knew he had a sub-2.00 ERA for the year. I mean, he was pretty much [a] lockdown [reliever]. He would come in, a little bit like [Tim] Crews. There wasn't a day when he wouldn't take the ball. He wasn't gonna throw any fear in anybody. But he just changed speeds enough, located his pitches really well, and it's kind of hard to think, "Well, how'd you have those numbers? How'd you do that?" He was literally lights out. And more than that, I'd say, he was lights out when the lights were bright.

Howell points specifically to Game 4 of the NLCS. "When I was suspended and they went into extra innings—that game where Scioscia hit the home run in New York—I believe he was a yeoman in that game. I can't remember exactly the games that he was in, but he came through in all of those. Brian was out there, pitching in a big game and holding down the Mets for three innings."

Howell is right in that Holton, with an effective curveball, came up big that night with Howell serving the first of his two-game suspension for having pine tar in his glove. No, Holton didn't pitch three innings, but the right-hander did thwart the Mets in his one inning of work replacing ineffective starter John Tudor. The Dodgers, in a must-win game, trailed 3–2 after five innings thanks to back-to-back homers in the fourth—a two-run blast by Darryl Strawberry and a solo shot by Kevin McReynolds. In the sixth, McReynolds greeted Tudor with a double, and Gary Carter tripled him home—a deep drive over centerfielder John Shelby's head—for a 4–2 Mets lead.

In came Holton and his curveball, and the right-hander immediately struck out Tim Teufel. A walk to eighth-place hitter Kevin Elster put runners on the corners, but Holton got Mets ace Dwight Gooden to ground to shortstop for an inning-ending double play. Carter, the runner on third, was left stranded. Holton was pinch-hit for in the next half inning, and lefty Ricky Horton worked two scoreless frames before the Dodgers rallied and won in 12 innings. But had Holton not done the job in his one inning of work—with Carter already on third base and none out when he came on—Los Angeles might not have come back.

The following afternoon (in a day game), Holton was summoned in the eighth inning with New York threatening. Down 6–4, the Mets had two men on with one out. But Holton, with a steady diet of curveballs, got the next two outs, including an inning-ending fly out to left off the bat of Gary Carter (who'd already had four RBIs in the first four games). He then worked a 1-2-3 ninth inning to send both teams back to Dodger Stadium with Los Angeles now ahead three games to two. Incidentally, Holton, with the save, was the third Dodger to record a save during the series, joining Peña and Hershiser.

Holton had closed the regular season with 17 2/3 consecutive scoreless innings, a streak spread out over his final 10 appearances. Through his first two playoff appearances, the streak had continued. It finally ended at 21 2/3 innings the next day in Game 6—the third straight game in which Holton was called upon—when he gave up a double and was pulled, and Ricky Horton allowed that runner to score, a run charged to Holton. The Mets, who'd built a big lead against starter Tim Leary, won 5–1 to even the series.

Holton finally got a day of rest—in fact, nobody in the bullpen was needed in Game 7—when Hershiser spun a shutout to give the Dodgers the NL pennant. But Holton was back out there in the famous Gibson game. He came on in the sixth and proceeded to retire Carney Lansford, Dave Henderson, and Jose Canseco in succession on only eight pitches. In the seventh, Holton walked Dave Parker but got the next three outs, including Mark McGwire on a weak tapper in front of the plate. Two innings later, Gibson would stun Oakland with his game-winning homer.

Holton never pitched in another game for Los Angeles, as he was traded in the off-season in a deal that brought Baltimore slugger Eddie Murray to the Dodgers. But he was definitely clutch in 1988. "And that wasn't the only thing," Howell continues. "You look at the whole year. Just looking at his numbers, he was doing that the whole year long. He didn't come in and have any blowouts. He didn't come in and give up a lot of runs—or give up a lot of runs for somebody else. He really had a year for the ages. I mean, that was an amazing year for him. And a good guy. He was a great guy to have down in the bullpen. He was just a super guy. I mean, we all loved him. He was awesome."

The 1988 NLCS went to a seventh game on October 12, but it was no contest. Hershiser, making his fourth appearance of the series, pitched a shutout to finish off the Mets 6–0. As *Boston Globe* columnist Bob Ryan remembers, it was Hershiser, Hershiser, Hershiser in that series. Ryan wasn't exaggerating. After his eight and one-third innings on October 4, Hershiser worked seven more innings on October 8, recorded a one-out save on October 9, and went the final nine innings of the series, finishing with a 1.09 ERA and the series MVP award.

Ryan also remembers that everyone in the press box was stunned. "[Earlier in the series] it just seemed that there was no hope for the Dodgers. But, of course, it was Hershiser's year. It was Hershiser's moment. Everything was Hershiser, Hershiser, Hershiser. And it continued into the World Series," Ryan says now.

Mickey Hatcher admits today that some of the Dodgers, including himself, were shocked that they were able to knock off the mighty Mets. But as far as Franklin Stubbs is concerned, the Dodgers weren't going to be denied, thanks to Scioscia, Gibson, and Hershiser. "Probably the biggest thing that stands out [in that series] is Mike Scioscia's game-tying home run," recalls Stubbs.

I think it was Game 4, when we were down. If we lose that game, we end up going down 3–1. So, that was a huge blow for us . . . and then Hershiser coming into that game to get the save and John Shelby making the good running catch coming in. To me, that was the turning point of the whole thing for us. Then the next day, Kirk Gibson hits the home run against the big Hawaiian lefty, Sid Fernandez. That kinda got us over the hump. I knew David Cone was gonna throw a great game in Game 6 because we'd got him the first time he pitched—so I knew he was gonna throw a great game, and he did. But fortunately for us, we had more pitching than they did. Their pitcher [Ron Darling] kind of ran out of steam a little bit in Game 7, and we took advantage and closed the door.

For Hatcher, being able to clinch the series in front of the home crowd at Dodger Stadium was an incredible feeling. It was emotional for him too, as he'd missed out on playing in the World Series with the Twins in 1987 and the Dodgers in 1981. For Joey Amalfitano, it had been a longer wait; the third-base coach had last made it to a World Series in 1954, when he was a rookie infielder with the New York Giants. Because he signed a bonus contract for $35,000 when he became a professional player in 1954, Amalfitano was known as a "bonus baby" and spent the first two years of his pro career sitting on the bench with the Giants. Under the terms of the bonus baby rule in those days—a rule instituted in 1947 and abolished in 1965—teams were required to keep on the 25-man roster for two full seasons players who were signed to a contract in excess of $4,000. Otherwise, the team would lose rights to the player's contract. Amalfitano never did play in the 1954 World Series, won by the Giants in a four-game sweep over the heavily favored Cleveland Indians.

"It was great," Hatcher says of clinching the pennant at home. "It was absolutely great. The fans were just great. It was unbelievable. And then we went to Tommy Lasorda's restaurant in Pasadena. It was just a great celebration of a bunch of guys who'd worked so hard, and we got there! I think we were just as shocked as anybody else. How did this team get to the World Series? We did it with heart, we did it with a lot of guys with experience. We grinded it out and it was just a very magical year."

"I remember that night too. I was very, very happy to get the chance to go to the World Series," Amalfitano says. "I remember I was sitting there in the top of the ninth, I was very solemn and quiet, which sometimes wasn't really unusual for me. But I remember Tommy saying out loud, 'Hey, look at Joe!'"

John Shelby also remembers that night very well. "I remember running through the crowd of people that ran onto the field and then celebrating the big victory in the locker room."

For Shelby, who'd been a member of the 1983 World Champion Orioles five years earlier, returning to the Fall Classic was nothing new. For Amalfitano, though, it was emotional. "It took me 34 years to get back to a World Series," Amalfitano says.

I was a player in '54. I never played, and shouldn't have played—because I didn't know how to play. I was there [only] because of a rule. I was on the Giants and not in the minors—where I should've been—because I signed a deal for more than $6,000, which meant I had to be on the team's 25-man roster. So, I basically sat on the bench in 1954 and 1955. And now to get a chance to experience this again, and be a part of it where I had something to do with it, because I was at third base . . . that was very, very special, and important to me. Very important to me. It was very important.

For Tracy Woodson, it was his first (and only) trip to the World Series. He recalls counting the number of outs before the Dodgers officially clinched the NL flag. "We had Hershiser on the mound. We got the lead and I think the whole team was ready to explode out of the dugout, knowing that we were gonna go to the World Series. The excitement was great. For some of us, that was [our] first time. It was exciting."

Waiting for the Dodgers were the Oakland A's, who'd swept aside Boston in four games in the ALCS. In the NLCS, David Cone had provided Los Angeles some bulletin board material, and as Joey Amalfitano remembers, Oakland supplied some ammunition just prior to the Fall Classic too.

"There was a comment that was made that they wanted to play the Mets because the Mets were a better team," the third-base coach says matter-of-factly, without any hint of bitterness. "There was a player on that club—I won't bring up his name—who said that. What we did was the advanced scouting report which [Ron] Perranoski and myself, and Tommy would oversee and we'd go over the opposing team."

Amalfitano doesn't care to mention any names, but he's referring to designated hitter Don Baylor, who before the World Series was quoted in the *San Jose (California) Mercury News* as saying the Dodgers were inferior to the Mets. As far as Baylor was concerned, he wanted to play the NL's best team—and that was the Mets. He was also critical of Jay Howell (a former Athletic), saying, "What's he ever done? He couldn't save games over here, so they got rid of him. We want him in the game, all right. . . . He can't handle [pitching with all the people in the stands screaming at him]. He couldn't handle it when he was in New York with the Yankees. I know; I played with him."[2]

Yes, Baylor played with him in New York, but that was a younger Jay Howell who hadn't yet developed into a major-league stopper. Baylor, the 1979 AL MVP with the Angels and a Yankee from 1983 to 1985, was teammates with Howell for only two seasons. While Howell had an ERA of 5.38 in 1983—when he was called upon by manager Billy Martin to make 12 starts and seven relief appearances—he thrived the following year in the Yankees bullpen by going 9–4 with a 2.69 ERA and seven saves in a career-high 103 2/3 innings. Traded to the A's after the 1984 season (along with Jose Rijo and three others) in a deal involving Rickey Henderson, Howell was an All-Star closer in 1985 and 1987 with Oakland, although he logged a 5.89 ERA while pitching hurt in '87. In his three seasons in Oakland, Howell averaged 20 saves a year.

"That was [the day] before the World Series [began]," Amalfitano continues, adding that he agreed with Lasorda's line of thinking to have the team meeting one day early.

> Tommy had the meeting the day before the first game, where we went over the other team. Normally, Tommy would have a meeting to go over the other team the day of the first game of the series. But Tommy felt that we'd concentrate more, we'd get [the Dodgers players'] attention more versus doing it on the day of the opening of the World Series, because it can get kind of dizzy. That was Tommy's doing, and I agreed with it totally—because it is an exciting time in your mind; I wouldn't say it's drifting. But you might be focusing in another direction. If you do it the day before, you get your family stuff in order, and now we got to go to work here.
>
> So, the three scouts were in the meeting, which was unusual because it didn't happen during regular-season play. They were there because Tommy wanted their input. But anyway, what I did was I made copies of the report for everybody, and I put it in a blue binder. And on the first page was this comment that was made, and I put that on the front page. When we started the meeting, I said, "OK, everybody, open up, we're gonna go over this together." As you read the first page, we went after it. We went to critique each guy. What did that have to do with it? Hell, I dunno. But you're looking for the edge. I guess in football or in college, they always put that stuff up.
>
> Then we went over their pluses and the minuses. Did that have anything to do with it? I dunno. But like I said, you're looking for every edge you can possibly get; that's happened in sports where maybe a

member of an organization says something about the opposing team. I guess more in football. But this fellow who said it, well, we just put it on there. Did that win the game for us? Hell, I dunno. That didn't swing the bat or throw a pitch or make a fielding play. It didn't do that. But I think if you're a competitor, and somebody says something about your ability, you might raise yourself up another step or two. I don't know about other people, but I know the way I am. I'm not a world beater in the game of baseball, but I like to compete. If somebody tells me I can't do something, I wanna try and prove them wrong. That's me.

When recounting this story, Amalfitano doesn't once mention Baylor's name but still remembers those comments. As for Baylor, he did remember those comments some 25 years after the fact, telling ESPN.com in 2013 that he'd wanted a second chance against the Mets. After all, Baylor was a member of the 1986 Red Sox who lost to New York in excruciating fashion two years earlier. After finally winning a championship in 1987 with Minnesota (against St. Louis)—and being in the World Series for the third straight year with a third different team—he was eager for a rematch with the Mets. "The Mets were the better team, and I wanted to play the better team," admitted the Oakland designated hitter in 2013. "I was with the Boston Red Sox in 1986, and I wanted another shot at them after they beat us. I wanted another shot at the Mets. It wasn't meant as a slap at the Dodgers, but they took it and made it bulletin board material. That's fine. I don't care."[3]

While Baylor wanted to face the Mets, not everyone in Oakland felt the same. A's closer Dennis Eckersley, for one, has said on several occasions since the 1988 World Series that he was excited about not having to go to New York. "I was happy the Dodgers won because they shouldn't have beaten the Mets. The better team was obviously the Mets," Eckersley once said, believing the A's would simply crush Los Angeles. "The Dodgers just played over their heads. I was happy when the Dodgers won because I thought they were the easier team to beat. I didn't want to go to New York."[4]

The Dodgers were heading to the World Series for the first time since 1981, but they'd be without their offensive leader. Gibson had a pulled left hamstring and a swollen right knee, and wasn't expected to play. "I hurt my hamstring in Game Five against the Mets and got a shot right after that game from Dr. [Frank] Jobe," he told *SI.com* some 25 years later. "I didn't play in Game Six, but I did play in Game Seven. Then I went to break up a double play and I slid funky because of my other leg, and that's when I stretched my medial collateral."[5]

On the morning of the World Series opener, Gibson thought he could play, but realized he couldn't when both of his legs hurt while he was jogging across his living room. He arrived at the ballpark early and had injections in both legs, but he was in so much pain that he didn't take part in pregame ceremonies or batting practice. "Gibson had that football mentality, where he was tough and could deal with any kind of pain or injury," hitting coach Ben Hines remembers. "And now we go to the World Series against Oakland. But he couldn't go in Game 1. And for seven innings of the game, he wasn't gonna play."

Gibson was expected to be a spectator all game, and he sat in the clubhouse—with a bag of ice on each leg—to watch Game 1 on television. Of course, he didn't stay there the entire game. Hearing Vin Scully say to the television audience that he wouldn't be playing, Gibson said, "My ass." By then, it was the eighth inning. He got up, got dressed, and went to the batting tee next to the tunnel which went to the dugout.

When Tommy Lasorda got word in the dugout that Gibson could play and wanted to play, the manager sent him into the game as a pinch hitter with two outs and a runner on base, with Los Angeles trailing by a run against the seemingly invincible Eckersley.

And with one swing, the series would turn in favor of the Dodgers.

CHAPTER EIGHT
TOMMY THE MOTIVATIONAL LEADER

Lasorda was known as a motivator, but if he was ever called into question for being a motivator, he put it all together in this year, I can tell you that. It won't work for everybody, but it worked for this team.

—Jay Howell, Dodgers closer

Man, the man [Lasorda] loved to win. He loved his players. I enjoyed playing for him. Great manager.

—Franklin Stubbs, Dodgers first baseman

Both managers in the 1988 World Series would wind up in the National Baseball Hall of Fame—Tommy Lasorda was inducted in 1997 and Oakland's Tony La Russa in 2014—but other than the fact that they are of Italian descent, the two skippers couldn't be more different.

"In addition to managing the team," baseball writer Phil Elderkin noted of Lasorda during the 1988 World Series, "Tommy is virtually another publicity man—out there every day like a guy on the back of an old-fashioned medicine wagon selling Dodger Blue, Dodger Pride, Dodger Personnel, and even Dodger Dogs. He never saw a player in an L.A. uniform he didn't like. Lasorda doesn't just answer questions; he goes swimming in them, diving fearlessly into uncharted waters for just the right adjectives. In three minutes or less he can make someone like reserve first baseman Franklin Stubbs sound like a candidate for the Hall of Fame."[1]

Indeed. Lasorda was known to motivate his players, telling them they were the greatest team in the world and telling each player that he was the best at his position. It was something that worked in 1988. "[Lasorda would tell me], 'You're the best shortstop [in the world].' You get to a point that you listen to him and you believe it," shortstop Alfredo Griffin once said.[2] Knuckleballer Charlie Hough, a Dodger from 1970 to 1980, once said that the Hall of Fame skipper was "kind of a psycho for believing in yourself." As Hough explained in 2017, "When you play this game, every one of us runs into a stretch where nothing goes right. He would just convince you that you're going to make it go right. He would always say, 'Nobody can believe in you if you don't, so when you walk out to the mound you have to believe you're the greatest pitcher in the world.' And he would say, 'Don't tell anybody, though.'"[3]

Pitcher Tim Leary remembers how Lasorda played a huge role in instilling all these positive thoughts into everybody's minds on that 1988 team. It became a whole team with the mind-set of believing in themselves. The alternative, Leary says, would have been detrimental. "Negative thoughts ruin a lot of sports careers, as all you hear is heckling," explains Leary. "So, you have to tune that out and tell yourself, 'I can execute and beat him,' nonstop! Strong minds win. That was a very, very *big* part of the '88 team's mind-set. Lasorda played a big part in that."

Lasorda, known for never berating his players in front of reporters, was also never regarded as a manager who relied on statistical analysis the way that La Russa did. The Dodgers manager, instead, had a reputation of managing on hunches. Lasorda, for instance, might pinch-hit, hit-and-run, and bunt where you didn't expect him to. Or he might pull a pitcher on a hunch. "I know writers who don't think Lasorda could manage anything as complex as a pushcart," Elderkin added in his 1988 commentary about the Dodgers' skipper. "It's hard to argue, though, with the fact that Tommy has won six division titles in the last 12 years. No other big-league manager has done that."[4]

La Russa, meanwhile, was seen as a manager who seemed to do it all, getting his teams to play above their capabilities. "Tony La Russa is the un-Lasorda," baseball historian George Will once said, depicting La Russa as a skipper who made more use of statistical analysis than any other. "He's a meticulous planner. To La Russa, counting on adrenaline is not good planning."[5]

La Russa, known as a manager who motivated without screaming or hollering at his players, took teams with injuries and produced. He was known for taking teams with difficult-to-manage players and making them positive and contributing factors. He was innovative with his lineups; he wasn't afraid to pinch-hit. La Russa, for instance, wouldn't hesitate to replace right-handed hitting Dave Henderson with a left-handed-hitting pinch hitter if the opposing manager brought in a right-handed reliever. He wouldn't be afraid to get Mark McGwire, a slugger, to put the bunt down when the opportunity arose. "Tony was great at handling egos," A's outfielder Dave Parker once said of his manager. "Very smart. He had to be, because we had an All-Star team. He brought us altogether and made [us] all a team. . . . He was the most prepared manager I played for."[6]

La Russa was also the one who converted Dennis Eckersley, a veteran starter who'd thrown a no-hitter in 1977 and won 20 games in 1978, into a reliever. He even took the advice of pitching coach Dave Duncan and decided to use Eckersley for only one inning at a time—the ninth inning. In 1988, Eckersley rewarded La Russa with a league-leading 45 saves. "The thing with Tony," Eckersley once said, "is that when you're on the other side of the field, you think he makes too many moves. But when you're on his team, you understand that the moves help the bullpen, which makes all the pitchers better. He knows what he's doing."[7]

Because of the way he used his bullpen with the A's teams—going with lefty-lefty matchups and righty-righty matchups—La Russa has been credited with refining the way bullpens operate, pioneering the use of the specialized bullpen. While he wasn't the first to employ the tactic, the modern concept of using the closer just for one inning and just in save situations stems from the way he used Eckersley. "He understood the role of the closer before anyone else; he knew how important the bullpen was to a club," Eckersley said of La Russa, praising his manager's vision. "No one could have foreseen back then what it would evolve into one day. But I do believe it is what it is because of La Russa."[8]

Yet it was Lasorda, a two-time NL Manager of the Year (1983 and 1988), who made all the right moves in the '88 World Series. Not only did he motivate his players into believing they could win; Lasorda also made moves that worked out. Take Game 4 in Oakland. When he employed the hit-and-run, the move worked out enough times for Los Angeles to manufacture sufficient runs to take a lead into the late innings. When

Lasorda then trusted his closer to record the final seven outs for a pivotal save in a one-run game—a call his Oakland counterpart likely wouldn't have made—the move again worked out. It was that type of a postseason for the Dodgers skipper.

As sportswriter Joel Bierig noted in the *Chicago Sun-Times*, Lasorda's moves even worked out in the NL playoffs. Bierig pointed to one specific lineup change Lasorda employed early in the Mets series that wasn't injury related. "He put Mickey Hatcher at first base after Franklin Stubbs failed to advance baserunners in the first playoff game," noted Bierig following the World Series, referring to Lasorda's benching of Stubbs in the NLCS after his failures in two bunting situations against the Mets' Dwight Gooden in the series opener. "Not only did Hatcher move runners, he moved mountains [by hitting .300 with a team-high eight RBIs in the postseason]."[9]

And an instance of Lasorda having no problem pulling his pitcher if he felt he needed to make a change no matter how early it was came in Game 1 against Oakland. The Dodgers trailed 4–2 in the second inning, but Lasorda pinch-hit for starter Tim Belcher and handed the game to his bullpen for the next seven innings. Once again, that move worked out as the bullpen kept the A's off the scoreboard and Kirk Gibson's miraculous ninth-inning homer won it for Los Angeles.

Boston Globe columnist Bob Ryan covered mostly the local American League Red Sox—and interleague play didn't exist during Lasorda's time as a major-league skipper—but the veteran writer is familiar with the former Dodgers manager. Ryan covered the 1988 NLCS in its entirety for the *Globe*, and upon reflecting back on that series 30 years later, recalls that Lasorda's best move was never backing away from Orel Hershiser in big moments. "So much about that year was Hershiser," says Ryan today.

> He had enough sense to keep running Hershiser out there, including out of the bullpen. I still have an image of him after the Gibson home run. Yes, I can still see him, his hat off, his arms up skyward, and all that. It was part of his shtick, if you will, by that time. I actually met him when he was in Albuquerque in 1972 when I was writing a book on minor-league baseball. He was the manager of the best minor-league team in the last 50 years. And *that* is no exaggeration. Go look up the

'72 Albuquerque Dukes. So, I was always curious and interested because of having seen him back then.

While Ryan no longer remembers all the specific moves that Lasorda made during the 1988 NLCS, he does recall one thing. "'Go get 'em, Bulldog!' I think that was the best move he made, not forgetting where Orel Hershiser was."

Tracy Woodson, one of the Dodgers' Stuntmen in 1988, remembers pinch-hitting for Stubbs in Game 4 of the World Series in Oakland. With runners on first and third in the seventh—and just one out—Woodson hit a grounder to shortstop. But because Lasorda had called for a hit-and-run on the 1-and-2 pitch, A's shortstop Walt Weiss's throw to second base wasn't in time as Steve Sax, the runner on first, was running and had gotten to the bag. So, Oakland only got the one out at first base, and a big run scored from third. The Dodgers went on to win 4–3 to take a three-games-to-one lead. "Tommy just made all the right moves in the World Series," Woodson says now. "He had a lot of hit-and-runs that were right on. In that situation, Sax was running on the play—and all I had to do was put the ball in play. We won that game by a run. It was huge."

Jay Howell offers a unique perspective, having also played for Billy Martin (Yankees), Yogi Berra (Yankees), Tony La Russa (Athletics), and Bobby Cox (Braves). "Lasorda had a big-time fire," Howell says today. "La Russa was like that. Bobby was like that. I had Billy Martin. He had a huge fire. They all did. Those four. Temper. Fire." As for Lasorda specifically, Howell remembers that the Dodgers' Hall of Fame skipper was as good a prankster as there was when it came to managers.

"Tommy used to keep it light during spring training. Tommy's deal was he wanted to have fun in spring training," Howell recalls.

I was not accustomed to that. I had no idea coming into a Dodger spring-training camp the difference, of feeling like you had [stand-up comedian and actor] Don Rickles talking to you in the morning. And Lasorda would start the day off with a story, a joke, a prank. It didn't matter to him. He was gonna make it fun. He'd call a meeting and everyone's sitting there. He'd end it with a story, a joke, and you just start laughing, and then you hit the field.

It was very, very different from anything that I'd ever encountered on any team. He was consistent about it too. I remember he always had a situation going on with his GI tract. Always, for whatever reason. It might've been his diet. There was usually the situation going on where he had excess gas and usually when he let one, it wasn't a bouquet of flowers, putting it mildly. At times, he'd call it "crop dusting" when he'd walk down the plane, and he'd love to do that after a win and you were traveling. He'd walk down the aisle of the plane and then stop and say, "I like what you're doing. I love your approach at the plate; it's changed," and while he's talking, he's just letting these silent-but-deadly farts go on the plane. You could tell whenever he was doing that. I mean, you knew when he had game, it was pretty rough. He could just blow out the whole back of a plane. He loved to do that.

While the Dodgers' spring training in 1988 was defined by Gibson walking out prior to a game because of a prank played by pitcher Jesse Orosco—and later telling the rest of the Dodgers that he was in town to win and not to clown around—Howell acknowledges that Lasorda himself was a big part of the practical jokes in the clubhouse. "Lasorda would have a little urinal in his office when you walked into the clubhouse in spring training at Vero," Howell says, giving an example of one of Lasorda's pranks.

There was a little toilet. It was just very small, just a little toilet. On an occasion when he was feeling particularly toxic, he'd tell some of the veterans, "Hey, get the guys together. Watch this. I'm gonna go back into my office. Get one of the rookies, and tell him I wanna talk to him."

The veterans would go get somebody and say, "Hey! Tommy wants to talk to you. He's in his office." We'd follow the kid. He'd walk through the office and stand at the door. The urinal would be in the back. The door would open. Tommy would say, "Son, I just wanna talk to you a little bit about what it's like being a Dodger. I'm gonna tell you what I expect out of you when you wear the Dodger Blue. Come here, son, I can hardly hear you." The kid would then walk into the middle of his office. And there's Tommy, door open. "Come here, I'm talking to you." He'd tell the kid, "Come here a second. You see that toilet paper roll over there? I've been throwing a lot of BP I can hardly move my arm. My elbow's killing me. Would you pull me off some toilet paper?" He'd have to lean over Lasorda's legs to start pulling the toilet paper. The room smells like a toxic waste dump, and the kid's eyes are watering as he's pulling the toilet paper out. Tommy would just keep going. He wouldn't quit. "No, I need more! I need more than that!" The kid would keep pulling the toilet paper up until he had a whole wad of it—until he realized it was a joke. And we'd all start laughing. That was the kind of thing that happened. That was typical.

But the urinal prank wasn't the only thing. Lasorda also pulled off the traditional three-man lift annually with rookies—or unsuspecting visitors—where he'd get bullpen coach Mark Cresse involved. Continues Howell: "Mark Cresse would say, 'Yeah, I've been doing a lot of weight-lifting. I'm much stronger this year. I swear to God. I can lift three guys if you all lie down on the ground. I was doing it this past winter and I had three guys who were 250 pounds each and I could grab the middle guy—you'd interlock your arms and legs—and I could lift everybody off the ground.'" The veteran players, meanwhile, would make the prank more believable by collecting a phony pot of money. One of the rookies would get on the floor with two veterans. Cresse would then pretend he was going to lift up all three men, but instead the team would douse the unsuspecting rookie with all sorts of nasty things.

"The veterans would say, 'Oh, bullshit! No way! There's no way you can do that! I'll bet you a hundred bucks!' And so the betting would start. Tommy would take Scioscia, and say, 'Okay, Mike. You lie down. I need two volunteers. I need somebody. How about you?' They'd pick a veteran and a rookie," says Howell, explaining the prank.

> Scioscia would say, "No, you need to have the lighter guy in the middle and the two heavier guys. That'll be more difficult. Gotta be more difficult." So, the two veterans would get on either side. The guy's in the middle. They interlock the arms and legs. Get them all ready. And [Cresse] walks up to grab [the rookie's] belt. He loosens the belt. And everybody comes in with mustard and mayonnaise and ketchup and shaving cream, and you just cover him—spray him all down. Now he's got shaving cream all over his face, and that's the meeting. "Okay, boys, let's hit the field." And I mean, it was always a good time.

Then there was also the story of how, one year during a spring-training game, Lasorda pulled a prank on Mickey Hatcher, who was then with Minnesota. He cut up Hatcher's trousers and had the remains run up a flagpole during a Dodgers–Twins game. "It was a good time to start in the morning," continues Howell. "Tommy was like that. It was consistent and deliberate. It was a pretty funny clubhouse. And then you had Gibson with the eye black. 'This isn't gonna happen.' He comes in and says, 'No wonder you guys finished last last year. You think this is funny?' And it put a little damper on it. It slowed it down."

All the joking and pranks aside, Howell adds that Lasorda did an outstanding managerial job in 1988.

> I can't say enough about Lasorda guiding that '88 team. I think a good part of that was he was very positive and he allowed the chemistry to work on the team. And Lasorda had these nicknames for everybody. He called Orel Hershiser the Bulldog. He called the bench players the Stuntmen. Those players played a huge role in the playoffs and World Series. Without them, we wouldn't have done it. Lasorda had built them up as the Stuntmen of LA. That stands out. Lasorda had these names that built up the bench players and they felt like they were a unit and they came together for us in the playoffs and the World Series.

When pitcher Jerry Reuss received an interview request to discuss Lasorda, at first he was skeptical—because he wasn't around in 1988. However, Reuss was gracious enough to accept the request and he offers some perspectives on his former manager.

> I wasn't a part of the '88 team. I knew some of the people, some of the people involved, with the '88 team, but I left in early '87. By the time they played the World Series in '88, that's two complete seasons—well over a year and a half. And in baseball terms, boy, do people change a whole lot. I [had been] gone for a while. Personalities change.
>
> I don't know what happened in '88. I just know about him for the eight years that I played for him. I imagine because of the personnel, he had to manage differently. Generally speaking about Tommy, like a lot of other managers, he had all the information he needed. It wasn't done like the way it is now, at least from what I perceive. Tommy managed by the seat of his pants, and he made some guesses, and more times than not, his guesses were right on. He had a unique way of gauging his personnel and what they could do. That's why he'd play things pretty close to the cuff on a daily basis. There are other managers who did things a lot differently—what they did was chart things out, figure out what the matchups were going to be, and then play the game before the game was even played. That wasn't the case with Tommy.

An example, of course, came in the ninth inning of Game 6 of the 1985 NLCS, when Lasorda went with a hunch and refused to intentionally walk Cardinals slugger Jack Clark with two men on and first base open. Instead, Lasorda allowed reliever Tom Niedenfuer, working his third inning in relief of Hershiser, to face him. Two innings earlier, Niedenfuer had struck Clark out. So, Lasorda wanted Niedenfuer to face Clark again with the Dodgers one out away from forcing a seventh game—instead of walking him and going after Andy Van Slyke, who at the time was batting .100 in the playoffs. Clark made the Dodgers pay by smacking a three-run homer, the Cardinals won the pennant, and Lasorda was second-guessed for that decision—until he guided the 1988 team to the championship.

If anyone tries to second-guess Lasorda now, Steve Sax wants to hear none of it. "Oh yeah," says Sax matter-of-factly.

> You know what? I mean, everyone's an expert when it doesn't go your way. [When] you make a move, there's a chance it's not gonna turn out right; it doesn't mean it was the wrong move. It just didn't work out.

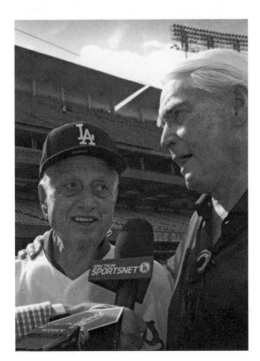

Fred Claire catches up with Tommy Lasorda on Old-Timers' Day at Dodger Stadium in 2017. *Fred Claire*

Tom was a right-handed pitcher. Jack Clark was a big home-run hitter. I don't know what the numbers were with those guys; they didn't use sabermetrics back then. You know, Jack Clark hit a home run that probably still hasn't come down. That's the way it goes sometimes. Everybody wants to be an expert after the fact. You wonder how many people want to put money on it and call it before the fact, but you don't see that a lot. You know, we won the World Series and Tommy was our manager. I won two World Series with Tommy, and he [is in] the Hall of Fame. I think that speaks volumes.

Mickey Hatcher, who was given a chance to play regularly in the World Series after spending the season as one of the Stuntmen, can't say enough about the job Lasorda did in 1988. Given the roster he had to deal with, says Hatcher, Lasorda deserves to be in Cooperstown based on his work with that team. "If you look back at any managers in the game of baseball, yeah, when you got the players to win it, that's great," Hatcher says now. "But Tommy probably managed his ass off that year with all the players that he had to deal with. I'm sure it was a flip of the coin a lot of the times he had to make the lineup card out. But we got through it. Any other team in baseball that won it, can't look back and say how special it was, [the way it was special] with us. They can never say that."

PART THREE

THE A'S SERIES

When I came in, [Gibson] told me he can't play. He was really suffering, and he couldn't do it. If he had half a chance of doing it, he would have done it, but he said, "I just can't do it. My leg is really hurting me." So I figured that was it. Every inning I'd go into the clubhouse and stand at the door of the trainer's room and say, "How are you feeling, big boy?" Maybe he'd feel better and come back out, and each time he put his thumbs down and I'd go back out.

—Tommy Lasorda, Dodgers manager,
speaking to ESPN.com in 2013

CHAPTER NINE
GIBSON'S HOME RUN

*I told Kirk that in all my years with the Dodgers, that was my greatest con-
tribution, getting you off the rubbing table.*

—Vin Scully, Dodgers broadcaster calling the play-by-play for
NBC-TV, speaking to *USA Today* in 2013[1]

*It was an exciting time, an exciting year. That first game at Dodger Stadium,
with Kirk Gibson hitting the home run, really set the tone. I think probably
what was so special was nobody expected the Dodgers to win that year—having lost to the Mets [10 out of 11] games, and then beating them to get into
the World Series. So, it was a magical year.*

—Charlie Blaney, Dodgers farm director

The Oakland Athletics, winners of 104 games during the 1988 season,
were widely expected to beat the Dodgers in the World Series. Oakland,
led by young mashers Jose Canseco and Mark McGwire as well as the
pitching of ace Dave Stewart and reliever Dennis Eckersley, had been the
best team in baseball throughout the course of the season. "The intimida-
tion factor started when we walked out on the field, and then it continued
when Dave Stewart grabbed the ball," Dave Henderson once said of the
Athletics and the team's ace, who every fifth day stared down hitters from
beneath his cap before blowing them away. "He had that devilish stare.
He'd look down on you and say, 'There's no way you're gonna beat me.'"[2]

In fact, in terms of regular-season wins, this A's team was the greatest ever seen by the Oakland fan base. The 104 victories represented the most in franchise history since the club was located in Philadelphia in 1931, when the Philadelphia Athletics went 107–45 before losing to the Cardinals in the World Series. Following that seven-game defeat, the team didn't win another pennant in Philadelphia, and when the franchise relocated to Kansas City in 1955, the A's never won more than 74 games a year or finished higher than sixth in the eight- (before expansion) to 10-team (post-expansion) American League. When the team relocated again, this time to Oakland in 1968, the A's saw more success. When MLB adopted divisional play in 1969, the A's finished second in the newly created AL West for two years in a row. Oakland, thanks to a star-studded roster that included Hall-of-Famers-to-be Reggie Jackson, Rollie Fingers, and Catfish Hunter along with All-Stars Sal Bando, Joe Rudi, and Vida Blue, then ran off a streak of five consecutive AL West titles from 1971 to 1975.

Surprisingly, the highest regular-season win total for Oakland's back-to-back-to-back World Championship teams from 1972 to 1974 was 94, which the 1973 club accomplished by going 94–68. (Ironically, the 1970s Oakland clubs that won more games didn't even advance to the World Series. The 1971 A's, who won 101 games, were swept in the ALCS by Baltimore, winners of the same number of games. The 1975 club, which went 98–64, was also swept in the ALCS, by the 95-win Red Sox.)

These 1988 A's, with Canseco and McGwire, were expected to capture multiple championships of their own. Led by Eckersley and Canseco, they got off to a fine start in the postseason by sweeping Boston in the ALCS. Eckersley saved all four games to earn series MVP honors, while Canseco, the major-league leader in homers and RBIs, contributed three big flies—with each either tying the game or putting Oakland ahead.

Since interleague play wouldn't be introduced until 1997, Los Angeles and Oakland never met during the 1988 season, but the A's were still expected to win the World Series easily. Even if the Dodgers' pitching staff could shut down the Canseco-McGwire duo, there were still hard-hitting veterans such as Dave Henderson, Dave Parker, and Carney Lansford to do some damage. Although Don Baylor didn't provide much pop—only seven homers while batting .220 in 92 games—he could be counted on in the clutch. The Dodgers, without the injured Gibson, who was bothered by the right knee and the left hamstring, didn't seem to have a prayer.

And while the Dodgers had outstanding pitching, so did the Athletics, whose staff led the AL with a 3.44 ERA. Stewart, an ex-Dodger, was their ace, going 21–12 with a 3.23 ERA and completing 14 of his major-league-leading 37 starts. Eckersley, meanwhile, was dominant the entire season coming out of the bullpen. But Oakland had several other mound contributors. Bob Welch, another former Dodger (traded in the off-season to Oakland as part of a three-team deal involving the Mets), went 17–9 with a 3.64 ERA in 36 starts. Rick Honeycutt, yet another ex-Dodger (traded in August 1987 to Oakland in a deal that sent Tim Belcher to Los Angeles), recorded seven saves while working as a left-handed specialist in the A's bullpen. After struggling during mid-season, Honeycutt had notched a 2.10 ERA in his 19 appearances over the final two months of the season.

Mel Antonen, then an AL beat writer for *USA Today*, remembers how stacked that Oakland club was when asked today to reflect back about those Athletics. "They had a lot of pitching," Antonen says.

> They had incredible starting pitching. They had, obviously, a great bullpen with Dennis Eckersley, Gene Nelson, and Rick Honeycutt. They had speed at the top of their order, and they had good power with McGwire and Canseco in the middle. I mean, they just had it all. High-average hitters, Carney Lansford. Good defense, Walt Weiss. Top-notch bullpen, Dennis Eckersley. Starting pitching, I believe Dave Stewart and Bob Welch were their leading pitchers that year. My point is, they had a little bit of everything. They won 104 games and won their division by 28 games, I believe [actually, 13 games]. They were just so unstoppable because they had everything. I mean, Carney Lansford was an incredible hitter. But then they had the power of Mark McGwire and Jose Canseco. Dave Henderson hit .304. Don Baylor was their DH. I mean, they had world-class everything! [Terry] Steinbach was their catcher. They just had a lot of everything.

Jay Howell, who had come over to Los Angeles with shortstop Alfredo Griffin from Oakland in the Welch deal, acknowledges today that it felt odd to face his ex-teammates in the World Series less than a year after the trade. "It was strange. Bob Welch. Rick Honeycutt. There were a number of Dodgers on the A's, and vice versa. Alfredo Griffin, me, Belcher," says Howell, who despite having bone chips in his elbow in 1987 still tied for the A's club lead with 16 saves. "It was a little strange for me because I'd left Oakland, came over to LA. I had surgery—I'd left Oakland having surgery on my elbow—but it was not major. I had a bone spur and I was pitching with pain there. I was really successful and had a good year. It was kind of interesting playing against players that had the familiarity with the Dodgers and us having familiarity with the A's. And I knew some of the tendencies with some of the hitters, obviously. So, that was interesting."

Howell wouldn't see any action in Game 1 on the night of October 15, 1988, at Dodger Stadium. Belcher got the start and, in what turned out to be an abbreviated outing, gave up a second-inning grand slam to Canseco. He was removed for a pinch hitter after just two innings, and Tim Leary, normally a starter, took over. The A's must have been delighted to see Leary; in 1986 when the right-hander was with Milwaukee, the Athletics pounded him in his three starts against them for 12 earned runs in 14 innings (a 7.71 ERA). Over the course of his career, Leary would be 1–10 against Oakland with a 5.71 ERA in 15 regular-season appearances.

But Leary in 1988 was a different pitcher. Coming off a horrendous 1987 in which he went 3–11, he knew what he had to do to ensure a comeback season. "I knew I needed to, number one, pitch in winter ball, [and] number two, work on the shoulder exercises that [team physician] Dr. [Frank] Jobe had designed," Leary recalls. "I found that I had a weakness in the infraspinatus muscle [one of the four rotator cuff muscles]! So, I lifted three-pound weights in the very specific way. All four exercises. Then, moved up to two sets! When I got to two sets of 12 reps, I moved up to five pounds [and] one set of eight reps. And over time, got up to two sets of 12 reps with five-pound weights." (In weight training, a rep, or repetition, is one complete motion of an exercise. A set is a group of consecutive repetitions.)

When the calendar turned to 1988, Leary felt confident in his pitches.

And that was while the '87 season was finishing and in October when I started playing for Los Potros de Tijuana in the Mexican Winter League. The combination of getting very, very strong, and pitching nine innings every five to seven days, plus running, abdominal work, etcetera, led to a 12–1 winter, with 138 innings and much more confidence in all of my pitches—especially the two-seam fastball down and the split-finger fastball! I could attack any hitter with just those two pitches and get groundballs and strikeouts—and jam shots. For left-handed hitters, I also used a cut fastball, a four-seam fastball "in," and some low-and-away semi-screwball changeups! I was a new and improved pitcher! The best I'd ever been. I had a great spring, made the rotation, pitched a three-hit shutout versus San Diego in my third start with 11 Ks, and was feeling strong!

Leary would win 17 games before faltering down the stretch. But in the third inning of Game 1 against Oakland, Tommy Lasorda called on the right-hander, and Leary—a forgotten hero in that opening contest—responded with three scoreless frames to keep the Dodgers close, including a big strikeout of Terry Steinbach with two on to end the fourth.

As a Brewer, Tim Leary struggled against the A's. In the 1988 World Series with the Dodgers, however, the right-hander worked three clutch innings in Game 1 as Los Angeles rallied and won on Kirk Gibson's home run. Those three scoreless frames, says Leary, were the most important innings of his career. *Milwaukee Brewers*

The Athletics, thanks to Canseco's grand slam and eight strong innings by Stewart, led 4–3 going into the bottom of the ninth. With Oakland three outs away from victory, Eckersley was called upon to try and close things out. Eckersley was nearly automatic in 1988; the Hall-of-Famer-to-be registered 45 saves during the season and surrendered just five home runs in 72 2/3 innings. And now, Eck was gunning for his 50th save of 1988, including the postseason.

But while the game was going on, something was happening behind the scenes for the Dodgers. During the late innings, the injured Gibson had been getting ready for an at-bat.

Ben Hines remembers that night vividly.

> I thought it was a miracle because for seven innings of the game, he wasn't gonna play. He set up in the trainers' room and he kept hearing Vin Scully say that he wasn't gonna play. He kept hearing Vinny say, "Kirk Gibson's not gonna be in this game tonight." Well, I'd go up and check on him about every inning. Tommy [Lasorda] would send me to see if he had anything. Finally, when I went up in the eighth, [Gibson] said, "I think I've got an at-bat for you. I'll give you an at-bat in the ninth." He saw that there was gonna be a spot for him with Eckersley on the mound. He said, "I can give you an at-bat in the ninth."

All of this was happening without the knowledge of anybody in the stands or in the A's dugout—or even in the press box. After recording two quick outs, Eckersley faced ex-teammate Mike Davis, who was pinch-hitting for Griffin, with infielder Dave Anderson now standing in the on-deck circle as a decoy; Lasorda didn't want the Athletics to know Gibson was ready. A year earlier, Davis had hit .265 with 22 long balls for Oakland. In 1988 with the Dodgers, though, he'd batted just .196 with two homers. Eckersley, who had pinpoint control, inexplicably walked Davis, setting up the dramatic Hollywood moment with the limping Gibson coming up to bat.

As both Eckersley and Davis recalled some 25 years later, the A's stopper was thinking of a guy with legitimate home-run power—which Davis had shown in 1987—instead of a Dodger who finished 1988 below the Mendoza Line. "I was giving him too much credit," Eckersley told *SI.com.* "I had respect for his power. On that last pitch, I was outside, way outside. It was brutal. I was remembering his home runs." Concurred

Davis: "I wasn't expecting a walk because Eck didn't walk many batters. . . . Eck was probably thinking of the guy that he played with in Oakland. But this was different. I was having a bad year."[3]

Eckersley also was pitching carefully to Davis because he had to have seen the light-hitting Anderson standing on deck. Why let a 20-homer guy like Davis beat you when you could pitch around him and face the less-dangerous Anderson instead? But, of course, as soon as Davis walked, Anderson retreated back to the dugout as Gibson emerged. "If Davis gets on, wait 'til you see the crowd's reaction," Tracy Woodson told Mickey Hatcher on the Dodgers bench. As Gibson limped to the plate, the 55,000-plus fans at Dodger Stadium rose to their feet cheering.

Eckersley, speaking to *SI.com* in 2013, remembered Gibson taking his sweet time to get into the batter's box. "It took Gibson forever to get up to the plate. FOREVER," Eckersley recalled. "It was grueling waiting for him to get to the plate. We assumed he wasn't going to play. So I was surprised. I had a long time to think about Gibson coming into the game. You could have written a book in the time that it took him to get ready."[4]

Batting in the ninth spot of the batting order—for reliever Alejandro Peña—the hobbling Gibson fouled off the first two pitches. He then hit a weak grounder down the first-base line and limped toward the bag—but the ball curved foul. Next came a backdoor slider on the outside corner, which Gibson laid off for ball one. Gibson fouled another pitch off, and when Eckersley missed outside for ball two, Davis stole second base. Now, all Gibson had to think about was shortening his swing and trying to get a base hit to score Davis.

He worked the count to 3 and 2 before taking a short swing and sending a backdoor slider out over the plate into a spot five rows deep in the right-field seats. As Gibson hobbled around the bases pumping his fist, Dodger Stadium went crazy and CBS Radio's Jack Buck exclaimed into his mic, "I don't believe . . . what I just saw!"

Nobody had ever seen this type of ending in World Series play. Ever. Since World Series play began in 1903, nobody had ever hit a come-from-behind, game-ending homer to win a World Series contest. While there had been six game-ending homers in series history up to that point, Gibson's marked the first time that a final-inning homer had taken a team that was losing to a sudden victory. Tommy Henrich (1949 Yankees), against Brooklyn's Don Newcombe; Dusty Rhodes (1954 Giants), against

Cleveland's Bob Lemon; Eddie Mathews (1957 Milwaukee Braves), off the Yankees' Bob Grim; Bill Mazeroski (1960 Pirates), off the Yankees' Ralph Terry; Mickey Mantle (1964 Yankees), against the Cardinals' Barney Schultz; and Carlton Fisk (1975 Red Sox), off Cincinnati's Pat Darcy, had all hit game-ending homers in World Series play prior to Gibson's blast, but each of those six players had done so with the game tied.

In 1993, Toronto's Joe Carter would hit a come-from-behind, World Series–ending homer against Philadelphia—a three-run blast with the Blue Jays trailing 6–5—to win the series in Game 6. The Blue Jays' Ed Sprague, in the 1992 World Series, would be the second player after Gibson to hit a go-ahead homer in the ninth inning with his team trailing. Sprague's two-run shot in the top of the ninth in Atlanta came with Toronto behind 4–3. It should be noted, too, that two years prior to Gibson's blast, the Mets' Lenny Dykstra had, in the 1986 NLCS against Houston, become the first player in postseason history to hit a come-from-behind, game-ending homer. The 1951 NL tiebreaker series, which ended on Bobby Thomson's famous "Shot Heard 'Round the World" homer, counted as regular-season games—not postseason contests.

Although Gibson's game-winner is referred to today as a walk-off homer and the origin of the term *walk-off home run* has been credited to Eckersley, the adjective *walk-off* didn't attain widespread use until the late 1990s and early 2000s. When Gibson hit his game-winner, newspapers of the day would call it a "game-ending" homer. If such a dinger had ended a series, then it would be a "series-ending" (or "series-clinching") home run.

Boston Globe sports columnist Dan Shaughnessy once wondered how the term *walk-off* came about. "Walk-off was first used in reference to game-ending home runs, but now we see headlines and hear commentators talking about walk-off hits, walk-off walks, walk-off balks, walk-off hit-by-pitches, and walk-off errors," noted Shaughnessy in the *Globe* in 2005, although the walk-off balk has also been dubbed a balk-off. "Few of today's major-leaguers can remember when they first noticed the new terminology, but there's little doubt ESPN has put 'walk-off' into the mainstream of American sports talk."[5]

"I hate to take credit, but I guess it was me," Eckersley acknowledged in 2005. "It's not a good thing for a pitcher. You don't want to be known for giving it up. I'd hate to be the one talking about walk-offs like I was the master of 'em." According to *The New Dickson Baseball Dictionary*, the first walk-off reference appeared July 30, 1988, in the *Gannett News Service*: "In Dennis Eckersley's colorful vocabulary, a 'walk-off' piece is a home run that wins the game and the pitcher walks off the mound." Eckersley confirmed he'd said that. "That's right," the Hall of Fame closer continued, adding that ESPN was the one responsible for making the term popular. "It was always walk-off *piece*. Like something you would hang in an art gallery. The walk-off piece is a horrible piece of art. The Gibson one had a lot of play in it, but if it wasn't for ESPN, we probably wouldn't have any of this crap."[6]

But nobody at Dodger Stadium was concerned about any of that walk-off trivia; everybody had just witnessed an incredible moment with Gibson ending the game with that homer and pumping his fist. And while that's what everyone remembers today—Gibson going deep and celebrating limping around the bases—others recall that Oakland was just inches away from getting that final out to seal a victory. "So when he came up, I threw him nothing but fastballs," Eckersley recalled in 2013, referring to the fact that the A's game plan was to throw Gibson only heat. "The first couple of swings [were] feeble. He hit the nubber down the first-base line. Me, [first baseman Mark] McGwire and him were all standing in the same place. If the ball had been fair, I could have picked it up and tagged him. That could have been the last out, and this event would have never been talked about."[7]

Up in the NBC-TV broadcast booth, meanwhile, Vin Scully, who was also a Dodgers play-by-play announcer, prayed that Gibson wouldn't embarrass himself as the injured slugger limped up to home plate. "Please, God, don't let him strike out. He's had such a great year. He's led the team and worked so hard. And now that he's on the national stage, just don't let him strike out," Scully recalled to *USA Today* in 2013. "Never, ever, did I think he'd hit a home run."[8]

Steve Sax, the Dodgers' leadoff hitter, had a unique view of Gibson's homer. Standing in the on-deck circle and waiting to bat next, Sax thought the game might come down to himself against Eckersley. "I just remember at that time I was trying to figure out how I was gonna win the game off Eckersley, because Gibson, if he got on, it was gonna be in my hands," Sax recalls. "Then Mike Davis stole second base. I thought they might walk Gibson because first base was open. But they didn't. And he was throwing the fastball right by Gibson, and I don't know the reason he threw that backdoor slider that didn't break. That's the one that Gibson hit. But he was just throwing the fastball right by him, and he kept just barely fouling it off. I thought he was gonna get Gibson out with the fastball for sure. But he threw the backdoor slider, and Gibson hit it out of the park."

Rick Dempsey, who didn't play in Game 1, considers the homer to be one of the biggest in the history of the game. "Well, it was one of the most iconic moments in the history of baseball," Dempsey says now.

I can remember him in New York, coming in to catch a line drive—what should've been a base hit to left field—and full out diving and catching the ball . . . and him straining his hamstring doing that. Of course, we were glad that he made that catch. But everybody was concerned because we were now going into a World Series situation without our star player. But it happened and so coming into the World Series, whether he was gonna get a chance to play at all, with that bad hamstring, we didn't think we'd ever get a chance to see him.

But in that first game, when Tommy Lasorda called on him and he limped up to the batter's box, nobody in baseball felt like he was even gonna have a chance to swing the bat and get around on the ball. And the way he looked, off of Eckersley's fastball, he was late on it every time. The best swing he had, he chopped the ball down the first-base line and limped out of the batter's box. We just pretty much knew that that game was probably gonna be over with, very quickly. But then we also had a scouting report on Dennis Eckersley, that once he got to a 3-and-2 count on every left-handed hitter, he always threw a slider on the outside corner. We went over that in the pre-game meeting. We got to the 3-and-2 count, and he couldn't get around on the fastball. Eckersley threw him the changeup, which everybody knows kind of speeds up the bat a little bit. He threw that slider on the outside corner, and as soon as Gibby made contact, it was game over. We knew that ball was gone when it left the infield. It was just one of the most amazing home runs in the history of the game, to come back and beat the Oakland A's in Game 1. It was just inconceivable.

Hines, the hitting coach, recalls the late innings vividly.

When I went up in the eighth, [Gibson] said, "I think I've got an at-bat for you. I'll give you an at-bat in the ninth. I can give you an at-bat in the ninth." I really thought he thought he was gonna go in and hit in [Alfredo Griffin's spot], which was the eighth hole, but he didn't. Mike Davis went up [and batted for Griffin instead] and had one of the greatest at-bats he'd had all season, because he was not a walker. He swung at everything. And I don't know how he got a little plate discipline in that ninth [inning] of that first game of the World Series, and he laid off some pitches that he normally would swing at. And he had a 3-and-1 count, and boom! Eckersley threw him another backdoor slider that was outside, and he walked.

That set Gibby up with a chance—if Davis stole, he might score [on a base hit]—to at least tie the game. Davis stole second, and half of Gibby's at-bat it was a man on first base, and then the other half he had a man on second base. So, all he had to do is punch in a single someplace out there, and he'd at least tie the game. But the count got to 3 and 2, and one of our postseason scouts had come back with the information that when it gets to 3 and 2, Eckersley will throw you a backdoor slider, which meant that it comes from the outside corner and tries to catch a little bit of the outside corner.

So, Gibby stepped out of the box and tells himself that that pitch is coming. So, he knew he could wait a little longer to pull the trigger. And if you look at the side view when he was hitting, he took a stride but his hands didn't go anyplace. His hands stayed back with the cock still in his swing. And here comes the backdoor slider. Then he hit it, mostly with his arms and primarily with his hands and wrist, and he hit that home run. It wasn't like he really got his hips into it. It was mostly hands and wrist and arms. And he squared it up enough that it went into the bleachers.

Hines is also a fan of NBC broadcaster Bob Costas's description of the events leading up to Gibson's game-winner in Ken Burns's 1994 documentary *Baseball*. In fact, he thinks Costas—who was standing in the corner of the Dodgers' dugout in the final innings waiting to conduct a postgame interview—did an outstanding job breaking down Gibson's at-bat in that documentary. "I remember what Bob Costas told me later as he saw me going down and telling Tommy that Gibby was available," Hines continues.

I told Tommy, "Yeah, he says he can give you an at-bat in the ninth." And Tommy got real excited.

Then I had one of the bat boys just put balls on a tee, and let Gibson loosen up. And he did; he swung at the balls on the tee. You hear him up there. He'd swing and go, 'Ugh!' And he'd come back. And the bat boy would put [the ball] on the tee—I set the thing to just about the middle of the strike zone, and out in front just a little bit, so Kirk could swing easy. I didn't want him bending over. I told the bat boy, "You get all the balls and take them out of the bucket and put them on the tee." I had the bat boy put the balls up on the tee for Kirk, and Kirk would hit the ball and he'd go, "Ugh!" He was grunting and groaning.

That bat boy, Mitch Poole, still remembered that moment 25 years later. "I was sitting on the ball bucket and all of a sudden, [Gibson] stops, looks down at me and says, 'This could be the script.' Those were his exact words. I'll never forget them," Poole, who was also the Dodgers' assistant clubhouse manager at the time, recalled in an *SI.com* interview in 2013.[9] Hines, meanwhile, continues his recollection.

Bob Costas was down at the end of the dugout, kind of back in the shadows. [When] Costas heard that Gibson was going in to hit, he thought, "You couldn't write that script any better, about him getting into the game." Costas had a great review of that [on Ken Burns's *Baseball*]—he had a great, schematic breakdown of that, and it was really good—because he heard me tell Tommy that Kirk had an [at bat], and, hey man, he'd be ready for the ninth. Costas told me this later, "When I heard you tell Tommy that, I thought, 'You can't be serious! I saw the guy after taking a swing. He swings and grunts. He cries and moans after every swing! And he's gonna be in the game?!'" Bob Costas said there was no way that it was gonna happen. He said, "He can't even swing a ball off a tee!" Well, he went up and got that backdoor slider, on 3 and 2, and he hit a home run, and the rest is history.

But as dramatic as Gibson's homer was, Hines doesn't believe it was the reason the Dodgers went on to win the World Series. Instead, Hines feels that Orel Hershiser's dominance in his two starts later in the series was the real difference. "It may not have won the series—I think Hershiser's pitching won the series—but it definitely gave us a boost when we were down one run in the ninth, and came back and scored two," Hines says of the impact of Gibson's home run. "That was a big boost, and it gave us a 1–0 lead in the series."

But several Dodgers players thought Oakland was finished. "We were going to win the World Series," Dave Anderson told the *Los Angeles Times* in 2013 when asked what went through his mind the moment Gibson's fly ball left the yard.[10] Tim Leary, who threw three shutout innings that night, echoes Anderson's sentiments. "It was the most incredible excitement ever. We tore their hearts. It was like we won the World Series right there. Gibson's dramatic two-run homer to win the game put us in [a great position]. And with Orel pitching Game 2 and Game 5, we knew we just needed one other victory as he was unhittable in September and October."

Steve Sax, who was in the on-deck circle, also believed the Dodgers were going to win the series.

> Oh yeah. Well, things were going right for us. Things were breaking our way, especially when you look at the fact that we beat the New York Mets in the playoffs—who I think were a better team than the A's and that's not to impugn anything about the A's—but the New York Mets were, I think, a more talented and tougher team. But I felt we had a good chance to win it because our team was just on a roll. We actually gained momentum when we beat the Mets in the playoffs. That gave us a lot of momentum, and yeah, so I felt we could win.

John Shelby, normally a quiet man, even to this day doesn't like to say much about his own contributions. But when pressed to talk about the World Series, Shelby does acknowledge he realized the Dodgers would ultimately win it all when Gibson's high fly ball disappeared into the seats. "[I thought that] right after we won the first game," Shelby says. "[As for the home run itself, that moment was] indescribable. The World Series could have ended right there. It definitely gave us a tremendous boost, confidence, and an extra drive that we could beat the A's."

Franklin Stubbs wouldn't go so far as to say the Dodgers had the World Series won there—but he knew Los Angeles's chances improved dramatically with the victory, especially with Hershiser going the following night. "I thought when we came back in the first game and got that win, that was huge," Stubbs recalls. "I knew once we got past them, we had Hershiser going in Game 2. If we got a couple of runs, we usually were gonna win his games. So, that was huge for us to always get ahead. The first game was a big game for us. I thought it was the most important game. Once we got that one with the Gibson home run, I was pretty confident that we'd do a great job in Game Two. And I knew we were gonna win at least one or possibly two games in Oakland."

But not everybody thought the series was over. The Dodgers, after all, had to win three more. Joey Amalfitano, Mel Didier, Charlie Blaney, and Rick Dempsey share their thoughts on how they felt when Gibson hit the iconic home run.

"No way. No, no, no. No way. We had to win three more games," Amalfitano, the Dodgers' third-base coach, says. "No, you don't—at least I don't—think that way. I don't think it's wise to get your hopes up real high or become overconfident. Next thing you know, you're looking up at somebody else. But no, I did not think that way. No."

"No, no," added Didier in a phone interview in April of 2017, four months before he passed away.

> The players thought, "Oh, we won!" And I said, "No, we have three more games to go." This is something that not many people know, and I haven't told this story much. My wife and I were sitting on the third-base side, right next to the edge of the dugout. As soon as he hit it, and the ball started going, I jumped up, and my wife was with me. She said, "Where are you going?"
>
> I said, "Meet me in the office. I'm going into the dressing room. I'm going in there to tell the players to put the books up."
>
> We had the little pamphlet books that we'd written up, on all these players, on each player of Oakland—their strengths and weaknesses, all of it. Anyway, I said, "I'm going into the dressing room." I ran all the way up the steps, ran down and got into the tunnel. I went down and got into the office, and as the players came in, they were yelling and all that. I said, "I want you guys to put those God-damn books up. We've still got three or four more games to go. It might happen again. So, take them off, because when the writers come in, they're gonna ask you! Don't say one word! Don't say one word, because it could happen again! It may not happen the next game, but it could happen again!" So, they took all their books and hid them, put them up, before the writers got in. That's the way we handled it. But the players thought, "Oh, we won!" I said, "We have three more games to go. Anybody could find those books, so hide them! Take them and hide them. Don't tell anybody about this."

Blaney, the Dodgers' farm director, says anything can happen in sports, so don't take things for granted. "That certainly was a great highlight. No one expected Kirk Gibson [to even come up to bat]; he wasn't even on the bench until the ninth inning. I've been in the game long enough. You never take anything for granted, but it was certainly a momentum builder for the team and the city."

"No, nobody ever thought that far ahead [that we'd won the series]," says Dempsey, contradicting the comments of Leary, Sax, and Shelby. "This team was the perfect mental team for a series like that. We never got out of character. We always stayed one game at a time, one inning at a time. It was the anatomy of a perfect season; with the kind of players we had, the only way we could win was to do what we did."

Others, meanwhile, were simply stunned that Gibson did the unthinkable. "Unbelievable," says Tracy Woodson.

> I still get chills when I see it today. My friends would call me or text me, "Hey, I just saw you on MLB [Network]." Or whatever station where they're showing World Series highlights. You hear about Bobby [Thomson]'s home run and all these other home runs. There's no other home run [that was as impactful]. It was his only at bat. It was Game 1. He never played again in the series. I mean, he was hurt. You're facing the best reliever in baseball. You're facing the best team in baseball. It's unreal. Dodger Stadium . . . they didn't sit down for 15 minutes. I get asked a lot, "What was it like?" It was unreal. That's basically what it was.

Mickey Hatcher, who'd opened the World Series scoring with a two-run homer, only realized a comeback was possible after Davis had stolen second.

> I think we all talked about the scenario there. When Gibson was asked to go up to the plate to hit, everybody thought Tommy Lasorda was crazy. We still had an opportunity there, but if he got a base hit, we were gonna have to pinch-run for him. I think at that time we didn't really have that many players. I think the key was Davis stealing second base. Once he stole second base, I think everybody's feeling changed. It was now, "Hey, we've got a chance! Gibby might get a base hit here, we might tie the game, and we might have a chance to go into extra

innings." So, the big key was when he stole second. I think everybody then realized, "Hey, something can happen here." The last thing we thought, it was gonna end with Gibson hitting a home run. That was just an amazing game right there. I think it just took the air right out of Oakland.

Third-string catcher Gilberto Reyes wasn't on the World Series roster, but he was with the team for the first two games at Chavez Ravine before being sent to the Dominican to begin the winter-league season. He smiles when thinking back to Gibson's homer. "Awesome," Reyes says. "The feeling was awesome."

Scout Phil Regan, meanwhile, had left at the conclusion of the NL playoffs because of his winter-ball obligations. He shares some interesting perspectives of the homer in the context of other historical moments he's seen.

I was a fan of Gibson's because of the way he played. I remember when we made that deal [to sign] him, the big thing about him was he was such a hard-nosed player; he was like a Dodger player. He went into second base hard. He gave 100 percent. . . . He carried the team. That was the big thing. And I can remember this like it was yesterday. I was managing in winter ball. I'd left after the playoffs to go down and manage my team in Venezuela. When he hit the home run, no one could believe it. My phone started exploding. People were calling to say, "Did you see that?! Did you see that?!" It was really unbelievable.

Ironically, for a man who's witnessed numerous historic events in baseball in person, Regan wasn't around for Gibson's homer. But even if he'd seen it in person—as dramatic as that moment was—he wouldn't rank it number 1 in his book. "I stayed with the Dodgers until the 1994 season. In 1995, I was offered the job to manage the Orioles. That was the year that Cal Ripken broke Lou Gehrig's [consecutive-games-played] record," says Regan, referring to the Hall of Fame shortstop's major-league record of playing in 2,632 consecutive games from May 30, 1982, to September 19, 1998. Ripken surpassed Gehrig, whose record of 2,130 consecutive games had stood for 56 years, on September 6, 1995.

"Ripken breaking the record was unbelievable," Regan, who's now in the Mets organization, marvels today.

Just to see everything leading up to it. . . . As you went into different towns, the things that the ball clubs did. . . . At the end of a three-game series, we had to wait for him and hold the bus going to the airport; there might be 2,000 things that teams wanted him to sign. It was really a pretty amazing year. For me, the [Gibson] home run was tremendous. But I've gotta tell you this. I can see a guy coming up and hitting a home run. But it's pretty inconceivable for a guy to play the equivalent of 14 or 15 years and never miss a game. . . . I think he went on to play even more than that. We're going through some things with the Mets right now where guys are getting hurt [with first baseman Lucas Duda, outfielder Yoenis Cespedes, and ace Noah Syndergaard all on the disabled list at the time of the interview]. I'm still in baseball now, and I see guys getting hurt [and having to miss games]. To me, that's gotta be one of the greatest records. That's a record that I don't think will ever be broken.

Those were two of the greater events [in baseball history, but] I've been very fortunate in that when I was with Seattle [as the Mariners' pitching coach], I was in the ballpark in Boston when [Roger] Clemens struck out 20 to set a major-league record [in 1986]. In 1998, I was the pitching coach in Chicago with the Cubs when Kerry Wood struck out 20 to set the National League record. That was pretty amazing. The other thing is, [while with Detroit] I pitched against Roger Maris when he hit 61 home runs in '61. And I was the pitching coach in Chicago [again in 1998] when we went to St. Louis, and McGwire hit a home run on the first night off Mike Morgan to tie [Maris's single-season home-run] record [of 61], and then the next night he hit a home run off Steve Trachsel to break the record. I saw that one too. So, I just happened to be at the ballpark and see a lot of different things.

But Ripken's was pretty special.

For Chris Gwynn and Joey Amalfitano, though, nothing will top Gibson's homer, especially since the club never lost momentum and went on to knock off the Athletics in five games. "No, no, [there won't be anything] like that," Gwynn says.

That was his only at-bat in the whole series! One of the best things about that—as I remember—was we weren't favored to win anything. Orel got on a roll; he went 59 scoreless leading into the playoffs and then dominated in the playoffs. I know people talk about what [San Francisco's] Madison Bumgarner has done in the playoffs. He's pretty much dominated. I was telling a story a couple of years ago: "Yeah, he's done really well. But listen to this: Orel led us to the playoffs with 59 scoreless and then dominated in the playoffs—and we won the whole thing." I don't think we'll ever see too many performances like that. I mean, Gibby basically had one at-bat, and it probably was the most influential at-bat in the whole Series.

Amalfitano, who'd begun his big-league career as a player in 1954, says unequivocally that Gibson's homer is number 1 in his books. "For me, being in uniform, my most memorable nonplaying day in uniform is Gibson's home run. No question. For me, no doubt. I saw Willie Mays hit a lot of home runs. I saw Willie McCovey hit a lot of home runs. I saw Ernie Banks hit a lot of home runs. If you're talking about home runs or one game, one event—I've seen perfect games, I've seen no-hitters—this game, to me, again, as a nonplayer, and being a coach, that's the highlight of my time in the game."

When asked to reflect back some 30 years later about seeing Gibson come up to bat, veteran sportswriter Mel Antonen, who covered the World Series for *USA Today*, remembers being in the Dodger Stadium press box.

It was a sense of disbelief. I remember I was standing next to another reporter from *USA Today*. His name was Ken Picking. We were standing at the back of the press box, thinking that Oakland had won. We were both gonna be covering the Oakland clubhouse after the game, and so we had our stories laid out about who was going to do what, assuming Oakland won. Then Ken Picking, who was the lead American League beat writer at the time, looked down on the field from the back of the press box, and here comes Kirk Gibson walking out of the dugout. He just went, "Oh my gosh. Oh my fucking gosh. Oh my fucking gosh. Oh my fucking gosh."

He couldn't stop saying it. I go, "What's going on?" I looked down, and there was Kirk Gibson hobbling to the plate. We could all sense that this was gonna have a very dramatic ending, not that everybody thought, "Gee, Kirk Gibson's gonna hit a home run." But just knowing and covering Kirk Gibson as we had, you just knew that there was gonna be one final chapter, one final story in this game. We didn't know which way it was gonna go. But obviously it went the way with Gibson hitting the home run.

But I'll never forget the reaction with Ken Picking, just going, "Oh my gosh. Oh my fucking gosh. Look what's happening." Emotion took over a little bit. When reporters are on deadline, everybody is so focused on the game that I don't know if Picking was more worried about what would happen to his story or if he was really into it as a baseball fan and going, "Oh my gosh. Can Kirk Gibson hit a home run?" When you're on a tight deadline, the last thing you think about is enjoying the moment. You think about the consequences and how this is gonna affect you. There were two of us going to the Oakland clubhouse. Picking and myself. We were assuming that Oakland was gonna win that World Series game. So, we had our stories mapped out—it was the eighth and ninth inning—and we were just standing at the back of the press box, waiting for the game to be over. But Kirk Gibson changed everything.

When asked if he thought the series was over then, Antonen wouldn't say that. But he couldn't tell you when he realized Oakland was actually going to lose the series. Bob Nightengale, another veteran sportswriter, never believed the A's weren't going to come back.

"That's a good question," Antonen says. "I really don't know. I think there was a sense of disbelief. There was just a sense that Oakland was the better team, just like in 1990 when they got beaten by Cincinnati. Everybody thought, 'Gee, they're gonna win.' I guess after Game 2 or Game 3. I don't really remember any defining moment where I heard a quote or saw an anecdote, and thought, 'Gee, Oakland's gonna lose this series.'"

"I covered the playoffs, in both the American League and National League, and the World Series," says Nightengale, who at the time covered the Royals for the *Kansas City Star*. "[The Dodgers were] such an overachieving team; nobody expected them to get past the Mets—who'd beaten them up pretty badly during the regular season—in the NLCS. When they went to the World Series, I picked the Oakland A's to win that series in four games. When the Dodgers won the first game, I picked the A's to win it in five games . . . then six games . . . then seven games. I never believed that they could beat the Oakland A's. I expected the Athletics to come back."

Adds Antonen:

I just remember Dave Henderson of the Athletics saying after the Gibson home run, "You guys are making too big a deal out of this. This is just one baseball game. If someone had hit a home run in July to win a game, [nobody would be making such a big deal]. . . . Tomorrow's just another day." Oakland wasn't freaked out by it. Oakland wasn't tempered by it at all in any way, shape, or form. For the players, it was just another game. That was Dave Henderson's attitude. He never got too high. He never got too low. I'm sure the loss affected him. But I remember him saying that on a number of occasions: "It's just one game." To the media, it was drama, and obviously for the Dodgers fans, it was absolutely a once-in-a-lifetime moment.

Gibson's homer, for Antonen, was so iconic that he did a story on it 25 years later for *Sports Illustrated*. One thing that several of the A's have said is that they weren't surprised to see Gibson come up to bat. "We had a feeling that [Gibson] might pinch-hit. It wasn't like a big surprise," catcher Ron Hassey told Antonen. "He was on the roster, so they aren't going to put somebody on the roster that couldn't play. It's a great story to say that Tommy Lasorda fooled everyone and here comes Gibson in to pinch-hit. But we were prepared." Manager Tony La Russa echoed the same sentiments. "The number one question I get about the game is, 'Was it surprising to see Kirk Gibson get that at-bat?' And the answer is no. He's a true competitor."[11]

"There's just so much to that Gibson home run," continues Antonen.

When I did that story for *Sports Illustrated*, I didn't realize how much was going on and how much I missed. It takes a long time to develop a story, like the one that ran in *Sports Illustrated*. It was an amazing story from what the scout told the Dodgers about Dennis Eckersley, what Dennis Eckersley and Ron Hassey were thinking, what Lasorda was thinking. . . . There were so many things. It truly is an amazing, one of the most dramatic baseball experiences ever. It has to be, when you consider, it's dramatic enough to hit a game-winning home run, but to come off the trainer's table to hit a home run . . . is mind-boggling, to say the least.

What did Gibson do after that game? After his postgame interview with NBC's Bob Costas, he went home and did what he usually did—play with his 12-year-old son and his daughter. "My kids were always up late because it was one of the better times that I had to spend time with my kids," Gibson recalled in 2013. "It was festive for sure, but we just played around like we normally did. We did what most people do: We sat around and reminisced about the night. I always looked forward to coming home after a game and playing with the kids. They are still night owls because we always did that."[12]

Eckersley shared his thoughts in 2008 with Mike Lopresti in a story that ran in *USA Today*. "Time heals everything. When I look back and all is said and done, I saved more than 300 games since that moment. And we won it the next year. If that had been my only chance to win the World Series, I'd kick myself in the ass. All I can say is Kirk Gibson will have fond memories of that dinger but I'm in the Hall of Fame. I'll take the Hall. He can replay that home run until the cows come home."[13]

Based on the comments of Antonen and Gibson himself, it appeared that both the A's and Gibson treated the home run as just another day at the office. It was just one game. Jay Howell, naturally, would disagree. As far as Howell is concerned, the homer was, in fact, a once-in-a-lifetime moment and certainly had some lingering effects. "One other thing that was impactful to me was the day after Gibson's home run. Gibson hits the home run, and the next day we're in the locker room. On TV, it's the pre-game," says Howell.

They run this replay of the home run and they feather in the scene from [the 1984 sports movie] *The Natural*. And I think it was Scully who narrated it—I'm not exactly sure—and they may have gone back-and-forth with the verbiage from the movie. We're all standing there watching it. The music from *The Natural* is playing, and you could almost feel the hair stand up on your neck. And you're seeing [actor] Robert Redford [who played Roy Hobbs] adjust his helmet—and he's left-handed as well—and then you see Gibson getting into the box. And he adjusts his helmet. It's almost like it was identical. Then they go on a little bit further into the at-bat and they show a couple of swings and you hear the background of Scully and you hear the announcer in *The Natural*. It was really a phenomenal piece, phenomenal.

I remember watching that and I remember thinking, "Who did that? Who created that piece of work? It was amazing." I guess Costas and his crew. Maybe it was Scully. It was dynamite. And Redford hits the home run, it goes out, it takes out the lights, [you see] the sparkles from the lights, and he's jogging around the bases, and he grabs his helmet, he's jogging, and it shows Gibson, he's one-handing it, he's going around the bases and he touches his helmet. It was just unreal. We're all sitting there and the feeling I had was that we're part of something that's . . . nuts. [Whenever] I hear that music, I always think of Gibson. I think everybody on the damn team saw the damn thing. It was like, "Wow, look at that!" And then Hershiser goes out there and he whips off another shutout.

Howell is referring to Hershiser's three-hitter in Game 2, a 6–0 victory that saw the Bulldog himself go 3 for 3 with a pair of doubles. (With his five total bases, Hershiser alone had more total bases than the A's lineup, as Oakland managed just three singles—all by Dave Parker.) Game 2, unlike the opening contest, was over early. A five-run third inning—capped by Mike Marshall's three-run homer—put Los Angeles ahead 5–0, and Hershiser added insult to injury by driving in the sixth run an inning later with a two-bagger to cash in Alfredo Griffin.

With the shutout, Hershiser joined Sandy Koufax as the only Dodgers with two shutouts in the same postseason. Both did it in back-to-back starts. Koufax, inducted into the Hall of Fame in 1972, performed his heroics in the 1965 World Series, blanking Minnesota 7–0 in Game 5 and then 2–0 in Game 7 as the Dodgers captured their third title in seven years. In those two outings, Koufax allowed seven hits with four walks and 20 strikeouts. As for Hershiser, because he never put up big strikeout numbers, there was a tendency to not think of his stuff as being dominant. However, in his two shutouts—the first one coming in Game 7 against the Mets—Hershiser was certainly dominant, allowing a total of eight hits with four walks and 13 punch-outs. With Hershiser's 1988 performance, it was natural to compare the two Dodgers aces. Koufax had a lifetime 2.76 ERA, while Hershiser's was at 2.77 following the 1988 season. While Hershiser had gone just 14–14 in 1986 and 16–16 in 1987, pitching coach Ron Perranoski explained in October 1988 that it wasn't the Bulldog's fault. "He was as good in '87 as he was this year, but we didn't have the people like Alfredo Griffin to catch the ball."[14]

When the World Series shifted to the Oakland Coliseum for Game 3, Los Angeles seemed to be in trouble as John Tudor lasted only four batters before leaving with an injury. But the Dodgers, thanks to Tim Leary's three and two-thirds innings of three-hit ball and Alejandro Peña's three shutout innings, managed to get the game through eight tied 1–1. With one out in the bottom of the ninth, Mark McGwire ended an eight-pitch battle with Howell by homering off a fastball—the second game-ending homer of the series—and Oakland stayed alive with a 2–1 victory.

Fittingly, perhaps, it was the ex-Dodger Welch who started for Oakland (and fanned eight in five-plus innings) and the ex-Dodger Honeycutt who earned the victory with two perfect innings in relief. And it was the ex-Athletic Howell, who threw all fastballs to McGwire in the ninth, taking the loss. To some observers, McGwire's homer surely supported an earlier claim by Don Baylor that Howell weakened in pressure situations. "It's the ninth inning in Oakland, and I give up a walk-off home run to McGwire," recalls Howell now with a shrug. "So, now, they're back in the series."

But Howell wouldn't know then that he'd be called upon to face McGwire again in a key spot the following night with the series hanging in the balance. Would the young masher beat Howell again to even the series? Or would the much-maligned closer, who'd lost two games and gotten ejected in his three postseason appearances up to that point, redeem himself to put the Dodgers on the doorstep of the championship?

CHAPTER TEN

SCOUT'S HONOR
The Dodgers Scouts Come Through

I did a long piece on the Gibson home run on the 25th anniversary, talking to everybody involved. That one always stands out, just with the scout Mel Didier, Gibson, Vin Scully talking about how he kind of got Gibson motivated to come off the trainer's table. . . . Just that whole facet of that single at bat and what it meant [stands out].

—Bob Nightengale, *USA Today* writer

The 1988 Dodgers reached the pinnacle because the general manager brought in key players, the manager motivated the entire team of overachievers, and the players themselves came through in the clutch.

But the work that the scouts did shouldn't be overlooked. As *Sports Illustrated* writer Steve Wulf noted following the 1988 World Series, the Dodgers' scouting reports gave the club "a certain psychological advantage." Say you're A's leadoff hitter Luis Polonia about to face Orel Hershiser, who suddenly steps off the mound, pulls a laminated crib sheet from his back pocket, studies it for a moment, and then looks in for the sign. If you're Polonia, you might be wondering, "What does he know about me that I don't know?"[1]

The scouting reports for the 1988 postseason were prepared by Steve Boros, Jerry Stephenson, Phil Regan, and the legendary Mel Didier. Without those reports, would the Dodgers have beaten the Mets and then stunned Oakland in Game 1 of the World Series?

Joey Amalfitano, who was coaching at third base when Gibson homered off Eckersley, knows the impact of Didier's scouting report. "At
that moment, that time, when he stepped out of the box after there was
a 3-and-2 count on him, I was wondering what he was doing because we
had the tying run at second base," says Amalfitano today.

> He got back into the box. But at that moment, that time, I was saying
> to myself, "I wonder what he's doing" when he stepped out of the box.
> He was ready to hit, and yet he stepped out of the box. Then, when he
> hit the ball, I watched Canseco in right field, and he took, like, maybe
> two or three strides back, and then he stopped. And I thought, "By God,
> we just won this game."
>
> Mike Davis was on second; he scored. Gibby was on one leg; he
> looked like [the limping character] Chester [Goode] in [the Western
> television series] *Gunsmoke* [which ran on CBS from 1955 to 1975]. As
> he came to second base, and between second and third, I started going
> towards home plate. Naturally, all of our team, led by Tommy, came
> out of that dugout with a lot of energy and spirit and happiness. I'd
> gone about halfway but I decided to go back to third base, because in
> my mind, I said, "Well, I wanna be the first guy to congratulate him!"
>
> Also, I really did think, at that moment, this one was gonna go down
> in history. And it sure has, because I get to see it, not completely, every
> World Series now, because they always play back some of the highlights
> of the World Series, and that was one of them, one of many. But that's
> what I was thinking about. How can I think of all that? Really, when
> he stepped out, I said, "I wonder what he's doing. Let's get on with this
> game and find out if we can tie or win this thing." Then when he hit it,
> I watched Canseco, and his body language kind of indicated to me that
> the ball was out of the ballpark. So, that made us a winner.
>
> I just took off and went upstairs immediately after I shook his hand.
> It was just hectic out there. Everybody was at home plate, around Gibby.
> I just took off and went upstairs. My wife, Kay, who was at the game,
> told me the fans were still in the stadium; they were just standing up
> and acknowledging this great feat that had just appeared before them,
> recognizing it and appreciating it with an ovation. Gibby, I understand,
> had to come back out on the field.
>
> The next day, after everything calmed down, I went to him and asked
> him what he was doing when he stepped out of the box. He was collect-
> ing his thoughts on the meeting we had the previous day on the Oakland

club. One of our three scouts, Mel Didier, was the one that pointed out in the meeting, because Tommy at the end of the meeting after we went over the Oakland club, he'd asked our three scouts—Mel was one of them and the others were Steve Boros and Jerry Stephenson—if anybody had anything to add. And Mel Didier told us, "If Eckersley got you 3 and 2, and you're a left-handed hitter, the game was on the line—which that all came to be at that time, at that moment—he'd throw a backdoor slider."

So, again, why did Gibby step out? He was collecting his thoughts. His thoughts went back to that. You know what that says to me about Gibson? Aptitude and retention was really high for him. In anything we do in life—anything, I don't care what it is—you have aptitude and retention, and you have a chance to do something good . . . in anything that's important to us. You become good at it. In his case, he wanted to be good at it. And he had a great career.

Mel Didier was the scout who gave the Dodgers the scouting report on Eckersley. Undoubtedly, that was one of the proudest achievements of Didier's career, given that it led to the Dodgers' improbable—and last—World Championship in 1988. However, the veteran scout, who in 2017 was with the Blue Jays organization as a senior adviser in player development (and in his 64th season as a professional baseball scout or administrator), was most proud that he helped start three expansion clubs.

Didier had a chance to share his memories just months prior to his passing at the age of 90 on September 11, 2017. "We got to the World Series, and on the Friday, Tommy Lasorda asked the scouts [to talk to the team]," he recalled in April of 2017 from his home in Phoenix.

We'd been scouting the various teams. I had Oakland; that was my club. He asked us to come in and visit, and talk about our reports, and we did. We had to give the reports on the defense and the offense of the Oakland club. Oakland was a really, really good club. I mean, they had solid pitching; they had Lansford at third, they had guys like Parker and Canseco and Henderson in the outfield, and McGwire at first base.

But actually, Eckersley was the key; he was the guy who shut you [down]; he did this time and time again. I'd watched him about 25 games at the tail end of the season, and just picked up [his tendencies]. He didn't do it, like, 25 times when he came into the [ball game]. But he did it three or four times in key situations. He threw a backdoor slider

Mel Didier, who helped build three expansion clubs during his seven decades in baseball, was a scout with the Dodgers in 1988. He finished his career as a senior adviser for the Toronto Blue Jays, serving in that role from 2009 until his death in 2017. *Toronto Blue Jays*

to key hitters . . . to left-handed hitters only, in the ninth inning. And if anybody got on, on second or third, and a left-handed hitter came up, and he got the count 3 and 2, he did this only about three or four times.

So, when Tommy let us talk to our club on Friday, I was the last one who spoke. I'd talked about the pitching, and then I turned around—I had all of the left-handed hitters sitting against the wall; that included Gibson, Davis, Mike Scioscia, those guys—and pointed at them. I said, "Let me tell you this. If you get in a tough situation, it's the ninth inning, and the winning or tying run is at second or third, you get the count of 3 and 2, you're gonna get the backdoor slider." And I said, "You can bank on it, podnuh." That's what I said.

So, anyway, that's what Gibson remembered. If you remember, he fouled off 13 fastballs. Thirteen of them. [Actually, four.] Ball one, then he'd foul one off, ball two, and then he'd foul off two more, and so forth. And they were all fastballs. As Kirk got into the box for that last pitch, he had two strikes. He stepped in, and he said, "Mel, I remember your Cajun accent . . . *you better remember it's gonna be a backdoor slider.*" He stepped back, and he said, "I heard your voice. *This is gonna be a backdoor slider.*"

He stepped in, and sure enough, Eckersley threw him a backdoor slider and, fortunately, he hit it for a home run. He could've popped it up. He could've hit it on the ground. You could still do that even if you knew what was coming. But he was capable of doing things that the ordinary guys can't do. He had the great speed, the size, the strength, and of course, he basically hit a long home run off of one leg and one hand, if you noticed. He did it off of one hand. He said, "As soon as [the ball] came out of [Eckersley's] hand, I saw the spin [of that slider]." And as he went around third base, he told Joe Amalfitano, "It was the backdoor slider!" He then just kept running. And he was good enough to make it happen. That was the big thing.

Naturally, Didier was proud that the players came through and won the World Series. After all, the 1988 Dodgers had to defeat two dominant teams. "The Mets and Oakland were the two best clubs in the two leagues, and we beat them both," he said. "We were hot. With the Mets, they were by far the better club with Strawberry and all those guys. And, of course, there was Oakland, with Henderson and all the guys that they had. Jesus, it was like an All-Star team. But we were hot. That's the way it happened."

As for his own career, Didier could have remained a Dodger for life if he had wanted to. "I was with the Dodgers for 16 years. And the only reason I left the Dodgers, I'll tell you this right now," he said matter-of-factly. "This is a true story. I remember the date; it was January 5, 1997. Buck Showalter had been asking me in the winter, in November, to go with him to the Arizona Diamondbacks and run the minor leagues for him."

In 1995, Arizona had been awarded an expansion franchise to begin play for the 1998 season. Showalter, who'd managed the Yankees from 1992 to 1995, was hired by the Diamondbacks in 1996, two years before the team was scheduled to begin play, in order to take a more active role in developing the eventual roster.

I said, "Buck, I'm not leaving." I said, "First of all, I have the best owner in the world, in Peter O'Malley. I have the best boss, in Fred Claire. And as long as they stay here, I'm gonna stay with them." So, that was it. But he came back at me three times, and said, "We need you. We need you to start this. You started two clubs."

See, I'd started two [expansion] clubs and really knew what it took. It's tough. It's the toughest thing I've had to do in baseball, and that's starting the Montreal [Expos] club. I started the Montreal club with

Jim Fanning, who was the general manager. I was scouting director and player development director. And then [the] Seattle [Mariners] . . . Lou Gorman asked me to go over there and start their club. I started their club as director scout and director of player development. So, when Buck came along, [I'd been] with the Dodgers for 16 years, and I was gonna stay with them. I mean, the O'Malleys were great to me, so great to all of our people. I was staying with these guys.

Well, on January 5, 1997, the phone rang, and I picked it up. It was in the morning. It was Fred Claire. He said, "Mel, I've got some bad news. Peter just walked in and said he sold the club." I said, "What? You've gotta be kidding!"

He said, "No, Peter walked in and said he sold the club."

And I said, "I resign right now, Fred." I never would've done that [had O'Malley not sold the club]. Fred was a great, great individual and a great, great boss. Peter was the greatest, the best owner I'd ever been around. He treated us really, really good. So, I said, "I resign right now."

I hung up the phone and called Buck Showalter. I said, "Buck, you've still got that player development deal open with Arizona, to start that club?"

"Yeah."

"I've started two, so I know better than anybody what to do."

He said, "Good."

I said, "Well, I've just left the Dodgers."

"I'll see you tomorrow at nine o'clock."

I met him the next day at nine o'clock, and I helped start that Arizona club. We built that thing and in four years they won the World Championship.

Didier's decision to leave the Dodgers was ultimately the right one. His recollection about the sale was partly right; in early January of 1997, Peter O'Malley announced his intention to sell the Dodgers—although the agreement to sell the club to Rupert Murdoch's Fox Entertainment Group didn't happen until early September. But it didn't take long for a major shakeup to occur after the sale to Murdoch's Fox Group, which ended the nearly half-century of ownership by the O'Malley family (1950–1998). In May 1998, the club's new Fox owners traded catcher Mike Piazza, a fan favorite, to the Marlins without Claire's knowledge. One month later, it was Claire's turn to go, as he (along with manager Bill Russell) was fired by the Fox executives, ending his 30-year tenure with the club.

As for Didier, he was proud when Arizona defeated the Yankees in the 2001 World Series, giving the franchise a World Championship in just its fourth year of play. Of course, it was a special accomplishment considering that many people who have worked in baseball for decades have never sniffed the playoffs. The expansion Diamondbacks, thanks in part to the ex-Dodgers scout, had reached the pinnacle faster than any other team in major-league history. It was remarkable considering that several teams—including Boston, Cleveland, and both Chicago clubs—had endured long championship droughts which were still active. At that time, the Red Sox (with their last title in 1918), White Sox (1917), and Cubs (1908) hadn't won a thing since the dead-ball era!

Didier, however, had moved on to Cleveland in 2001 to be a special assistant to the general manager. "The only reason [the Diamondbacks] won is because of what we did," Didier said in April of 2017, referring to the players that he helped bring to Arizona. Between Diamondbacks assistant general manager Sandy Johnson, ex-manager Showalter (who'd been fired in 2000), and Didier, the three of them handpicked virtually every player on that championship team, including pitching aces Randy Johnson and Curt Schilling as well as outfielder Luis Gonzalez, who'd homer 57 times in 2001. "But by 2001, I'd already moved on. I'd just moved on prior to 2001. But I take as much credit as anybody, because I got half of that team for them, I'll tell you that!"

A lot of credit has been given to Didier for the 1988 World Series outcome, as his scouting report proved valuable in the opening game. Didier, however, chose to credit the players. "With the '88 Dodgers, you talk about the hustle, the preparation, and that type of thing," he explained.

They were the best bunch of young men. Mike Scioscia was a great, great leader. All the guys we had were great. It was unbelievable. Mickey Hatcher. The pitching was really, really good. Leary won 17 games. The key guys that we had [stepped up]. Hershiser was unbelievable. He's the only pitcher who's ever pitched 59 innings without having a run scored against him. He was unbelievable down the stretch, in August and September and October. Our whole club got into a roll in late July and we just played like no one ever thought any of them could play. That was the difference. We came down the homestretch, podnuh, really, really tough.

Dodgers advance scout Phil Regan, who wasn't around when the World Series began, should receive credit for his work, too. Regan, who scouted the NL East teams for the Dodgers in 1988, was the one who submitted the reports on the Mets. A former Dodgers reliever during the 1960s—the right-hander had a 13-year career, including a stint with Los Angeles from 1966 to 1968—Regan went to the World Championship for the first time in 1988. As he recalls with a laugh today, being a part of the '88 team was something he would have never envisioned following his playing career.

After getting released by the White Sox in 1972, Regan retired and went to work for a school in a small Michigan town called Allendale, about 12 miles west of Grand Rapids. He was quite content as the school's baseball coach, with no intention of ever returning to the big leagues as a coach or scout. However, a phone call from an agent about eight years later changed things—and Regan was back in the majors as a scout and pitching coach. He's also, of course, the proud owner of a 1988 World Championship ring. "The '88 team was special," Regan recalls now. "Gibson was a tremendous player and sparked the team. Hershiser was outstanding. They had the right chemistry."

As for his role as a scout with the 1988 team—he'd joined the Dodgers in 1987—Regan remembers that Fred Claire believed in him to do the job, though it meant some added pressure to get it done. "My job was to have the National League East," Regan explains.

> I was to prepare reports on the National League East. Against the Mets that year, we [lost 10 of 11] during the regular season. We really had a tough time with them. My job was then to prepare the report on the Mets. Jerry Stephenson was our other scout in the National League, and he had the National League West. I guess one of the things that stood out was when Jerry Stephenson said, "Phil has never done an advance report before; would you want me to go and help him?" But Fred said, "No, Phil can handle that himself." And he sent Jerry on another assignment. So, that made me feel kind of good, but also a bit of pressure too!

During his time as a player, scout, pitching coach, and manager, Regan has seen his fair share of outstanding teams, ones that resembled the 1988 Dodgers. When posed the question about similar teams, Regan asks rhetorically, "Have there been teams that people thought had no chance of winning, and they still won? I think Kansas City has been like that [beginning in the mid-2010s]; they ended up winning [the AL pennant in 2014 and the World Series in 2015]. Most people probably thought they didn't have a chance. I think our club, the Mets, going into the World Series [in 2015] when it didn't look like we even had a chance . . . that's another one."

Regan, now with the Mets organization as their assistant minor-league pitching coordinator, then pauses for a moment before bringing up the 1969 Mets and 1991 Braves.

> There's a couple more that I can think of. In 1969, I was with the Cubs. By the end of August, we had, like, a nine-and-a-half-game lead on the Mets. [Actually, the Mets were 10 games back on August 14 before closing in to within 4.5 games on August 31. New York then took over first place on September 10 and won the division by eight games.] They caught us and went on to win the World Series. That was pretty much a miracle. I think another one was when I was with the Dodgers. At the [1991] All-Star break, Atlanta was just coming out at that time. They had Terry Pendleton playing at third base. We had a nine-and-a-half-game lead at the All-Star break. And I'll never forget what Joey Amalfitano told me, that Pendleton told him, "Joey, we're gonna catch you before this year's over. We're gonna catch you." Joey told me that, and the Braves did. There's been some teams like that that did some pretty remarkable things.
>
> But the Dodgers were special that year. They came together and they had the chemistry. To me, Tommy did a great job. The coaching staff was good. I think Fred Claire did an outstanding job. He was so personable. He's so thorough in everything that he does; I really admired him for that.

Regan was happy working for Claire but by the 1990s had decided he wanted to eventually be a field manager. Knowing he wouldn't get that opportunity in Los Angeles, he left the organization to become the pitching coach for Cleveland during the strike-shortened 1994 season. The following year, he finally realized his dream of managing in the majors, when he guided Baltimore to a 71–73 record. Alas, after just one season with the Orioles, Regan was fired and replaced by Davey Johnson. "It was a memorable year for me," Regan says. Baltimore had a strong finish, going 17–11 over the final month—and winning 9 of its last 10—to end the 1995 season with a respectable record. "It was my first year managing in the big leagues, in the United States. Overall, I thought it was a good year, an exciting year—but not good enough because we finished in third place in the division!"

After managing the Dodgers' Triple-A club in Albuquerque in 1996—where he had a chance to work with youngsters such as Darren Dreifort, Wilton Guerrero, and Roger Cedeno—Regan spent two years in Chicago as the Cubs' pitching coach before returning to Cleveland in 1999 to take on the same role with the Indians. While with Chicago and Cleveland, Regan returned to the postseason in back-to-back years in 1998–1999—though both teams were eliminated in the Division Series. By 2009, Regan had joined the New York Mets organization as the pitching coach of their Advanced-A affiliate club, the St. Lucie Mets. Today, he is still with the Mets as their assistant minor-league pitching coordinator.

Interestingly, Regan might not have gotten back to the majors following his 13-year pitching career—one that saw him go 96–81 with 92 saves for the Tigers, Dodgers, Cubs, and White Sox—had an agent not reached out about a full decade after he'd left the game. He recalls getting that opportunity fondly, one for which he is very thankful. Otherwise, who knows if he'd have ever gotten back into the pros—and eventually get that World Series ring in 1988?

> After I got out of baseball, I was 35 years old. I'd been with the Cubs and was then traded to the White Sox. I was released by the White Sox [in 1972], and Roland Hemond was the general manager in Chicago. He'd asked me if I wanted to go to Japan. I said, "No, I really don't wanna go to Japan." So, I went home. I was offered a job at a small, Division II school, called Grand Valley State University. It was a small school that was just starting up. They offered me several jobs. I taught a class in baseball, I was the athletic fundraiser, and I coached the baseball team. I did several things there.

It seemed like Regan would be at Grand Valley State forever. He was perfectly happy being where he was and had absolutely no reason to leave. Besides, it wasn't as though anybody was calling him offering him a major-league job.

After about, maybe, eight or nine years there, I'd never heard a word from anybody in baseball about coming back in. Nor had I even given it much thought, really. But I got a call one day from an agent out of Chicago that I'd known when I was pitching there. He said, "Phil, I have a player that has lost his fastball. I remember you had a good sinker when you were here in Chicago. I think if he's gonna continue in baseball, he needs a sinker. He needs to learn that pitch. Would you be willing to work with him?" We were in our fall practice at the time with the college team. I said, "If he wants to come here in September, yeah, I'll work with him." I didn't know who it was. So, I then said, "Well, who is this?"

He goes, "It's The Mad Hungarian, Al Hrabosky."

I said, "Holy! That's kinda interesting!"

He came in and stayed at my house for three or four days to work out. He practiced with us. We worked on some things. Then, he said, "I'm going down to winter ball." I think he was going to Venezuela to pitch winter ball there. He said, "Would you mind calling some teams and telling them what I'm doing, what I'm working on, and what I've done?" I told Al that I could do it. I mean, I knew Jim Campbell in Detroit and Roland Hemond in Chicago.

Neither general manager, however, expressed interest. "Then I was reading in the papers that Seattle was looking for a left-handed reliever," continues Regan. "I got on the phone and called Danny O'Brien, [whom] I'd never met in my life. I started talking to him and telling him about this kid working on the new pitch. 'He's going down to winter ball. I'm just giving you this information. You might wanna check on him, see how he's doing.' Danny and I started talking. He said to me, 'Well, what are you doing?' I told him, and we talked for about 30 minutes. And he said, 'Phil, I might have a job for you. I'll get back to you.'"

Regan didn't hear back for four months. Then, at the end of January, the phone rang. It was O'Brien.

He said, "Phil, I want you to come with us and be our advance scout. I want you to come to spring training with us and be [pitching coach] Frank Funk's assistant in spring training. I want you to go down to our Triple-A club for a week during the season. And I want you to do instructional league with us. What do you think?" I'd never scouted before in my life. I said I needed a couple of days to think about it. I'd been in school now for almost 10 years. I talked it over with my wife, and we decided, "Well, let's try to do something different."

So, I ended up taking the job with Seattle. I think about a year-and-a-half later, the Dodgers called Seattle and they were looking for an advance scout. They wanted me. Al Campanis wanted me to go to the Dodgers. [The Mariners] told him, "If we don't promote Regan by the end of the year, you can talk to him." They refused permission at that time. Then a short time later, they fired the pitching coach in Seattle. So, I became the pitching coach there and stayed for about four years. That's how I got back into baseball. I was just calling teams to tell them about the Mad Hungarian. And all of a sudden, I had a job in the major leagues! Talk about a huge break for me!

I stayed with Seattle for about four years and then I left there on the last day of the season. The next day—the day after the season ended—Al Campanis called me and offered me the scouting job. So, I took that, and I stayed with the Dodgers for about nine or 10 years.

All these years later, where's that 1988 ring? And didn't he win a championship or two while with Walter Alston's 1960s Dodgers along with Sandy Koufax and Don Drysdale? Well, Los Angeles did win World Championships in 1963 and 1965—beating the Yankees and Twins, respectively—but Regan didn't join the Dodgers until 1966. And while the 1966 Dodgers did win the pennant, Regan says with a laugh, "Well, the ring with the 1988 Dodgers was my first championship ring!"

But let me go back to 1966. I was traded from the Tigers to the Dodgers [in December 1965 for infielder Dick Tracewski], and we won the pennant the last game of the season and went into the World Series. We didn't get into first place until September [11th]. We went into the World Series and we lost four straight games to the Orioles. Mr. [Walter] O'Malley [the Dodger owner at the time] was really anxious to get that ring. We knew that you get a championship ring for being the National League champions anyway and being in the World Series. But he said, "Well, losers don't get rings." And he gave us a watch! So, yeah, that ring in 1988 with the Dodgers was the first World Series ring I got! I keep it [along with] the [2015 NL Championship] ring with the Mets.

Being with the Dodgers in both 1966 and 1988, Regan makes a natural comparison between the two clubs. The way he looks at it, a championship team is about a group of guys coming together and pulling on the same rope. Then, hey, something magical might happen that year.

Phil Regan, who pitched for the NL pennant-winning Dodgers in 1966, was back in the organization as a scout when the team won it all in 1988. *National Baseball Hall of Fame and Museum, Cooperstown, NY*

It happened with the 1966 pennant-winning Dodgers, and it happened again 22 years later when Los Angeles went all the way.

> When you win a championship, it just seems like everything has to fall into place. The year that we won in 1966 with the Dodgers, we acquired Ducky Schofield [on September 10th from the Yankees]. The last month of the season Ducky Schofield just played unbelievable at third base, filling in for us, to help us win that pennant. I don't think he qualified to participate in the World Series because he wasn't on the roster at the right time, but for that last month he really played hard. And you need that. You need everyone on a team to do their part, and come through. Then you will have some surprises, some guys that [you don't expect to will] come through. You got to get along together and pull together.
>
> [The '88 Dodgers] did that. Hershiser relieving in the playoffs . . . that's another thing that was unbelievable. Of course, Hershiser's pitching was just outstanding. . . . It was a team that wasn't expected to win, but they won.

A'S SERIES MOMENTS

Nobody but our team believed that our pitching could hold down the Mets' or the A's offense. Or realized the heart and soul of every player—[for example,] Orel getting a save on zero days' rest—[to help us win a ball game]. But we did it.

—Tim Leary, Dodgers pitcher

The A's had gotten back into the 1988 World Series with Mc-Gwire's walk-off home run, and were poised to even things up the following night with ace Dave Stewart, the majors' only back-to-back 20-game winner, taking the mound. The Dodgers, meanwhile, would be fielding a depleted lineup in Game 4, with right fielder Mike Marshall sidelined with spasms in his lower back.[1] Marshall, who'd contributed a three-run homer in Game 2, had led the club with 82 RBIs and was second with 20 home runs during the season.

With Marshall unable to start (although he'd appear as a ninth-inning defensive replacement for Mickey Hatcher), Lasorda was going with a batting order of Steve Sax (.277), Franklin Stubbs (.223), Hatcher (.293), Mike Davis (.196), John Shelby (.263), Mike Scioscia (.257), Danny Heep (.242), Jeff Hamilton (.236), and Alfredo Griffin (.199). Five of the starting nine, including a DH that was required in the American League ballpark, had batting averages below .250 during the season. Also, with both Gibson and Marshall sidelined, Shelby was now the Dodgers' biggest power threat with his 10 regular-season homers—and the starting

163

lineup had a total of 36. Their DH (designated hitter), Heep, had zero. Here, in fact, were the home-run totals of the top five hitters in the batting order of both lineups:

Dodgers	Athletics
Sax 5	Luis Polonia 2
Stubbs 8	Dave Henderson 24
Hatcher 1	Jose Canseco 42
Davis 2	Dave Parker 12
Shelby 10	Mark McGwire 32

As if that wasn't bad enough, Lasorda would lose Scioscia to an injury before the end of the night when the veteran starting catcher twisted his right knee on an attempted steal of second base. Of course, there was also John Tudor, the Game 3 starting pitcher, who had an ailing left elbow and was done for the series.

The Dodgers had just finished a meeting in the clubhouse, and Lasorda turned on the TV—only to see Bob Costas saying on the NBC pregame show that the Dodgers might have been the worst team ever put on the field in World Series history. "I wasn't going to have a meeting that night," Lasorda recalled in 1998. "But then [coach Bill] Russell came over and told me that Mike Marshall couldn't play. And that really burned me up. So I had a meeting and did a little screaming and hollering. And then I turned on the television and Costas comes out and says this may be the worst team ever put on the field in World Series history. That's when I said, 'Can you believe this guy? Can you believe it?'"[2]

Joey Amalfitano remembers the doubters. "I guess there were some people that said that," he says matter-of-factly today.

> Some people said that we had no business being there. But we had some good players. Proof of the pudding is the catcher Mike Scioscia, who's managed, I think, now for 18-plus years with the Angels—with one team! That's very important, and I think that should be acknowledged by the media. That's quite a feat, to be with one team for that many years. But Mike Scioscia was kind of like a player-coach. He had that mentality, which he [has shown] after his playing days.
>
> And we had Mickey Hatcher, who I'd have to say was kinda like [right fielder] Hunter Pence, who's with the Giants. Plays with a great deal of

energy. [Always] plays to win, not that they all don't, but highly competitive, and very much alive in the dugout when he was playing—and not playing. He got into the game. Was he inspiring them? Well, I think with his comments during the game—what he'd say aloud—he was trying to maybe make the fellows think the situation out. He was invaluable for me. Then in the World Series, he shined. He did. He sure did.

Sax doesn't remember David Cone's newspaper column during the NLCS, but he does remember what Costas said prior to Game 4 in Oakland. "Bob Costas, the announcer, said this was the worst-looking World Series team he'd ever seen. Mickey Hatcher was hitting third. Kirk Gibson was injured. Mike Marshall was injured. And yet, our team still won. So, it was amazing that people were saying those things about our club, and our team had a lot of heart."

For Jay Howell, this scene in the clubhouse before Game 4 exemplifies how the team all rallied together that year:

This [is another example] of us being a unit, us being a team. The TV was on in the locker room. Bob Costas was talking about how this was probably one of the biggest lopsided games ever. "Vegas has it at huge numbers. Oakland, the Big Bash Brothers versus the Broken-Down, Beat-up Dodgers." Lasorda was standing in the middle of the locker room. He looked at the TV and said something like, "Costas, my happy ass! Do you hear that? Biggest lopsided . . . in World Series history, my happy ass! You don't have a clue! This team, we've got more heart! This team is gonna rise up and we're gonna take care of business." He was just yelling at the TV, and he went on and on about our team. He got everyone yelling. And we kinda broke the locker room right there. And we went out and started hitting. All those little stories about just how Lasorda had us as underdogs. But we had resources. We had the Stuntmen. It was, "No worries, we'll just go to the bench. We got a guy. We're fine."

Rick Dempsey remembers the doubters, but he also remembers believing the Dodgers would pull it off—even with their Stuntmen. Hey, they'd done it so many times throughout the course of the season. "Bob Costas called us the worst World Series team on paper in the history of the playoffs and World Series, and we kinda laughed about that, but it also motivated us at the same time," says Dempsey.

We went up against Oakland. It was a David-and-Goliath series. [The Athletics had] Canseco and McGwire, and they had a lot of great players. But we just knew how to play. And it was just the rarest thing in baseball for that particular group to get together. The formula that Fred Claire used to put this team together was just incredible. And we knew it. We knew on paper that we were not a great team by names and everything. But we also knew with the roles that we were to play, that we could be very effective. I think we proved it during the course of the season to take it as far as we can.

Heep, in the lineup at DH in Game 4, offers a diplomatic answer today when asked for his thoughts on Costas's comments. "I think he was just looking at our lineup. Without Kirk Gibson in the lineup, we weren't [the same team]," reflects Heep.

I can't even remember what we hit as a team during the series. But the whole idea, at that point, was there weren't a lot of teams that made the World Series that didn't hit. Now, we beat a very, very good Mets team in the National League Championship. And they beat us up pretty good in the regular season. Then we got hot, Mike Scioscia hit a big home run in one of those games that [helped to win] it for us, and then our pitching staff just did a good job. So, I mean, we got hot, and we just played together. The pitchers got hot at the right time in the playoffs and the World Series—and basically carried us.

The Dodgers stunned the sloppy A's 4–3 to take a three-games-to-one lead. Despite its depleted lineup, Los Angeles scored enough runs by taking advantage of several Oakland mistakes. Sax, who reached base on a leadoff walk against Dave Stewart, scored the first run when a routine pitch eluded catcher Terry Steinbach for a passed ball. Then, following an error by A's second baseman Glenn Hubbard in that same inning (which put runners on the corners with one out), Hatcher came home on Shelby's groundout—a soft liner that deflected off Stewart's glove and went to Hubbard, whose only play was at first base for just one out. (Had Stewart caught Shelby's liner cleanly, it would have been an inning-ending double play.) Two innings later, Stubbs scored when A's shortstop Walt Weiss let Mike Davis's liner bounce off his glove and into the outfield for a two-out error. Tracy Woodson, who pinch-hit for Stubbs later in the game, drove in Los Angeles's fourth run on a groundout—when Sax, the runner on first base, took off on the pitch to break up a potential double play. So, the Dodgers' four runs came on two groundouts, a passed ball, and an error. And to make things even wackier, even seldom-used Dodgers outfielder Jose Gonzalez—who batted .083 in 24 at-bats during the season—got into the game (though he struck out in his lone at-bat).

But the game's biggest moment came in the bottom of the seventh, and Howell remembers how Dempsey—who'd replaced Scioscia behind the plate three innings earlier—was instrumental in the victory. "We go to Oakland and it's the ninth inning that I give up a walk-off home run on a fastball to McGwire. It was a bit fun for Oakland. I had to answer to the media [afterward] and interestingly the next game it's the seventh inning and there's two outs and we got a one-run lead and Lasorda brings me in to face Canseco," recalls Howell.

With Dave Henderson already on second base, Howell walked Canseco to put two men on, bringing to the plate Dave Parker—who at age 37 was still a dangerous hitter. In his age 34 to 39 seasons with Cincinnati, Oakland, and Milwaukee, Parker would average 24 homers and 97 RBIs a year. He'd gone 3 for 4 in Game 2, the only Athletics player to get a hit off Hershiser. "Runners on first and second, one-run lead, it's the seventh, and I jam [Parker]. He hits a soft liner at Alfredo—remember, he had the thumb issue—and the ball clanks, and he drops it. And the bases are loaded," continues Howell.

And McGwire comes up. The stadium feels like it's moving. You can't hear anything. It's insane. I'm thinking, "Oh God." Dempsey walks out to me and says, "What do you wanna go with here?"

"I dunno. I mean, I dunno. He got me on a fastball. What are you thinking?"

He looked at me and he goes, "We're going with the exact same pitch. Just go with me. We're gonna shake off a bit, and we're gonna go right back to it. I guarantee you he's looking breaking ball."

I said, "OK." He shakes me off, and I shake my head. And I threw a fastball, pretty much the same pitch. Jammed him, popped him up to first base.

I'll never forget this. Dempsey said, "We're gonna go right back to it. There's no way he thinks you're going fastball again. No way." That was big, and he was confident. "That was the one to go with." He came through for me. I just threw it where he wanted it. But that's the kind of team—there's a time in the game right there where you've been burned, you're right back at it, same situation, late in the game, you've got this guy up who's hot, who's a fastball hitter—[where] you've got somebody that says, "Look, I got this. This is what we're gonna do." Very confident about it. And I went with it. I would be inclined not to do that, and was grateful. Jammed him, popped him up, and we ran through the eighth and ninth—and won that one by one run. That was the game they needed, to even the series.

Howell's two-and-a-third-inning save, at the time, wasn't unusual. He'd entered in the seventh inning and recorded the final seven outs. Two- or three-inning saves weren't all that unusual back in the 1980s, even during World Series play. Steve Howe had gotten a save in the 1981 Game 6 clincher for Los Angeles against the Yankees by pitching the final three and two-thirds innings. Bruce Sutter had recorded a two-and-a-third-inning save for St. Louis in Game 3 against Milwaukee in the 1982 World Series. San Diego's Craig Lefferts had notched a three-inning World Series save against Detroit in 1984, while counterpart Willie Hernandez had gotten a two-and-a-third-inning save in the same series. In the 1985 World Series, Cardinals rookie Todd Worrell had recorded a two-and-a-third-inning save in the opener in relief of ace John Tudor. Even in the league championship series, these seven-or-more-out saves weren't uncommon. In the 1987 NLCS, Worrell had even topped that performance with a three-inning save against San Francisco when manager Whitey Herzog called upon the right-hander right after St. Louis had taken a 6–4 lead. In Game 6 of the 1985 NLCS, Tommy Lasorda had given the ball to Tom Niedenfuer early in hopes of an eight-out save—although that one didn't quite work out.

Howell downplays his performance now, but those were seven ultra-stressful outs because Los Angeles had just a precarious one-run lead throughout his stint on the mound. Even after he retired McGwire, he wasn't out of the woods yet. In the eighth, Howell gave up a two-out single but struck out Walt Weiss on three pitches to put the Dodgers three outs away from the improbable victory. While lefty Jesse Orosco and righty Alejandro Peña warmed up in the ninth, once again it was Howell out on the mound. With one out, Dave Henderson singled, and Jose Canseco—the 1988 major-league leader in home runs and RBIs—came up as the potential winning run. With the count full, though, Howell struck out Canseco swinging for the second out. With the left-handed-hitting Parker coming up, bringing in the lefty Orosco would have made sense— but Lasorda stuck with Howell, who got Parker to hit a foul pop-up to third baseman Jeff Hamilton on the first pitch. Game over.

So, Howell, who'd been the goat just 24 hours earlier, gave Los Angeles a three-games-to-one lead despite facing at least the tying run with every single pitch. And he did it in the same ballpark where A's fans constantly booed him the year before when he pitched for Oakland—including at the 1987 All-Star Game, which was held at the Coliseum. "He did the job he had to do. That was a tough one. That was a real tough save," acknowledged A's manager Tony La Russa afterward.[3] Lasorda, meanwhile, had nothing but praise for his stopper. "After what happened [in Game 3], when McGwire got the home run, it was important for us to bring Jay back as soon as possible," explained the Dodgers skipper. "It's like a young man falling off a horse. You've got to pick him up and get him right back on that horse."[4]

While that seven-out save wasn't unusual then, the way La Russa used his bullpen in 1988 soon became a trend around baseball, and no pitcher was asked to get that many outs in a save situation (in a tight game) in World Series play until the mid-2010s. By the 1990s, managers predominantly used closers for only one inning; sometimes a star closer such as Yankees stopper Mariano Rivera might be asked to come in for a two-inning save, but those situations were rare. In fact, after Howell's fourth-game heroics in 1988, no pitcher logged as many as two and one-third innings to save a tight World Series game until Giants starter Madison Bumgarner's record-setting five-inning effort to close out Game 7 in 2014, a 3–2 victory over Kansas City. But of course, Bumgarner, normally a starting pitcher, was used to pitching more innings (although his relief outing came just three nights after he'd thrown a Game 5 shutout). By then, observers were criticizing the role of the modern closer, as the meat of the order in the opposing lineup might come up in the seventh or eighth inning—when the game is on the line—rather than the ninth, when a closer typically enters the contest. In the 2016 postseason, several managers went old school and began using closers for more than the typical one inning, including Cubs skipper Joe Maddon. In Game 5 of the

2016 World Series, Maddon asked closer Aroldis Chapman to pitch the final two and two-thirds innings to protect Chicago's 3–2 lead against Cleveland—even though 35 of his 36 regular-season saves were one inning or less. Chapman, whose longest regular-season save that year was a four-out stint (in late July), did nail down the save in Game 5, but the long outing hampered his performance in each of the final two games (where he was pounded for a 10.13 ERA in two and two-thirds innings). In the 2017 World Series, Astros manager A. J. Hinch asked Brad Peacock, normally a starter, to get the final 11 outs in Game 3 against the Dodgers. Peacock did just that—with three and two-thirds hitless innings—to close out Houston's 5–3 victory, the first save of the right-hander's major-league career.

True, two pitchers recorded three-inning saves in World Series play during the 1990s: Atlanta's Mike Stanton in 1992 and Cleveland's Brian Anderson in 1997. However, both saves came in blowout games and neither pitcher was his team's closer. When Stanton, normally a setup man, entered Game 5 against Toronto, the Braves were ahead 7–2 and the left-hander was asked to finish the game to keep the bullpen well rested. Likewise, when Anderson, a starter during the 1997 season, entered Game 4 against Florida, the Indians were leading 7–3 in a game that they'd win 10–3. (In Division Series or League Championship Series play, only one pitcher had such a save in the 1990s. Pittsburgh's Bob Walk, normally a starter, also pitched a three-inning save in Game 1 of the 1991 NLCS—but he came on with the Pirates comfortably ahead 4–0 with no runners on.) But a regular closer was never asked, in World Series play in the 1990s, to do the same thing Howell was asked in the 1988 series. There were even famous meltdowns when closers—even the game's best stoppers—were asked to go more than one inning for a postseason save. When Eckersley was asked to come on in the eighth inning to protect a 6–2 advantage (with runners already aboard) in Game 4 of the 1992 ALCS against Toronto, he allowed two inherited runners to score and then coughed up the lead in the ninth by surrendering a game-tying, two-run homer to Roberto Alomar. In the 1995 AL Division Series, Seattle closer Norm Charlton came on in the seventh to protect a one-run lead in Game 2, but gave up a game-tying homer to the Yankees' Paul O'Neill. Mark Wohlers, a hard-throwing star closer for Atlanta, was asked to record a two-inning save in Game 4 of the 1996 World Series, but allowed a momentum-changing, game-tying home run to Yankees catcher Jim Leyritz. Likewise, when the Padres asked NL Cy Young runner-up and 53-save man Trevor Hoffman—who from 2006 to 2011 would be baseball's all-time saves leader—to protect a 3–2 lead in the eighth inning in Game 3 of the 1998 series, he faltered and served up a go-ahead three-run homer to the Yankees' Scott Brosius.

■ ■ ■

After Game 4, the Athletics were dead. Both Eckersley, baseball's premier stopper, and Stewart, their ace, had faltered against the Dodgers. Now, they had to beat Hershiser, a pitcher coming off back-to-back shutouts, just to stave off elimination.

According to right-hander Tim Leary, he knew the series was over, especially with Hershiser on the mound for Game 5. And Oakland had to be demoralized when Mickey Hatcher homered for the second time in the series and Mike Davis surprised everyone by slugging a two-run homer of his own. With the lead and Hershiser on the mound heading into the final innings, Leary knew it was over.

But not Tracy Woodson, who watched Game 5 from the dugout. There was never any point when he thought the series was over—until it really was over. He had a point. With the Dodgers ahead 5–1 in the eighth, Stan Javier singled in a run to cut the deficit to three with just one out. Oakland had two men on with Canseco and Parker coming up; one swing could tie things up. "Hershiser, again, was on the mound. In the last inning, it was still a close game," says Woodson. "You just never know, especially with the lineup that Oakland had." Hershiser, though, regrouped to retire Canseco on a pop-up, and after a wild pitch advanced both runners, strike Parker out swinging. Oakland got a runner on in the ninth, but Hershiser fanned Tony Phillips for the final out—and Woodson and the rest of the Dodgers finally got to celebrate. "I think the relief comes when he strikes out the last guy," continues Woodson. "That's when you do know that it's over. You can't take anything for granted, because—and I hate to be cliché-ish—it is never over until it's over. A lot of times when you think the game is over, and then something happens, and you end up losing the game. But I think once you get the final out, then you can celebrate and enjoy winning."

Like Woodson, Leary didn't see a lot of action in October. He started only once in the postseason, a 5–1 loss in Game 6 of the NLCS. But Leary isn't disappointed; it was a great season for him personally, he pitched well in the World Series, and the year ended with a World Championship. "I had my run from the first game after the All-Star break up to September. Started to tire. As by October, I'd pitched 406 innings in a 12-month period because of 138 innings in Tijuana where I went 12–1 and led our team to the Mexican Winter League Championship," says Leary now. "Regained my arm strength, and command of a hard two-seam, sinking fastball, and a nasty split that I could throw either, one, for a strike, or two, for a lower-than-the-knees strikeout/groundout pitch. Then 30 innings in spring '88 [followed by] 228 innings during the season. Actually 396 innings in 12 months, with January 15 to February 15 as downtime! Plus some not-good innings versus the Mets, then the three most important innings of my life in Game One!"

"There were a lot of big moments in the World Series," adds Woodson.

> Mike Marshall's [Game 2] home run was huge, there's no doubt. We started to bury them a little bit. I mean, hell, we almost swept them—if McGwire doesn't homer in the bottom of the ninth in the 2–1 game. I think the icing on the cake was when Davis homered in Oakland—and he was an Athletic the year before. He only hit two home runs that year. He didn't have a very good season. That was another big one. But the one defining moment of that World Series is Gibson's home run because I think that buried Oakland—because they were going, "Holy crap, how could that happen?" It happened in the first game. And Gibson didn't hit again.

Ross Porter, a play-by-play announcer for the Dodgers, erroneously thinks Bob Costas's on-air comments about the Dodgers had come during the pregame in the clincher. He's right, nonetheless, about how Hershiser and the team came together. "The 1988 Dodgers were not highly talented, but showed great resiliency and Hershiser had an amazing September," Porter says now. "Bob Costas said on NBC before Game 5 of the World Series at Oakland, 'This Dodger lineup tonight may be the worst in World Series history.' A few hours later, they won the World Championship."

The Dodgers didn't have the best players, says Howell, but they made all the plays that they had to. "We were an assortment of injuries, bench players, and bleeding-at-the-mouth characters," says Howell. "Look at Mickey Hatcher. There was a key play in the series where he hit a [high chopper to third baseman Carney Lansford], and it was a bang-bang play at first, and he dove. He was gonna be thrown out. And he always just loved to dive at the damn bag, and we all would say, 'You're just a showboat. What are you doing?' He was so goofy and fun, and we'd rib him. And we were in Oakland, and here's the play."

Howell is referring to the series finale, where Hatcher had already homered in the first inning before hitting that high chopper three innings later. "[The] throw [from Lansford was] to the inside of the bag. [First baseman Mark] McGwire goes down and goes to swipe to tag, in plenty of time, but [Hatcher] dove. He dove and he was safe at first. He ended up scoring [on Mike Davis's homer]. But if he didn't dive, he's out. He would've been out."

Hatcher, who batted .368 for the series with five RBIs, could have been named the World Series MVP—but the award went to Hershiser instead. Still, that series was the highlight of 1988 for Hatcher. "[The most memorable part of that year was] definitely the World Series," Hatcher says today.

> Because I wasn't an everyday player so I was thrown into the mix, to try to be a leader, to try to be an everyday player. All I wanted to do was win a World Series so bad, so that was just a great feeling—because Tommy Lasorda [gave me that opportunity to play]. Gibson gets hurt, and I get the opportunity to go out there and fill in some big shoes. And to go out there and do that, and end up winning the World Series—and actually having a good series, that was the greatest thrill for me.

Not bad for a guy who was almost out of baseball a year earlier. Although his career would end in 1991, Hatcher remained in the game and won a second World Series ring as the Anaheim Angels' hitting coach in 2002. "I think the only thing I missed was the fact that we didn't win it in front of the Dodgers fans. When we won it with the Angels [against San Francisco], we won it at home with our fans. I wished that with the Dodgers I would've had a chance to win it at home with the Dodgers fans because it was just electrifying. It was a whole different atmosphere and everything. With the Dodgers, when we won it, we won it in Oakland.

"I mean, that was in Oakland!" Hatcher adds with a laugh. "It was great amongst the players and the team and what we accomplished. But it took the fans out of it. I just wish that that opportunity would've been great if we would've done it in front of our fans."

Left-hander John Tudor, who'd miss almost all of 1989 because of his injured elbow, offered some reflection in a 2016 interview with sportswriter Corey Stolzenbach. "It's the old saying, 'That's why they play the game. You never know what can happen.' And obviously, the A's had the big boppers, with McGwire and Canseco, and some pretty good pitching [with] Dave Stewart and Eckersley in relief," Tudor recalled. "But that Dodger team was just destined from the first day when Gibson hit the home run off of Eckersley. That just kind of set the wheels in motion, as they say."[5]

On the media side, there were some—including Bob Nightengale—who never believed Los Angeles was actually going to win. Even in the finale, Oakland had a shot in the eighth inning—and it was only when Hershiser struck out Phillips to end the series that the nonbelievers realized they'd just witnessed one of the biggest upsets in the history of the Fall Classic.

"I missed out on the World Series other than Game 1—when I went away with the [NBA Boston] Celtics to Madrid, [Spain, to cover the second annual] McDonald's Open basketball [tournament]," says *Boston Globe* columnist Bob Ryan. "But I remember when they came on the air, they said it was—meaning the Dodger lineup—'the worst lineup in the World Series.' Canseco hit that [grand slam] home run into the cameras in the first game, and then of course the famous Gibson home run, which nobody will ever forget. . . . [The Dodgers] were just an improbable pennant winner and champion."

Nightengale, then with the *Kansas City Star*, can be forgiven for believing Oakland would come back. After all, fans had witnessed miraculous World Series comebacks in recent years, with the 1985 Royals (against St. Louis), '86 Mets (against Boston), and even the '87 Twins (versus the Cardinals again) rallying when it seemed they were done. "When Canseco hit that home run, everyone [in the press box] thought, 'OK, the series is gonna be over in a hurry.' [But Oakland] kind of [sat

Rick Dempsey caught the final out of the 1988 World Series, but he's known more for being the MVP of the 1983 World Series with Baltimore. *Michael McCormick*

back] and let the Dodgers win that game. I think the series turned on the Gibson home run. It actually gave them life and made them believe they could do it," says Nightengale.

"I think it was a little bit of a surprise the way the Dodgers came on," adds Mel Antonen. "Oakland had a little bit of everything. They had McGwire and Canseco. Carney Lansford. Dave Henderson. Don Baylor. So, what the Dodgers did to Oakland in the World Series was amazing."

For Rick Dempsey, who caught the final out on Hershiser's game-ending strikeout, being on the field for the World Series–clinching out was special, even though he'd already won a championship with the 1983 Orioles—and was the World Series MVP in Baltimore's five-game victory over Philadelphia. The 1988 championship was a total team effort, and Dempsey was proud to be a part of it. "I platooned with Mike Scioscia," he says.

> Very, very good baseball guy. Very good catcher. He could call a ball game. He could work a pitching staff. We complemented one another all season long. We just knew how to help young pitchers. I look back to that era in my career; it all came together—all the things that I'd learned from all the championship teams that I was on. We brought it all to the Dodgers that season. We helped develop guys like Tim Belcher, Tim Leary. It was amazing. It really was, because when we needed to win a baseball game, we would all just put our heads together. We talked the game of baseball. We knew how to get through the lineups and that's really what it was.
>
> Those young pitchers that we had on that team—together with Orel Hershiser, who that year was the best pitcher in baseball, ever, for a full season—just got on a roll. We just got on a roll. We totally believed in ourselves. The Stuntmen knew we were almost unbeatable. It didn't matter how big our names were. Nobody had an ego on that ball club. We only cared about winning baseball. We had the most fun, ever, doing it.

Charlie Blaney, meanwhile, points to the job the homegrown talent did in 1988. During the latter part of his stint as the Dodgers' farm director, Blaney oversaw the development of five consecutive Rookies of the Year in the 1990s, with Eric Karros (1992), Mike Piazza (1993), Raul Mondesi (1994), Hideo Nomo (1995), and Todd Hollandsworth (1996) claiming the NL top-rookie honors. Naturally, Blaney is especially proud of the homegrown players who contributed in 1988, the ones who went through the minor-league system and became stars in Dodger Blue. "Having Steve Sax, who was with the team, and Mickey Hatcher, coming across from the Twins [after originally being a Dodger], Mike Scioscia, having come up through the system, [and] Orel Hershiser," Blaney says. "They were, I guess, the standouts of that team that the Dodgers grew their own, and were proud of it, and gave them an opportunity to perform, and they did."

One interesting tidbit that's been forgotten is that the Dodgers, already missing Kirk Gibson, played without a backup catcher in the series finale following Scioscia's injury in the fourth game. Fortunately, they got through the finale without losing Dempsey. Their backup catcher, Gilberto Reyes, actually arrived as they were celebrating on the field.

Reyes was not on the postseason rosters that October at all but traveled with the team during the NLCS and the first two games of the World Series. He was home in the Dominican Republic, watching Game 4 against Oakland on television, and saw that Scioscia was injured. Following that game, Reyes received a phone call from Fred Claire to see if he could return to the United States in time for Game 4 to be Dempsey's backup.

By the time Reyes arrived at Oakland Coliseum, though, the series had just ended. "They sent me to the Dominican after the second game, when we beat Oakland after the Kirk Gibson home run [and Hershiser's shutout]," remembers Reyes now.

> We were supposed to start the winter league over there. Then two days later, they called me back. But my flight got delayed a couple times—I think it was in Dallas and somewhere else. By the time I got there, it was the last inning. To be honest, I celebrated like I hit a home run. It was, "Oh my God. What a moment!" Tommy saw me—he and everybody else knew I was coming, but I was supposed to be there earlier—and said, "Where have you been, Gilberto?"
>
> Then I said, "I've been celebrating, Tommy!"
>
> I mean, everybody was happy. I think I was supposed to play the next [game] because [Scioscia] was hurt. So, I was supposed to be in the lineup. But I didn't mind because I got my World Series ring. Everything was fun.

CHAPTER TWELVE
CLAIRE THE ARCHITECT

It's really sad that Fred's not in baseball right now because he can bring a lot to the table. He's a great human being, a great person. I just wish another organization gave him an opportunity to be in their organization because he can bring a lot to a team.

—Mariano Duncan, former Dodgers infielder

With the Athletics trailing 2–1 in the 1988 World Series, everybody knew Oakland had to win Game 4. If the A's lost again, they'd be facing elimination when Orel Hershiser took the mound in Game 5. Hershiser, after all, had posted an 0.30 ERA since the beginning of September with 8 scoreless outings in his last 10 starts. Of course, it was the Dodgers prevailing 4–3, a victory that was a testament to general manager Fred Claire, who took over when Al Campanis was ousted in April 1987.

Claire, a former beat writer for the *Long Beach (California) Press-Telegram*, was in only his second season as a major-league general manager (GM). But it wasn't as though he didn't know what he was doing. He'd started out covering the Dodgers and Angels as a reporter before landing a job in the public relations department for the Dodgers in 1969. Within six years, he'd worked his way up to become vice president of public relations, promotions, and marketing. During his tenure in that position, Claire played a major role in creating the phenomenon of "Dodger Blue," a branding that still remains relevant to this day, as well as establishing the Dodgers' "Think Blue" campaign. While working in the organization and serving as Campanis's assistant, Claire had developed an understanding of the game—and now Los Angeles was on the verge of winning the 1988 World Series.

Phil Regan, a scout with the '88 Dodgers, recalls how he went from working for Campanis to working for Claire. "Al Campanis hired me away from Seattle—in 1987—to become an advance scout for the Dodgers," remembers Regan.

> I went to spring training and my first assignment was the Houston Astros. I was to prepare a report for spring training and, as an advance scout, give it to Al. I was a little bit worried about it because they said Al was really tough on advance scouts and he really went over your reports with a fine-tooth comb. On Monday, when they were gonna open the season, I'd sent my report to Al in Houston and I called him on Monday afternoon. I said, "Al, I just wanna check and see if you got my report." He said, "Phil, I've got it but I haven't had a chance to read it. I'll read it tonight, and I'll call you tomorrow." That night was the night that Al Campanis went on television and then got fired the next day. So, I don't know if he ever read my report—but I never heard!

Regan is referring to Campanis's controversial remarks about African Americans in baseball made during an interview on the late-night ABC News program *Nightline*. "So then, I started working for Fred. He was really an amazing person to work for because he valued your opinions," continues Regan. "You could talk and he'd listen to what you had to say. One of the things I remember was just how thorough Fred was on everything. If we were gonna make a trade on a player, he wanted us to check with anybody that had played with this person, that had been on the same team, that had coached him, even go back to his college coach and find out what type of a person he was, what his work habits were like. . . . That was kind of an amazing thing that I remember."

Getting back to Los Angeles's fourth-game victory in Oakland, several players that Claire acquired made a difference. Back in 1987, the same week that he took over as the GM, Claire signed Mickey Hatcher to fill the void left by third baseman Bill Madlock's shoulder injury. In May, Claire traded reliever Tom Niedenfuer to Baltimore for John Shelby (and reliever Brad Havens). In June, he signed free agent Danny Heep.

Claire then sent left-hander Rick Honeycutt to Oakland in August for a player to be named later, and that player turned out to be Tim Belcher, then a minor-leaguer. Then came the off-season. In a three-way deal with the A's and Mets, Claire acquired Jay Howell, Alfredo Griffin, and reliever Jesse Orosco. He also signed free agents Mike Davis, Kirk Gibson, and Rick Dempsey. "It was a tremendous winter, and Fred Claire did a tremendous job," Tommy Lasorda recalled in his 2007 biography. "He knew the pulse of the team. He knew I needed a guy to run things in the clubhouse. He knew we needed Gibson."[1]

Fast forward to Game 4, where Belcher got the win—his third of the postseason. Howell closed out the one-run victory—though to this day, the Dodgers stopper credits catcher Dempsey for that seven-out save. Hatcher, who'd homer twice in the series in place of the injured Gibson, had a key single in the first inning. Shelby drove in Hatcher later that same inning, Heep contributed a single in the second, and Griffin scored what proved to be the winning run. While Davis went hitless, he nonetheless filled in at right field when Mike Marshall couldn't play because of back spasms. And Davis was the one who'd drawn the key walk ahead of Gibson's famous Game 1 homer, and Davis hit a two-run homer of his own in Game 5. The Dodgers won the World Series 4–1.

"Fred had a lot to do with this," says Joey Amalfitano. "He's the guy who put this together. He's the guy who got Gibson. He's the guy that got John Shelby. They were two pieces of the puzzle. Were they big pieces? Yup, in my opinion. Oh yeah, in my opinion. Then he made a trade where he got Alfredo Griffin. He got Jay Howell. He got Tim Belcher. He made several trades to make that team, to put that team together. And they came on in '88. They all got on the same end of the rope and pulled on it together, and we all have rings."

Howell is still amazed today at how Claire had managed to pull off all those moves. "I don't know how he did it, but he just seemed to make some trades. I mean, worst-to-first is kind of a big deal." Actually, the Dodgers had finished fourth in the six-team NL West in 1987, but their 73 victories would have put them in last place had they been in the East. Overall, the 1987 Dodgers were 10th out of the 12-team league. The year before, Los Angeles, with the exact same record, had finished just a half-game ahead of last-place Atlanta.

"He brought in some players that I thought were really significant in terms of creating the body of the team. But it all goes back to Fred Claire and Tommy Lasorda. You've got Fred bringing these guys in, and then you've got Tommy creating the identity of our team," continues Howell, who also pitched for Cincinnati, Oakland, Texas, Atlanta, the Cubs, and the Yankees. "And I played a number of years on different clubs. I can tell you it was a good environment. That, I mean, is kind of what Fred Claire put together. I don't know if they consciously sit there and look at stuff like that. I don't know how GMs do it. I really don't. Is it luck? Is it the manager? Is it the right place at the right time? I dunno."

Mel Didier, like Amalfitano, remembered that Claire's moves in 1987–1988 really made that '88 team into a championship club. But he also credited the scouts for the team's success. "It was a hellacious team put together by Fred Claire and the major-league scouts, Steve Boros, myself, Phil Regan, and Jerry Stephenson. The four of us who [are] the ones who worked for Fred; we worked for him rather than just for the major leagues as scouts," Didier said in April of 2017.

Dodgers closer Jay Howell, shown here in a Reds uniform in his rookie year in 1980, pitched for seven teams in his career. *National Baseball Hall of Fame and Museum, Cooperstown, New York*

Fred really worked at it. We put together a plan. We started the season off with seven or eight moves. Kirk Gibson. Alfredo Griffin at short-stop; he'd been with Oakland. Dempsey, catching. Tim Belcher came over the year before. We had a number of key players who came to us, and they performed dramatically. Our centerfielder [John Shelby] came from Baltimore; he was outstanding. We got Hatcher back at the start of the [1987] season; he was a big addition because he provided a lot of pizzazz and a lot of hustle. So, we brought in a lot of key players, and they made the key plays.

Steve Sax echoes Didier's sentiments. The second baseman recalls that although the team had a significant number of injuries—including former ace Fernando Valenzuela missing two months of the season and the entire postseason—there were always other players who stepped up to fill the void. Not only were many of them brought in by Claire, as Sax recalls, they were also acquired before the Dodgers could be undermined by injuries. "With Fernando, his biggest time was during the earlier part of his career, when it was Fernandomania," says Sax.

He learned how to throw the screwball. We always had somebody to step up to replace the next guy. John Shelby, in center field, made a big difference for us. Tim Leary came up and pitched really well. Tim Belcher was also good. He had really good stuff. We had John Tudor. That was a good acquisition, getting John Tudor from St. Louis [in exchange for] Pedro Guerrero. So, our team was one that had to make changes, and we actually made the changes while we were in good standing. Not when our team was actually going south. We did them when we were neutral or going north. I think Fred Claire made some good moves that year.

Third-string catcher Gilberto Reyes would be traded to the Montreal Expos during spring training in 1989, but he still considers Claire a friend today. He also recalls that Claire always made moves to improve the ball club in 1988. "We never asked for something that we didn't really need," Reyes says today.

I mean, everything was there. Fred Claire was completely with us from the beginning, all the way up to the very last out. We needed something, we got it. Whenever we wanted something, we got it. We always got somebody when we really needed. We got Jay Howell. We got guys in trades that year. Whoever came in, he came ready to play ball. Whoever came in, he was ready to compete. He was there for the team. No matter if he was there for just one out or just for a double switch and didn't get to hit, he was there for the team. It was completely, really fun.

Claire not only brought in key players, he also hired analytics experts and improved communication throughout the organization. As Hershiser once said, "It was Fred who gave us the first edge of being progressive, and aggressive."[2] Veteran sportswriter Bill Plaschke, in a *Los Angeles Times* piece on Claire some 30 years following that Dodgers championship, noted that the general manager changed the culture of the front office by holding regular conference calls with everybody from minor-league batting coaches to scouts. Claire, as Plaschke noted, would also often wander the Dodger Stadium tunnels to talk to players about not only baseball but also their families.[3]

Unfortunately, Claire, who was fired in 1998, is largely forgotten. He's probably best remembered by fans today as the man who, in November of 1993, traded Hall-of-Famer-to-be Pedro Martinez—then a rookie setup man in the Dodgers' bullpen—to Montreal for second baseman Delino DeShields, who batted .241 in three disappointing seasons with Los Angeles. In 1997, owner Peter O'Malley sold the club to Rupert Murdoch's Fox Entertainment Group, and things went south in a hurry. In May 1998, the club's new Fox officials traded future Hall of Fame catcher Mike Piazza to the Florida Marlins without the knowledge or involvement of Claire, who then publicly announced that he didn't make the deal. One month later, with the Dodgers struggling, Claire was fired, replaced by former manager Tommy Lasorda.

As Claire reflects today, he learned a lot during his 30 years with the Dodgers and wishes to share this message with everybody he encounters: keep learning in life because the knowledge you gain will never go to waste. "Being a general manager for many years and working in baseball— along with my years spent in teaching—I've found one thing to be true," Claire says today. "All the work I did, all the study I did, all the research I did, never went to waste. You know why? The reason is I learned from it. Knowledge is power. It's true." It is true. Claire didn't go directly from being a sportswriter to making trades; he'd studied the game all along throughout what he calls "a meaningful transition of 20 years" from 1969, and it paid off when he took charge of player personnel in 1987.

Claire never worked again in the front office of a major-league club after being let go by the Dodgers. Instead, he did some work as a columnist and analyst for MLB.com, and also as a radio host. He wrote a book about his 30 years being a member of the Dodgers' front office. He did consulting work for companies involved in sports from his home in Pasadena, got on the board of directors of the Rose Bowl Operating Company, taught classes at the California Institute of Technology and the University of Southern California, and became chairman of a sports analytics startup known as Scoutables.com—a platform offering machine-generated scouting reports and data-driven insights about every major-league player.

But as the seasons went by, it seemed Claire and his accomplishments with the Dodgers were forgotten. Also forgotten were his PR days when he was directing the team's marketing efforts when the Dodgers first hit the three million mark in attendance and established a period of record-setting attendance figures. Prior to 2017, his contributions for building

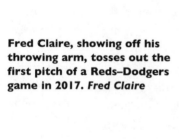

Fred Claire, showing off his throwing arm, tosses out the first pitch of a Reds–Dodgers game in 2017. *Fred Claire*

the 1988 world champions had never been publicly honored, his face had never been shown on a video board at Dodger Stadium, and he'd never thrown out a ceremonial first pitch.

Things changed during the 2017 season, when Claire was finally invited back to Dodger Stadium for Old-Timers' Day in June, and the former general manager was asked to throw out the ceremonial first pitch of the Dodgers–Reds game. Wearing a home white jersey with the number 88 on the back and the name "Claire" above it, an emotional Claire waved to the crowd as he was being announced before walking to the mound to throw out that first pitch to Mickey Hatcher, the first player he acquired as Dodgers GM. "The Dodgers [asked] me to throw out the first pitch and [I was also] introduced with the Old-Timers. It was an unforgettable evening . . . a memorable experience for me and my family," Claire says.

But these days, Claire's main focus isn't on baseball. He's been receiving treatments for cancer at City of Hope hospital, an independent research and treatment center in Duarte, California, for cancer, diabetes, and other life-threatening diseases. It's a cancer in his neck that required surgery in October 2016. Having seen the impressive work by the center's doctors, staff, and volunteers, Claire organized a golf tournament that

It was an emotional afternoon for Fred Claire being back at Dodger Stadium on Old-Timers' Day in 2017. *Fred Claire*

took place in August 2017—the inaugural Fred Claire Celebrity Golf Classic at Oakmont Country Club in Glendale, California—to raise money for the City of Hope.

Claire's goal was to raise $250,000, but he wound up exceeding that figure. "My cancer started with a spot on my lip, and if I had protected that area from many days in the sun, that may have led to a different outcome," Claire said in May 2017. "If I can help just one person with this message of the dangers of the sun and need for protection, it will be very rewarding to me."

At this time, the former Dodgers general manager's time is occupied by his efforts to continue to help the City of Hope with a second Fred Claire Golf Classic in August 2018 to benefit the Duarte research and treatment center. He was a participant on the City of Hope float in the 2018 Rose Parade to help call attention to the hospital. "In going to the City of Hope for the past year and a half and seeing so many patients in need of good care, patients of all ages, it's important to me to do everything I can to help in any way possible," Claire says. "The science of treating cancer patients is changing every day, and everything we can do to assist with the needed research is important to meet the needs of both current and future patients."

Part Four

AFTER 1988

[As I look back at 1988 all these years later], just that moment—Kirk Gibson's home run in the World Series—stands out way above the rest. Everything else was just a blur compared to Gibson's home run.

—Bob Nightengale, sportswriter

CHAPTER THIRTEEN
SAYING GOODBYE TO LA

Peter O'Malley, the owner of the Dodgers, and Fred Claire, the general manager, are just amazing people. I think that every player that had the opportunity to go through the Dodgers organization really appreciates the professionalism that those guys had, just believing in us.

—Mickey Hatcher, Dodgers Stuntman

Teams that win championships don't stay together forever. Sometimes, they get broken up immediately after the championship was won. Ask fans of the 1997 Florida Marlins how they feel, when within a short few months of winning the World Series, almost all of their key players were sent out of town as ownership conducted a massive fire sale. Outfielder Moises Alou was dealt to Houston just two weeks following the series. Pitching aces Kevin Brown and Al Leiter were traded to the Padres and Mets, respectively. Closer Robb Nen was gone, shipped to San Francisco. Center fielder Devon White was traded to the expansion Diamondbacks. Jeff Conine, an original Marlin and one of the expansion franchise's best players during its inaugural 1993 season, was dealt to Kansas City. In May 1998, slugging right fielder Gary Sheffield, catcher Charles Johnson, and third baseman/outfielder Bobby Bonilla were also traded.

While the 1988 Dodgers didn't do anything close to what the Marlins would do a decade later, the team also didn't stay together. One month after the championship was won, second baseman Steve Sax was the first to leave, signing a free-agent deal with the Yankees. By Opening Day of 1990, numerous players had either been released or traded, or had moved on to other organizations. Key contributors such as RBI leader Mike Marshall and 17-game winner Tim Leary were traded. Prospects like Mike Devereaux and Gilberto Reyes were also dealt to other teams. Jesse Orosco wasn't re-signed. Danny Heep was released. Pitchers Brian Holton, Ken Howell, John Tudor, Alejandro Peña, and Ricky Horton were gone. Stuntmen Tracy Woodson, Dave Anderson, Mike Davis, and Franklin Stubbs were also gone.

But Sax, whose place in Dodgers history is pretty unique, was the first. A three-time All-Star in seven-plus seasons in Dodger Blue, Sax is a member of the last two Dodgers World Championship teams. In fact, he has the rare distinction of winning a World Series ring and then capturing Rookie of the Year honors *the following year*—he was a member of the 1981 championship team before being recognized as the NL's top rookie in 1982 as he hadn't played enough games to get that rookie tag removed.

Sax, of course, was also the first player to break up the durable Dodgers' infield of the 1970s of Ron Cey (third base), Steve Garvey (first base), Davey Lopes (second base), and Bill Russell (shortstop)—a quartet that played together for more than eight years, a major-league record. Lopes was traded to Oakland three months following the 1981 World Series, and Sax became the Dodgers' everyday second baseman.

Of all the accomplishments Sax had with the Dodgers, he's most proud of being a member of Los Angeles's last championship clubs. "Of course. No doubt," Sax said in June 2017, four months before the Dodgers returned to the World Series, when asked if 1988 holds any significance to him.

It's the last time the Dodgers were there. I mean, it's been 30 years since the Dodgers last won. I don't believe the Dodgers have even been to the World Series, let alone won it. And this is a team that was expected to be fourth in our division that year; the sports pundits had us picked fourth in our division. We win the division. We only beat the Mets one game the whole year—and then we had to play them in the playoffs. And we beat them, and then we beat the Bash Brothers, the Oakland A's, after that. So, it was quite a year.

Steve Sax was a three-time NL All-Star during his seven-plus seasons with the Dodgers. *Michael McCormick*

It wasn't all smooth sailing in 1988, adds Sax, but several players stepped up and had outstanding seasons. "We had injuries that year," Sax says today.

> Kirk Gibson was injured part of the year. He was new to our team. Mike Scioscia hit a big home run off of Dwight Gooden that continued our chances to beat the Mets in the playoffs. We just had a year that was

incredible. Orel Hershiser, 59 scoreless innings to pass Drysdale. John Shelby played great center field for us and provided a lot of offensive punch for our team. That made a big difference as well. Alfredo Griffin came up and shored up the shortstop position. So, we had a lot of different things happen to our team that had to go right for us. Or else, we don't win it. We did a lot of the right things and everything fell into place for us. Tim Leary won 17 games that year for us. He went down to Mexico in the off-season and was working on that split-finger fastball that really made a big difference for him that year.

The Dodgers had a significant number of injuries in the Fall Classic, with Gibson getting only one at-bat and Marshall playing hurt in the latter part of the series. Even Scioscia went down with an injury, leaving the Dodgers' lineup thin. But through it all, Sax, a free-agent-to-be, remained healthy and batted .300 in the series. In the off-season, the second baseman opted to leave for New York, and on November 23, 1988, he inked a three-year contract with the Yankees worth $4 million.

A two-time AL All-Star in New York (1989 and 1990), Sax says today there's no hard feelings for his leaving Los Angeles. In fact, he sees former GM Fred Claire quite a bit these days, as both reside in Southern California. "I see him periodically," Sax says when asked if he still keeps in touch with Claire and the other ex-Dodgers on the 1988 team. "I saw him [at Dodger Stadium] for the Old-Timers' Game [in 2017]. People live in different parts of the country. It's hard to stay in touch on a day-to-day basis. But when you see each other, it's like nothing's lost. You're always gonna be brothers. It's binded you into history. It's binded you into a future that will never go away. So, it's a great thing."

Following his three-year stint in New York, Sax played for the White Sox (1992–1993) and Athletics (1994) before retiring from the game. He was back in uniform again in 2013 as the first-base coach in Arizona, joining ex-teammate and Diamondbacks manager Kirk Gibson for one season. But between 1994 and 2013, Sax enjoyed his time not being in uniform as he pursued several different endeavors.

I got into broadcasting for a bit when I retired—did three years with Fox. Then I became a financial consultant; that was 10 years with the Royal Bank of Canada as a wealth adviser, a wealth manager. And then I sold my business and became a full-time [motivational] speaker and executive coach. So, that's what I do now; I'm a speaker and a coach. I also work in radio and TV for MLB Network. It's a fun thing to do; I work on my own time. I do radio three to four days a week, and I do some TV for MLB Advanced Media. It's great. I'm enjoying it.

■ ■ ■

Stuntman Danny Heep was released by the Dodgers four days before Christmas 1988.

Although he batted only .242 and was a reserve player in '88, Heep proved early in the season that he could thrive when a starring role presented itself. From late April to mid-May, when John Shelby was sidelined for three weeks with a strained abdominal muscle, Heep took over in right field and batted .438 with six RBIs.

Heep, known for his smooth swing and excellent batting eye, fulfilled whatever role Tommy Lasorda had for him in 1988. A star pitcher during his days at St. Mary's University in his hometown of San Antonio, Texas—where he notched an 0.69 ERA with 11 saves in 1978—Heep even pitched for the Dodgers on July 30, in a blowout game versus Houston. With Los Angeles trailing 12–4, he came in and worked the final two innings. Although he allowed two runs (on a two-run homer by Ken Caminiti), Heep still recorded six outs to help protect the bullpen.

After being limited to a pair of pinch-hitting appearances in the NLCS against his ex-Mets team, Heep batted .250 with a double in eight at-bats against Oakland in the World Series. "We weren't dominating anything at that point. I think we won 88 games [actually, 94]," Heep says from his office in San Antonio, taking time out of his coaching schedule to spend a few minutes to share his thoughts about 1988.

> But we had a really great pitching staff. We all knew that if we could make the playoffs, if we could get in there, anything could happen. We had a great pitching staff, and they were the ones who really [got it done]. Orel coming up and pitching all those innings was what turned the tide for us. When Gibson got hurt, we didn't really know what was gonna happen. We were gonna be a little short-handed, and then all of a sudden a couple of the Stuntmen had to go play in the World Series that didn't get a lot of at-bats during the season. But Mickey Hatcher

did a great job, and so it worked out. But our pitching staff picked us up; they really did shut them down.

Alas, two months following the World Series, Heep was released. In February 1989, he signed with Boston, and received the most playing time he'd ever had in his career. In 320 at-bats, he batted .300 with only 26 strikeouts and a career-high 49 RBIs. He also smacked 17 doubles, which tied a career high set back in '85 with the Mets. Unfortunately, in 1990 Heep suffered through back problems and required surgery. He returned just in time for the playoffs, and the division-winning Red Sox included him on their postseason roster. Boston, however, was swept in the AL playoffs by Oakland.

In the off-season, Heep signed as a free agent with the White Sox, who sent him to Triple-A Vancouver to begin the 1991 season. He was traded to Atlanta in May for minor-league infielder Kevin Castleberry without ever playing for Chicago. After hitting .417 in only 14 games with the Braves, Heep was asked to accept a minor-league demotion in June. Heep's wife was pregnant with their daughter at the time, and he realized it was time to retire and spend more time with his family. He called it quits, ending a career that saw him bat .257 with 30 homers and 229 RBIs in 883 games.

Shortly after his retirement, Heep was hired as an assistant coach for the Cardinals baseball team at the University of the Incarnate Word (UIW), a private Catholic college in his hometown of San Antonio. He took over as the Cardinals' head baseball coach in 1998, a position he still holds today. In 2016, Heep surpassed 1,000 career games as UIW head coach, and 2018 marks his 21st season on the job. A three-time Conference Coach of the Year (2005, 2008, and 2011), he helped transition the program through promotions from NAIA to NCAA Division II in 2000 and to Division I in 2014.

When Heep takes one final moment to reflect back on 1988—and his role on that team—he feels he was fortunate to have been on some very good teams during his career. After all, he was a member of four division champions during his 13 years—and that doesn't even include the 1991 NL champion Braves, for whom he played 14 games. It also doesn't include the 1981 Astros, who made the playoffs in a special split season thanks to a players' strike. (Heep didn't play in the 1981 postseason; Houston lost to Los Angeles in the divisional round.) He was also a member of a Mets team that won 98 games in 1985—owners of the NL's second-best record behind only the 101-win Cardinals—but failed to make the playoffs because the wild card didn't exist back then.

"Obviously you can't ever win enough rings," Heep reflects.

It actually means more to you after you're done. When you're playing, you're kind of still wrapped up in the deal. But as you get older, you start appreciating things more. You start really understanding how hard it is to win championships. And I was fortunate to be on two World Series teams. Not a lot of people are able to say that. I was never a superstar. I was kind of a guy who just got 200, 300, or 400 at-bats a season. I seemed to have had good tastes; I was always playing on winning teams. When I was with the Astros, we went to the [1980] National League Championship Series and lost to the Phillies. Then when I went to the Mets, we went to the World Series. I went to the Dodgers, and we went to the World Series. I go to Boston; we win our divisional championship [in 1990]. So, I mean, every team I played on was a really good team. That was fun. I'm really proud of that. Winning championships, they can never take that from you. I still have the rings; that's something I was very fortunate to be a part of.

■ ■ ■

As for Franklin Stubbs, the writing was on the wall soon after the 1988 World Series. Just six weeks following the series clincher in Oakland, his career hit a snag as Fred Claire pulled off a major trade in an attempt to upgrade the first-base position. Desperate for some offensive help, Claire acquired slugger Eddie Murray from Baltimore in December to play first base, meaning Stubbs was out of an everyday job again. Stubbs requested a trade then, but the Dodgers didn't move him in 1989. "Mr. Claire, I think you're afraid to trade me," Stubbs finally told the GM.

"No, Franklin. I have no fear," Claire responded. "I want to try to be responsive to players. But I'm not going to trade players upon request. My obligation is to trade players—or move players—for the best possible talent. I want to get the best value I can get back for you in any trade. It's not as if I don't hear you. It's not as if I don't sympathize with you. It's just that you have a desire and I have an obligation."

Franklin Stubbs, the starting first baseman for the Dodgers in the 1988 World Series, played for the Brewers in 1991–1992.
Milwaukee Brewers

Claire finally granted Stubbs his wish in April 1990. After appearing in only 69 games with the Dodgers in 1989—being in Tommy Lasorda's starting lineup just 22 times all year—Stubbs was traded to Houston for career minor-league left-hander Terry Wells (who'd pitch in only five games for the Dodgers). In what was a career year for Stubbs, he batted .261 with 23 homers in 146 games while splitting time between first base and left field with the Astros in that one season—the year before Hall-of-Famer-to-be Jeff Bagwell took over first base in Houston and then occupied that position for the next 14 seasons. Then Stubbs moved on to Milwaukee for two years (1991–1992). Stubbs didn't appear in the big leagues in 1993—playing instead for Boston's Triple-A club in Pawtucket—and spent '94 in the Mexican League. He returned for one final season in the majors in 1995, batting .250 in only 62 games for the Detroit Tigers.

While things didn't end well after he left the Dodgers, Stubbs still cherishes the time he spent in Los Angeles. "The championship means everything," Stubbs says when asked what 1988 means to him. "When you're a little kid and you think about playing professional sports in any-thing, your whole goal is to get to a world championship and get on that stage. For us to get on that stage and be able to perform, it was everything because that was what I grew up wanting to do."

■ ■ ■

Jay Howell—a three-time All-Star and the Dodgers' saves leader from 1988 to 1991—stayed with the organization until the end of the 1992 season. Although the club contended in 1991 despite Howell dealing with a sore elbow for much of the year, Los Angeles never won another division title while he was still with the franchise. "It was a great team. A lot of unsung heroes, that's for sure," says Howell about the 1988 team. "That's the way I remember it. I just remember it as a very unique, weird circumstance where Hershiser would have a year that I don't know we've ever seen a pitcher dominate like that. I know we've seen some really good pitching over the years, but there was a time that he was unhittable."

Whenever the names Hershiser and Gibson are brought up in conver-sation, Howell has fond memories and plenty to say. "They talk in sports about a perfect game," Howell says.

> What's equivalent for a hitter for a perfect game? Four home runs. But there's only been a few four-home-run games. I mean, I think it's actu-ally less than a perfect game. Think about *that*. What's it like to throw [59 shutout] innings? What's that in terms of rarity? I dunno. Is that equivalent to, say, a World Series one-handed home run against the best closer in the game to win it when you're crippled? Maybe. I mean, that was the weird thing about the season when you look back at it. Hershiser does the impossible and breaks a record that you really never thought would ever, ever be broken. Then, you have Gibson, who couldn't even play, hitting a home run against the best in the game at closing out games. And even the pitch—it's not like it was a meatball right over the middle either. So, you have these two events—one taking much longer than the other, but still . . . I dunno.
>
> For me, Gibson was a powerful person. He was just a very powerful teammate. So was Hershiser. When you were struggling, it's nice to go to a pitching coach. But you had Orel Hershiser there. He was not self-ish with knowledge. Orel was very easy to tap as a resource. I know there

are certain guys on teams who are loners that kinda keep to themselves. They don't share. You can't say that about Orel.

But after the departure of Gibson—who signed with Kansas City as a free agent in December 1990—the ball club was different. Howell noticed, for instance, the rookies weren't necessarily listening to the veterans anymore and he brings up an example from the 1992 team. "There's a [Sheridan's] horse in Chicago that when you come into town and go into Wrigley, you drive right by it," Howell says, referring to the statue of Civil War general Philip Sheridan and his horse at the intersection of Sheridan Road and Belmont Avenue, which is roughly a mile away from Wrigley Field. "When you're in a pennant race, you come into Chicago, you paint the balls on the horse the color of your team."

Howell is referring to a tradition where NL teams had their rookies climb up to the base of the statue under the veil of darkness and paint the horse's balls with the team colors. The Dodgers would paint them blue, the Reds would then come to town and paint them red, and so on. There was a police officer that worked at the ballpark who participated in a mock arrest. He'd go into the locker room the following day after batting practice and ask to see one of the rookies, and then tell him he was being arrested for defacing public property. This rookie hazing tradition continued until the city of Chicago stepped in and stopped it in 2009.

In 1992, the Dodgers were in last place, but the veterans still wanted to make sure the rookies continued the tradition.

> I believe the Giants had been in town just before us. We drive by [the horse] the first game of the series. The call-ups are on the team, on the bus. One of the veterans—I believe it was [reliever] Roger McDowell— stands up and says, "Boys, one of you rookies, we're gonna ask the [clubhouse attendant] and get a can of spray paint—spray paint Dodger Blue. You're gonna go out there tonight and you're gonna get those gonads painted. Take care of it—because that's what you need to do." We go in, we tell the clubbie, "Okay, put the can in one of the rookies' locker." Then after the game they were instructed to go out, get into a cab and go, and take care of it. I don't remember whose locker it was put in.
>
> The next day, we're on the bus and we drive by, going to the ballpark, and they're not done. They're not painted. There's some talk on the bus, like, what's the matter with these rookies? "What's going on? I mean,

you've gotta take care of this. Tonight. Get another can, and make sure it gets taken care of." They were instructed again.

Disgusted that the rookies didn't do as they were instructed and not trusting that they would, Howell and McDowell, along with pitchers Kevin Gross and Tim Crews, decided to apply Dodger Blue paint to the horse themselves on the second night in town.

We left the bar. It was late. We got the can of paint and we were gonna take matters into our own hands. These rookies were gonna pay. They are gonna pay. We get out of the car and the statue is up, kinda like on a tripod about five feet high. You've gotta climb a bit to get to it. We walk up there. I put my hands down, lift them up. We all follow. We're now on the grass, and there's the statue. Roger starts climbing up. He climbs up, pulls the top [off the can of paint], and says, "Oh my God. The spray nozzle's not on the can. We're screwed." Roger gets down on his hands and knees in the grass. It's late at night. And we're looking for the cops. This doesn't look good. Four Dodgers were on their hands and knees. We're feeling in the grass all the way back to the sidewalk where we entered the historical monument.

But suddenly McDowell found the spray nozzle in the grass.

Roger yelled, "We've just won! Here it is!" He pulls it right out of the grass, he puts it on top of the can, he climbs up there, and he sprays it. He goes wild. He just sprays them all. Dodger Blue. We jump in the cab and come back.

The next day on the bus, we're all standing looking out the window at our work like we're looking at a Picasso as we drive by. Roger McDowell tells the rookies, "This better never happen again." In the future, they better get it done and pass down this tradition as it was passed down to us. It needs to happen.

Howell brings up this story to illustrate how the game has changed since 1988. Back then, rookies paid attention when the veterans were trying to teach them about life in the big leagues. But from the late '80s on, it seemed rookies stopped listening to the veterans. Or they were lacking the instincts dealing with the fundamentals of the game. Howell isn't the only one who saw the transition beginning then; others have noticed similar things with young players coming up. "That was the end of the generation of players where you had to know the game as a position player and as a pitcher to advance in the game," longtime All-Star closer Doug Jones, now a minor-league pitching coach, once reflected, referring to 1988 as the end of an era in baseball.

> If you didn't, you didn't play. You were lucky to get on a team. Nowadays, they've got extra coaches on the bench; they've got young kids that have never learned all the nuances of the game. On every pitch, they're changing the outfield positions, they're moving the infielders on the counts, and they go through each batter . . . because [the younger players now] don't know. They've got to be told where to go. And that's at the major-league level. . . . When I first saw the big leagues in 1982 [with Milwaukee], everyone on the team knew exactly what everybody was doing, where they're supposed to be and why, and where I should be at any given situation and what my positioning was, what the scouting report was on everybody. They all had this stuff basically as common knowledge. Nowadays, there aren't enough players that have that common knowledge of the game and they have to be helped and walked through it. . . . But that's just the nature of the game today.[1]

Hall of Fame second baseman Joe Morgan, an ESPN baseball analyst, once elaborated during a 1995 Dodgers–Phillies telecast about younger players lacking an understanding of the game's fundamentals. He cited the example of how players in the 1990s didn't execute the fundamentals of situational hitting enough. "One of the things that I've noticed that has changed in the game is situational hitting. . . . There's a left-handed hitter hitting [with a runner on second and none out]. First pitch, he ends up flying [out] to left field. It's like, 'What are you doing?' Sometimes I wonder if they really know that they're supposed to pull the ball on the ground," Morgan said, referring to how players didn't know they were supposed to advance the runner by hitting to the right side.

> We take it for granted because we know that's the way the game is supposed to be played. But sometimes I wonder if these players actually know what they're supposed to do in certain situations. . . . They swing the same whether there's a runner at third with one out or bases loaded with two outs; it's all the same. They have the same swing for every situation. I think that's something that has really changed in the game.

I really believe you need to get back to [the] basics; somewhere along the line we need to get back to knowing exactly what you're supposed to do in every situation.[2]

During Morgan's 22-year playing career—from 1963 to 1984—the veterans didn't allow the rookies to do whatever they wanted; the young players coming up had to learn the right way. But beginning in the late 1980s? Young players were no longer intimidated by anybody, and they just played the way they wanted to play. "They're not impressed by anyone—or their credentials," adds Morgan.[3]

Howell remembers being frustrated with the rookies on the 1992 Dodgers. "And those rookies . . . ," Howell continues.

We ended up then going into Atlanta [at the end of that same road trip]. They had a shoe store [in downtown Atlanta] that was called Friedman's Shoes. The owner there would sell these shoes to the sports teams. He'd have these unusually large shoes—a lot of tennis shoes and dress shoes. They'd send a van to the hotel to pick up the players and bring them over there. They have these wild-ass shoes . . . shoes from the '70s, the '60s with the big heels, and we go over there and pick out these Saturday Night Fever–type shoes with these tall heels that are just absolutely ridiculous. Some of them had felt with fur, you name it. Just ridiculous. We had the size of all the rookies that were supposed to paint the monument and then Roger cut their pants about mid-calf with scissors, took their shoes, and put the platform shoes in.

As we flew back to LA and walked through the airport, the rookies had to wear those shoes. That, I think, went on for a good number of years. But the Friedman's Shoes was a tradition. You came to Atlanta, and the rookies were gonna wear those. It's good, clean fun. I remember being real disappointed with the rookies. You know, the game's changed, but it hasn't. It's still the game. Some of that stuff, I don't know if they're still doing.

Howell reflects for a moment and then talks about one major change: realignment, which took Cincinnati out of the NL West. "The leagues [and] the divisions [have changed], and you've got interleague. A lot of that, I'm sure, has gone by the wayside. Right? I mean, the rivalries are different, no doubt. When I was with the Dodgers, it was Dodgers–Reds," he says, referring to the Los Angeles–Cincinnati rivalry that was at its fiercest in the 1970s and carried on into the late 1980s. Those days—in the pre–wild card, four-division era prior to 1994—that rivalry was a much bigger deal than Dodgers–Giants. Howell continues,

> There was really just no love there. That's changed. That's no longer. There's only so much you can do. You're not hurting anybody. The rookies were built up and they needed to be humbled. In the Dodger organization they were groomed to be spoiled, and it was our job as veterans to make sure that that didn't happen. We made sure of that. And with LA, it's typical. You read your press clippings and your organization is promoting you before you even set foot on a big-league field. I guarantee you that all teams go through this to try and make sure that they don't have a bunch of prima donnas.

The more Howell talks about 1988, the more he smiles. It's not every day where he gets to recount those memories.

> Hershiser and the rest of us . . . we just kind of rallied around Lasorda [and his motivational speeches]. We ended up beating the Mets and going to the World Series. We were the biggest underdogs. Belcher gives up a grand slam and we come back and win it on Gibson's home run. That's the way that team was. People had each other's backs. It was good times. A lot of the times everybody has their own take. Everybody has their own takeaway from impactful moments. It's fun for me to recount them. To a lot of people close to us, it's boring. So, we don't get to do that that often. So, it's fun to reflect back on that today. [For me, the main takeaway is that] strange things *can* happen if you've got the right chemistry.

■ ■ ■

Mariano Duncan began his 12-year major-league career as a shortstop with the 1985 Dodgers, appearing in 142 games and finishing third in the Rookie of the Year voting. While he played in 109 games in 1986 and 76 in 1987, he was demoted to Triple-A Albuquerque prior to the start of the 1988 season, along with outfielders Mike Devereaux, Chris Gwynn, and Jose Gonzalez, and infielder Tracy Woodson.

While Devereaux, Gwynn, Gonzalez, and Woodson all received call-ups during the year, Duncan never got the call—and didn't receive a World Series ring as a result. At the time he wasn't thrilled about the decision, but when reflecting back some 30 years later, Duncan feels that things worked out after all. "That year, 1988, was a really good year for the Los Angeles Dodgers," Duncan says today. "Even though I can say it was a bad year for me, it was a really good year for the organization. In 1985 I became the starting shortstop for the Dodgers and then 1988 was the year that I got sent down to Triple-A. For me personally, it was something that I'd never dreamed of, being in the minor leagues again that year. But you know, in baseball, sometimes a lot of things happen for a reason."

Now the hitting coach of the Triple-A Iowa Cubs, Duncan acknowledges that being traded in 1989 to the Reds worked out well for his career. "When you play in Los Angeles, it's a big city with so many superstars and movie stars and all that stuff," Duncan explains.

> The city is totally different in Cincinnati. When they traded me to Cincinnati in 1989, it was like my whole career changed because by being sent down in 1988 and not having the opportunity to play in the World Series, this really bothered me a little bit.
>
> But when I got traded to Cincinnati, it looked like I started a new life. Everything was different. I had new teammates, new people, and a new environment. Having the opportunity to go there and having [manager] Lou [Piniella] name me the starting second baseman in 1990 and having the opportunity to have a good year—I remember that year I hit .306 and led the league in triples—and helping my team go to the playoffs and then go to the World Series. And beating the Oakland A's, a team that nobody believed we were gonna beat. . . . Not only that, we swept that team in four straight games. That's something I'd never dreamed [about] before. At the same time, it made me very happy that I was starting all over again after being sent down in 1988 and going to Cincinnati. For me, it was like I was starting all over again.
>
> There's a big difference between LA and Cincinnati. But that 1990 team, we didn't have too many superstars. We played together as a team. I remember that team, every time that we played away games, as soon as we got off the plane, we used to go there and try to eat together and spend some time together. Again, it was something I'd never dreamed [about, being] on a team like that. No superstars. But we played the game together, we helped each other, and we picked each other up.

As for the Dodgers, Duncan doesn't have one bad word to say about the organization. In fact, he has nothing but respect for Fred Claire, the man who traded him to Cincinnati.

> You know, Fred spent many years in the organization. He worked in the front office, and he did a lot of stuff in the minor leagues for the Dodgers. When he became the general manager [in 1987], I was the first one to say, "He deserves to be the GM because he [has] spent so many years in the organization and he knows everybody in the organization, all the players, all that stuff." When I heard the news that he had become the GM, it made me happy and excited because he deserved that kind of job. That guy is a great human being and a great, great man. I've spent some time with Fred. He's a great baseball man.

While he doesn't own a ring with Los Angeles, Duncan does have championship rings with the Reds and Yankees—and still puts them on at special events with those clubs. "I still wear the rings," he says when asked about them. "As a matter of fact, [I wear my '96 Yankees ring at] their Old-Timers' Game. And every time I go to those events, I always wear my ring there." And while his LA playing career ended in 1989, Duncan reminds us that he did return to the Dodgers as the first-base coach from 2006 to 2010 and, as a coach in minor-league baseball today, looks to pass on his baseball knowledge to the young players trying to make it to the majors. "When I look back, I know that I had a great career," Duncan reflects.

> I played for 12 years in the major leagues and I accomplished something very special even though I didn't have the opportunity to play in the World Series in 1988. But I guess I'm happy and very lucky at the same time. I had the opportunity to play in the World Series for three different teams. Winning in 1990, [losing] in 1993 [with Philadelphia], and winning in 1996 with the Yankees. It makes me very excited because so many players—so many superstars—played the game for so long and never had the chance to play in one postseason. Or even one World Series. I was very lucky. For me, to play in three World Series, and win two and lose one.

Whatever he learned at the major-league level, Duncan wants to pass on that knowledge now.

This is one of the reasons why I'm still here in the game; this is my 15th year of coaching. I spent 8 years coaching for the Los Angeles Dodgers—3 in the minor leagues and 5 in the major leagues. Now this is my 7th year of coaching for the Chicago Cubs, [and] whatever I learned in the major leagues, I try to teach those kids everything in the minor-league level right now. [My goal is] to try to make those guys make their dreams and make sure those guys can be good baseball players and that way they can have a great career in the major leagues.

■ ■ ■

Reserve outfielder Chris Gwynn, who played in the majors for parts of 10 seasons, stayed with the Dodgers until December of 1991—when he was traded to Kansas City in a deal involving first baseman Todd Benzinger—but he returned to Los Angeles for two more seasons in 1994–1995.

Born in Los Angeles almost exactly one year before Sandy Koufax blanked Minnesota in Game 7 of the '65 World Series—Chris was born on October 13, 1964, while the Dodgers' 1965 championship was won on October 14—Gwynn was selected by his hometown Dodgers in the first round, 10th overall, of the 1985 amateur draft out of San Diego State University.

After batting .279 in 362 at-bats in Triple-A Albuquerque in 1987, Gwynn was promoted to the Dodgers in August—and he had quite a spectacular major-league debut on August 14. Facing San Francisco, the 22-year-old Gwynn went 3 for 4 with a pair of RBI singles as Los Angeles defeated the eventual division-winning Giants, 4–3. Unfortunately, he'd collect only four more hits the rest of the season to finish with a .219 batting average. Following a second consecutive productive year in Albuquerque in 1988—where he batted .299 with 37 extra-base hits in 411 at-bats—Gwynn was a September call-up and got in 11 major-league at-bats. Although he didn't play much, it was a learning experience for Gwynn as he watched the '88 ball club play hard day in and day out en route to the World Championship.

Perhaps best known for being the younger brother of the late Hall of Famer Tony Gwynn, Chris Gwynn has some fond memories of 1988. "For me, the most memorable part of that season," Gwynn says, "is mainly just being brought up in the middle of the pennant race, and every game meant something. So, that was great. I think the team was playing really well all year. They may not have started the year that great, but they hit their strides and it was great being on the bench, honestly." According to Gwynn, he and the other call-ups learned a great deal from watching the veterans. "Just being prepared, the preparation that goes on before a series—from defensive positioning to what guys were throwing and what [pitches] they featured, and watching them go out and execute the game plan. Good for any young kids to see that."

Gwynn didn't play in the postseason, but he traveled with the team and was there the night Gibson hit that famous World Series home run. "I just remember one of our scouts came in and I remember him saying what Eckersley liked to do when he was behind in the count and what he liked to do when he was ahead," Gwynn recalls today. "I remember him saying that Eckersley liked to throw a slider to left-handed hitters when he was behind. So, that's what I meant about executing the game plan—I mean, Gibby could barely run and he was on the [trainers'] table the whole day getting treatment. And Tommy decided to roll the dice that one time, and boom! It came up seven, eleven!" Gwynn pauses for a moment for a laugh before continuing. "It was unbelievable just watching that whole thing. It was enough to keep you motivated to do the things you needed to do to be a professional—and be successful."

■ ■ ■

Tommy Lasorda retired as Dodgers manager in July 1996, a month after suffering a heart attack. However, he'd stay on in the organization as the club's vice president following his retirement and, as of 2017, was in his 68th season in one capacity or another with the Dodgers organization. Lasorda's 1,599 managerial victories, as of the end of the 2017 season, ranked 20th all-time in MLB history—and will be surpassed by Mike Scioscia in 2018. Among the players, Ramon Martinez would be the last member of the '88 team to leave, signing with Boston as a free agent following the 1998 campaign. Orel Hershiser, who'd left after the 1994 strike-shortened season, returned to Los Angeles for one final year in 2000. Jesse Orosco, who signed with Cleveland in December 1988, returned to the Dodgers in 2001–2002.

■ ■ ■

Tommy Lasorda, shown here with Sheryl Claire and Fred Claire, was in his 68th season with the Dodgers organization in 2017. *Fred Claire*

Legendary Vin Scully, the voice of the Dodgers for 67 seasons beginning in 1950, finally retired from the broadcast booth in 2016. Ross Porter, Scully's longtime broadcast partner, didn't stay in the organization quite that long, but he did have a terrific run of his own with the Dodgers and was gracious enough to share a few thoughts about 1988. For 28 years beginning in 1977, Porter was the Dodgers' number 2 television and radio voice next to Scully—and he also had a 14-year run as the host of *DodgerTalk*, a pregame and postgame show on LA radio.

Sadly, though, Porter was abruptly let go by the Dodgers in 2004—when the club was under the ownership of Frank McCourt—and hasn't been the voice of any major-league team since then. Asked if he has stayed in contact with anybody from the '88 ball club, Porter acknowledges he's been in communication with the two primary catchers. The former Dodgers broadcaster also stated, matter-of-factly, that although he's been back to throw out a ceremonial first pitch and make a guest appearance as the public address announcer, he has rarely returned to Chavez Ravine since being pushed out in 2004. "Rick Dempsey plays in my charity golf tournament every November," Porter says. "I talk on the phone with Mike Scioscia once a year. I don't attend any games at Dodger Stadium because several people involved in my firing are still there."

Porter's departure from the Dodgers didn't mean he was ready to retire. The veteran broadcaster stayed busy on various announcing projects and worked for Fox Sports West at one point. More recently, when California State University, Northridge, contacted Porter in 2016 to see if he'd be interested in doing play-by-play for their baseball games, the longtime announcer gladly accepted the job. In 2017, Porter was in his second season calling baseball games for Cal State Northridge, broadcasting games from Matador Field and saying into the microphone, "Thanks for joining me on GoMatadors.com."

A couple of major differences between this job and the Dodgers gig? All of the Cal State Northridge games are online—at GoMatadors.com—as the school's campus radio station doesn't carry their games. And, of course, the attendance. For a big game against UCLA, for instance, Cal State Northridge might draw somewhere in the neighborhood of 500 fans, a far cry from the large crowds at Dodger Stadium, which averaged 36,793 fans in 1988.

When asked about 1988, Porter points to the fourth game of the NLCS as the biggest of the year. With the Dodgers trailing two games to one but the score tied 4–4 after nine innings, remembers Porter, manager Tommy Lasorda made a gutsy decision—one that would pay off. "Tommy Lasorda told Ron Perranoski to get Orel Hershiser up in the bullpen after that game went to extra innings," recalls Porter. "Ron did not agree with Tommy, saying if Orel relieved and went longer, Hershiser, who had pitched the day before on three days' rest, might be unable to pitch Game 7. Kirk Gibson homered in the 12th to put the Dodgers ahead, 5–4. New York loaded the bases with one away in its 12th, but Jesse Orosco got Darryl Strawberry to pop up, and Hershiser retired Kevin McReynolds on a fly ball to end it. Tim Belcher pitched a strong Game 5 to win, and Hershiser shut out the Mets in Game 7."

■ ■ ■

For third-string catcher Gilberto Reyes, the 1988 championship was the high point for his major-league career. Unhappy with the prospect of returning to Triple-A again in 1989, he spoke to Fred Claire about his status that spring. The Dodgers, at the time, still had the tandem of Scioscia and Dempsey, so Claire did Reyes a favor by trading him to the Montreal Expos on March 27th. Alas, Reyes spent the majority of the 1989–1990 seasons in Triple-A Indianapolis and appeared in his final big-league game in 1991 at the age of 27. He finished his career just above the Mendoza line—at .202 in 258 at-bats—though he did remain in the game until 1999, toiling in the minor leagues and in the Mexican League for nine different teams.

These days, Reyes isn't involved in baseball, but he enjoys what he's doing. During his playing career, he helped pitchers such as Hershiser. Now, he helps patients; for example, he helps carry people out of their beds and into their wheelchairs. And hey, he seems to enjoy his current profession even more—after all, he's making a true difference in people's lives. After leaving baseball, Reyes has been making a positive impact in the lives of many individuals, including children, trying to inspire them one day at a time.

"Personally, I'm doing great. I went back to school," Reyes says now.

I am a medical assistant. I've been doing this for 10 years. Before that, I worked with autistic kids for four years. I love to make a difference in those kids' lives. The ones we took care of, they were neglected or sexually abused. They were all a mess. Fifty percent of those kids had a chance to go to foster homes. We made a difference [in] their [lives]. Gave them a second chance. That made me feel good. And then, I've been working in the hospital. I'm a patient caretaker. I'd always dreamed about [being] a doctor. Now, I'm almost like a nurse. It's pretty good.

But things weren't always good. Although he performed well defensively when he received his chance to play regularly with Montreal in 1991—Reyes led MLB by throwing out 53.1 percent of would-be base stealers in a career-high 83 games that year and wound up seeing more action than Expos veterans Mike Fitzgerald and Ron Hassey—the problem was he couldn't hit. (To give some perspective, future Hall of Famer Ivan Rodriguez, third in the majors that season in throwing out base stealest, cut down 48.6 percent with Texas.) Reyes batted just .217 with nine extra-base hits, 19 walks, and only 13 RBIs—an offensive showing that undermined an Expos team that had three other regulars batting below

.240 (Tim Wallach, Delino DeShields, and Andres Galarraga). In his book reviewing the season, analyst Bill James called Reyes the best defensive player on the team, but the Expos had already acquired catcher Darrin Fletcher in a trade that December and brought back future Hall of Fame backstop Gary Carter, a fan favorite and ex-Expo, for the 1992 season.

But hitting wasn't his biggest problem; Reyes's off-the-field problems soon derailed him and he never played again in the majors. "Outside baseball, I was too happy, drinking alcohol," Reyes, who was known to drink beer before games and whiskey afterward, acknowledges today. Those around him certainly knew. "This is a kid who had the best arm of any catcher in the Dodger organization, by far, and could have been a backup catcher in the big leagues for a long time," Kevin Kennedy, then the Dodgers' minor-league catching instructor, recalled in 2013. "But he was too carefree."[4]

The Expos sent Reyes to an alcohol rehabilitation center twice in his short stint with the organization. But he was suspended in 1992 for 60 days by Commissioner Fay Vincent for violating his aftercare program and baseball's drug policy, and Montreal released him in May.[5] After not playing anywhere in 1992, Reyes spent 1993 with Colorado's Triple-A club in Colorado Springs before playing in the Mexican League through the rest of the 1990s. He did have a 17-game stint with Montreal's Triple-A club in Ottawa in 1996, but he never did get back to the majors. He then managed several Mexican teams beginning in 2001 as a 37-year-old, as well as the Dominican Summer League Mets in 2006.

But he trusted the wrong people, which took him right out of baseball again. In late December 2007, Reyes was going broke, so for $2,000 he agreed to help a friend move some furniture between New Mexico and Colorado in a pickup truck. And so, Reyes was driving along thinking the truck contained only furniture—when it slid off an icy freeway in northeastern New Mexico and crashed, revealing that the cargo also contained 420 pounds of marijuana. He had no idea about the drugs, and felt stupid to trust the friend.

Nonetheless, Reyes was arrested for drug trafficking—and spent 15 months in jail—but after a trial ended in a hung jury, the charges were dropped in 2009. When he was in the New Mexico jail, he led Bible study, performed laundry duty, and worked in the kitchen. "I'm really happy I rolled the truck. I didn't know there were drugs in there. But I'm happy it happened because those drugs never made it to the drug dealers on the street," Reyes said in 2009 in an Associated Press story while maintaining his innocence. "It was hard in jail, trying to have hope, but it was a good experience too. I helped people through Bible study. I didn't know how to peel potatoes. Now, I can cook for 150 people. I was a chef."[6]

Reflecting back today on his life in jail, Reyes focuses only on the positive memories. "The people in the jail finally found out that I was on the Dodgers, and I was a world champion. But they didn't make me a target. They asked me for stories about the Dodgers. I gave them stories. They didn't do anything to me. So, that championship season saved me in there."

Now, he's at peace with his journey in life following 1988, and enjoys his new career as a certified nursing assistant. "I got my family back. Outside baseball, I was too happy, drinking alcohol. So, I got my life together," Reyes says today. "Fifteen years ago was my last drink. Everything looks great. Everything is great. I can't complain about life. I have four grandkids that I love—they are four, three, two, and two. I have a day care over here. We're babysitting, me and my wife. We've got a day care right here. Right now I'm working at St. Joseph's [Hospital] South over here in Riverview, Florida. It's about 25 minutes away from Tampa. It's pretty good."

Of course, Reyes is a big hit at the hospital. "Some of the patients are really big baseball fans; they're baseball addicts. We'd start talking, and when I said I played for the Dodgers, they would say, 'Oh, I can't remember you!'" he says with a laugh. "They would say, 'Oh my God! What's your name?' or 'Who are you?' They start Googling me, and [when they realized who I was] they would say, 'Oh! Why [didn't] you say anything? You were a real player!' Oh, I didn't have to say anything, you know."

Reyes laughs when he tells the stories about the patients making a big deal about his being a Dodger. But he gets serious when he talks about helping the youth, about how he can use his experience to encourage them to make the right choices in life. "I go to schools and talk. I go to universities and chat with people. I sit in the middle and it's like a class for them. I'm the focus guy. And they start asking me all kinds of questions. I tell them the way it is. I haven't had a chance to do it in baseball yet. I mean, I did it a long, long time ago but not recently. It's something I'm looking forward to [doing], talk to a bunch of kids who think they have it all but they don't know what they have yet. You know?"

During the time he was in jail, none of his ex-teammates had any idea because he wanted to keep a low profile. But now, he's back visiting some of the spring-training and major-league ballparks where he can run into some of those old buddies who are still in coaching. "I go with my wife to different ballparks every year. I do this just to travel with her, usually around spring training," Reyes says.

> The players don't know me because they're all too young. But it's nice to know the coaches remember me because I played with them.
>
> For example, when I saw [then Nationals manager] Dusty Baker, he went crazy. "Gilberto! My God! How are you doing?" I went to Washington [for a ballgame] and I stopped by to say hi to Dusty. I went to the other side to say hi to Juan Samuel, the [Phillies'] third-base coach. I played with him too. Every single team has coaches that I played with, or played against. That's something that I make sure I do, go all the way down and say hi to them. It makes me feel part of the game. But sometimes, I get depressed because I could've been there [in a big-league dugout as a coach] if it wasn't for my [past mistakes]. At the same time, I thank God that if I continued with my [choices], I wouldn't be talking to you today. I'd be dead now. I would've continued drinking and doing drugs and all that. You know, the more you have, the more you want. That's my story.

After going through quite a journey, Reyes is brought back to 1988 and the third-string catcher just smiles. "All the players on that team, all 25 players, really enjoyed playing that year. Even the ones who were sitting. They were great. Orel Hershiser. Kirk Gibson. Mickey Hatcher. Tim Belcher. Tim Leary. All of those guys were great."

■ ■ ■

Like Gilberto Reyes, reliever Brian Holton's baseball journey wouldn't last long following 1988. Traded to the Orioles for slugger Eddie Murray that off-season, Holton never adjusted in the American League. He struggled in his two seasons with Baltimore and pitched his final major-league game in 1990.

"There's the adjustment of going from the National League to the American League," Jay Howell says, trying to explain Holton's lack of success in Baltimore. "The American League is a tougher league to pitch in. Just from the standpoint of you've got another bopper, you've got a DH. That's just math. I don't care how you look at it. You got another bat. Take the pitcher out or take a cold guy off the bench, and you're facing a thumper. That's why I hope they never get rid of it, the DH. I think it makes baseball interesting."

Following his two-year stint in Baltimore, Holton returned to the Dodgers organization and toiled in Triple-A Albuquerque in 1991–1992—notching a 5.75 ERA in 29 games in '92—before retiring from professional baseball. For many years, none of his teammates knew what happened to him. And like Reyes, Holton experienced more downs than ups along the way.

Fast forward to the summer of 2017, when *Los Angeles Times* writer Bill Plaschke finally tracked Holton down in suburban Milwaukee. Plaschke couldn't be reached for comment, but he did run a story in the *Times* discussing Holton's post-baseball life at length that August. "It hurt," Holton told Plaschke, referring to the trade that sent him to Baltimore. "We had just won a World Series, and I wanted to get my ring at Dodger Stadium, but instead I got it in the mail from Federal Express." Unfortunately, Holton no longer has that ring; he pawned it to stay out of bankruptcy.[7]

Howell was shown the article shortly after it came out.

Reading the article, how upset he was about not getting his ring. . . . You'd feel like you were a big part of something, in terms of your contributions. The way that he contributed, I get it. I totally get it. You kind of feel underappreciated, I guess. But [as far as] the team deciding to trade you, that's baseball. That happens all the time. If you had an opportunity to make a trade and get an Eddie Murray, would you do it? What would you have to give up? The club was trying to get better and they obviously valued the player coming back. That's baseball. There's nothing you can do about that. There's always disappointment in a trade. Always.

The reality is that when there's a trade, the team that gets you, they want you for a reason. It's not like the Dodgers didn't want you, so they traded you. Sure, that happens, but that's not the majority [of the cases]. For the Dodgers, I imagine at the time they were saying, "We've got some young pitchers that are gonna be ready." They had John Wetteland. They had some young cannons. Pedro [Martinez] was in the minor leagues right then, I think. You had Pedro [whom the Dodgers signed as an amateur free agent in June 1988]. You had John Wetteland. There were a couple of other arms. You're gonna replace bullpen arms with young arms that are coming up, so that's good. You need that bat, so you make a deal. And it's hard to tell a player you're thinking in that regard. "Oh, this is what our thinking was." That doesn't always happen and it doesn't always play out the way that you think. As far as Brian was concerned, he was traded and was wanted. So, it goes both ways. But I totally get why he was upset not getting his ring.

That ring wasn't the only thing Holton lost, according to Plaschke. Substance abuse, prison, homelessness, and unemployment would be a part of his long journey after professional baseball. After he retired, Holton became addicted to alcohol and pain medication, and his marriage eventually ended in divorce. He was arrested in 2007 and spent time in a Wisconsin prison when he didn't make child-support payments for his two children. His post-baseball journey also took him to a substance-abuse program and a homeless shelter. To make a living over the years, Holton did odd jobs such as selling mulch, working in a mailroom, unloading trucks, and running various stores—a far cry from the job he had in baseball retiring mashers and RBI men like Jose Canseco, Mark McGwire, Gary Carter, and Howard Johnson.

As Holton told Plaschke, he's living off savings and a major-league pension—but the good news is the former right-hander believes his life is turning around. Now staying with a longtime friend, Holton plans on getting back on track. And he still watches Dodgers baseball today and roots for the team to do well.[8]

Tim Leary, who was traded in July 1989 along with Mariano Duncan to Cincinnati for left fielder Kal Daniels and rookie utility infielder Lenny Harris, remembers Holton's passion for football too. "Brian once told me his story of driving from the Pittsburgh area [where he grew up] to the Rose Bowl [in Pasadena] for the Super Bowl that the Steelers were in. It was around 1980," Leary recalls fondly. "He's a great guy." The Steelers beat the Rams that January day in 1980, giving the city of Pittsburgh the unique distinction of winning championships both in baseball and football for the 1979 season. Holton, 20 years old at the time, was coming off a strong sophomore season in professional baseball, going a combined

10–5 with a 3.07 ERA for Single-A Lodi (California) and Double-A San Antonio. Nine years later, Holton himself was a champion.

Does 1988 mean anything to Holton today? As he explained in that *Times* story, that number gave him hope when he lay in a Wisconsin hospital bed preparing for knee-replacement surgery. "On my [medical] chart, for whatever reason, there was the number 88," Holton recalled. "I saw that and said, 'Doc, this surgery is going to turn out just fine.'" But when reflecting back on that year, Holton felt he didn't receive enough credit. "I was kind of overshadowed. They always talk about the stars from that season, and rightfully so, but I'm like, 'Hey, I also had a pretty good year,'" he told Plaschke.[9]

Jay Howell understands how Holton feels. In the pre–social media days, middle relievers across baseball simply weren't highly regarded. But Howell, like the rest of his teammates, appreciated Holton's contributions while acknowledging the game has changed since 1988. "The thing about it is that back in the '80s, you had 10-man pitching staffs—so you had five in the bullpen, maybe six, but mostly five," explains Howell.

There's one interesting thing that's changed in the game, if you think about it. Now, there's 12 or 13 pitchers and the idea of having a "lamb" in your rotation doesn't exist anymore. And that's one of those sacrifice games where you sacrifice the lamb. For example, say you had an extra-inning game on Saturday, and then you played a doubleheader on Sunday—and you've burned out your bullpen. Everybody's tired. You're the starter on Monday. Now it's Monday's game, and as the starter, the manager will look at you—and everybody on the club and in the bullpen will look at that starting pitcher—and say, "Don't be a lamb." If you go out there and you start breaking down, and there's a big inning, that manager's not coming to get you. You're out there. And that's what will destroy their ERA. They've gotta go seven or eight innings. Well, there's much less of that today. I don't think that that happens nearly like it used to. The era of the lamb, I think, is gone. They'd call up a guy from Triple-A. Bring in a guy, a fresh arm—and then send the guy down. They don't just leave a guy out there anymore, to sacrifice him, if you will.

Brian was a guy that could go out there and go five innings. Then you had the other guy in [Tim] Crews, who could give you three. They could do it every other day. They could do it every day! Brian didn't throw hard enough that his arm would be killing him that much. He could go five innings and he could give you something the next day. Good curveball. He'd pitch five innings and it wasn't like he needed two days to recover. He was okay. Pretty much the same with Crews. But Crews threw harder and I think Crews was just a toughness factor.

But Brian was a craft. I mean, he had a curveball. He didn't hang it. And it didn't have a hump in it. His went down—and he didn't telegraph it. He had a good curveball. And that was his value; the fact that he could go three innings today and he'd still be available the next day—and that's why Lasorda loved him. Lasorda had two of them, in Crews and Holton. No, they didn't get the recognition, but who did? In that day and age, who's paying attention to middle relievers? Nobody. A middle relief pitcher was out there to save a starting pitcher when you're losing a game, and you're just filling in innings. But I wonder how many of those were potential wins?

Howell points to the absence of Holton as perhaps one of the reasons Los Angeles lost many close games after 1988. "I think we had a lot of come-from-behind wins in 1988. But in 1989, we lost a very high number of one-run games. The reason I know is because I pitched in a lot of these games," reflects Howell, who in 1989 set the Dodgers' single-season saves record with 28.

I'd warm up and the phone would ring, and it would be that I'd be in the game if we tied it. And it seemed like we lost a bunch of those one-run games. I want to say, like 20-plus one-run games. Maybe more than that. I remember at the time thinking, "Hey, that's why." I was warming up all the time, and I was thinking, "Man." But there was a huge number of one- and two-run games where we didn't come back and we lost. But in 1988, we didn't. Was it because of Holton and Crews? I dunno.

After Howell left the Dodgers, he thought about that whole situation and came to the conclusion that Holton was a big piece that was missing post-1988.

When I look at the Braves in '93 with what they did having [speedy center fielders] Otis Nixon and Deion Sanders [where one would start and the other would be on the bench], there were a lot of one-run games that were won because the first guy would get on in the ninth, and they'd then pinch-run Deion. And Deion would then steal second. That's why there were a bunch of one-run games that were won there—for that reason. And that bullpen in 1993, we held them close, so that somebody could get a rally going late, so you could pinch-run Deion. Or Otis. It was an incredible weapon.

As a player, it dawned on me in 1993 that [the Dodgers] somehow missed that after 1988. In 1988, we won a bunch of those close games. After that, it seemed like we lost a bunch of close games. Was it because of the middle relievers? I dunno. I don't know that. You look at baseball and you say, "Well, was it because you didn't have timely hitting?" You could go into any number of ways to figure that out. But you pose the question: Could it be? I dunno. I'd need somebody to actually do analytics on it to figure out how many of those games they were responsible for. There was a good bit. They held us in. They kept us close. Every good manager appreciates that. So, Brian Holton . . . everybody loved the guy. He was just a perfect guy.

Everyone got along in 1988. But with Sax gone, with Holton traded (and thus weakening the bullpen), with Leary dealt away, along with other players being let go, the club wasn't the same anymore.

■ ■ ■

Leary was disappointed he was traded in the summer of 1989 but says '88 will always be special. Born in Santa Monica, California, Leary grew up rooting for the Dodgers—and for one magical season he won a championship ring with his hometown club. He has fond memories every time he puts on his ring today. "I didn't wear it for years," he says, taking a short break from his online insurance licensing course to reminisce. Yes, Leary does do private pitching lessons today, but he also moonlights as an insurance sales agent. "I wanted to keep it special. But I feel like a superhero when I wear that thing, especially [all these years] later!"

Leary thinks back now and reminds us that the old adage about pitching winning championships proved to be true when Los Angeles upset both the Mets and Oakland. "So many people see offense, when, in every sport, 'defense wins championships; offense wins games'! That saying has been around since long before me!" Leary explains. "Hockey, soccer . . . best goalie and defense wins! Football, same. Basketball, for all of the

Tim Leary, who grew up a Dodgers fan in Santa Monica, was a world champion with his hometown team in 1988. *National Baseball Hall of Fame and Museum, Cooperstown, New York*

offense, the better defensive team—and free throws, which in my opinion is a result of defense—wins! As, if a team can't put up points—or runs— then 'timely hitting' is what wins! Baseball is pitching, defense, and timely hitting! Game 1 of World Series epitomized that. And Orel, especially in September and October!"

While Leary went 10–5 in the second half of 1988, he also slumped after mid-September. With 17 victories by September 12, Leary had four starts remaining and a shot at a 20-win season. But fatigue set in, and he didn't win another game. "By September, the toll of so many innings finally caught up with me as my delivery got a bit out of synch," he says. "By October 1st, I'd pitched 406 innings from October 1987 to October 1988 and wasn't very effective against the Mets. But thankfully, I matched up well against the A's as I used my fastball inside primarily for their right-handed hitters and still had good velocity! As it turned out, the three scoreless innings that I pitched in Game 1 of the World Series were the three most important innings of my life!"

Even though he was facing the tough Oakland lineup on the big October stage, Leary was ready to pitch when he replaced starter Tim Belcher. "I never had a chance to be nervous," adds Leary. "As soon as I walked in the bullpen, the phone was ringing." After his three innings of work, Leary was in the clubhouse in shorts and shower shoes—and then Gibson pulled a Roy Hobbs. "When Kirk hit that home run, I jumped up, put on my uniform pants and shirt, and ran out to the field. For an hour, no one could sit down. It was the most incredible excitement ever!"

While he never came close to duplicating his 1988 numbers the rest of his career—being a combined 21 games under .500 with the Reds (1989), Yankees (1990–1992), Mariners (1992–1993), and Rangers (1994)—Leary is satisfied with what he'd accomplished in baseball. "I was a .300 hitter in my first 100 at-bats [actually, .290]," Leary says. "I had a stolen base in 1984, a save in 1987, and Orel and I [combined for] 40 wins in '88."

Interestingly, in 1988 Leary, the Dodgers' strikeout leader, finished with more strikeouts than Hershiser—at 180 to 178—despite pitching 38 1/3 fewer innings. Leary also had six shutouts through August 21—and none after that—while Hershiser's five consecutive September shutouts allowed him to end the season with an NL-best eight. As a footnote, Leary saw Hershiser break the consecutive-scoreless-innings record held by Don Drysdale, who'd set the mark thanks to six straight shutouts from May 14 to June 4, 1968. Leary, as a nine-year-old, attended the June 4th game and saw Drysdale blank Pittsburgh 5–0. "Orel and I had 40 wins in '88 with 15 shutouts [actually, 14]," recalls Leary. "His September and October was the greatest pitching of all time!" Of course, Leary erroneously included Hershiser's final start—10 scoreless innings against San Diego—as a shutout, but that outing actually wasn't a complete game and thus doesn't count as a shutout either.

When reminded that he fanned Will Clark in that 1987 save against San Francisco and that Mookie Wilson was at the plate when he stole that base in 1984 with the Mets against Atlanta, Leary can only smile. "Pete Falcone was pitching. High leg kick. I missed the sign. Thought hit-and-run was on. When I got to third base, [third-base coach] Bobby Valentine said, 'What are you doing?' I said I thought the hit-and-run was on," Leary says before stopping for a laugh. "I ran decent. But so many unique things happen in baseball—especially in the majors."

And Leary, who still lives in Santa Monica today, was a world champion with his hometown team. That, in itself, is unique. Not too many ballplayers can say that.

■ ■ ■

Rick Dempsey also laments the fact that 1988 seemingly has been forgotten. He's surprised too that their general manager didn't get another executive position in baseball after he was fired by the Dodgers in 1998. "It's kind of quietly gone to the wayside," reflects the veteran backstop, who himself left Los Angeles following the 1990 season.

> Fred Claire didn't even last in baseball like he should have. He was one of the best people I ever met in this game. He had a love and a passion for the game like very few people have. And for him to kind of be, I'd say, maybe pushed out of baseball and the role that he played, it's just one of those things that happens in the game. I don't know how it could possibly happen, but it did.
>
> But I guess it's the price you've gotta pay for the miracles we enjoyed in 1988. We would've all loved to make it last forever, but things change and people are forced to move on to elsewhere. I hated to see Fred Claire out of the game because he was a unique and special person. I mean, wow. He did the incredible. He did the impossible that one season, and we're just gonna live with it, enjoy it for the rest of our lives, and move on.

CHAPTER FOURTEEN
GONE TOO SOON
The Forgotten Reliever and All-Star Infielder

[Tim Crews] was a guy who had not extraordinary stuff. He had a nice sinker and he could get people out. Other than that, he wasn't a guy who was gonna tear up the radar gun. He wasn't a guy who had a special changeup or a trick pitch. He just battled and it was just kind of who he was. I mean, even the way he pitched, it was the same way. He'd go right after hitters.

—Jay Howell, Dodgers closer

[Mike Sharperson] worked so hard, and that was your goal. The goal was to get to the major leagues, and then once you got there, as you're playing, you realized there was more to it than just getting there. It was winning that World Series, fighting for it. I was just so blessed. We were blessed—both of us—to achieve it. Not only get there, but win it. There have been so many great players that played the game, Hall of Famers, who never got a chance to play in a World Series. So, we were blessed. And coming from the same hometown, Orangeburg, from a small town in South Carolina. It's ironic, isn't it, that both of our teams beat the Oakland A's in the World Series? I was fortunate to play in the 1990 World Series. [Reds outfielders Billy] Hatcher and [Eric] Davis got hurt, so I got a chance to play. I don't remember what Mike's [postseason] stats were or how much he played, but it didn't matter. We got there, and we won it, and nobody can ever take that away from us.

—Herm Winningham, MLB outfielder

W hen looking back at the late 1980s Oakland ball clubs, it seemed manager Tony La Russa had an All-Star lineup at his disposal. Sadly, the A's won only one World Championship between 1988 and 1990 despite capturing three consecutive AL pennants. Even more sadly, though, is that less than 30 years later, several of the players from those A's teams have passed away: pitcher Bob Welch (2014, at age 57, of a broken neck resulting from an accidental fall in the bathroom of his home), centerfielder Dave Henderson (2015, at 57, of a heart attack), utility man Tony Phillips (2016, at 56, of an apparent heart attack), and DH Don Baylor (2017, at 68, of cancer). All were instrumental to the A's success in 1988, and all except Baylor (who retired following that season) would help Oakland win the World Series the following year. Although "Bash Brothers" Jose Canseco and Mark McGwire—and Rickey Henderson when he returned in 1989—made most of the headlines, those other players also played significant roles for the A's.

News of each death rocked the baseball world. "I am in total shock," Canseco posted on Twitter the day news of Phillips's death was announced. "Played golf with Tony Phillips last week [and] he was driving the ball over 300 yards." Baseball writers and other former teammates and coaches, likewise, were saddened and stunned by the news of his passing, just as they were with the deaths of the other three former A's. The always-energetic Phillips had "seemed so healthy and full of life," added Canseco.[1] Undoubtedly, A's fans have fond memories of Phillips making the final play in Oakland's four-game sweep of San Francisco in the 1989 World Series, where he speared Brett Butler's bouncer at second base and tossed the ball to Dennis Eckersley for the last out.

Less than 27 years later, Phillips was gone at the age of 56.

The 1988 World Champions, meanwhile, had two separate tragedies to deal with just a few years following their victory—involving two players who were still active in the game.

Much like the 1989 Athletics, Los Angeles reached the pinnacle as a team effort—as the 1988 Dodgers' World Championship also didn't happen because of just one or two players. Sure, Hershiser and Gibson are remembered for their heroics, but the championship wasn't won because of just those two players. The Stuntmen contributed for the most part when they were called upon. The bullpen came through in the postseason after a brief hiccup in the NLCS. Even players who had just a few at-bats or pitchers who gave the ball club regular-season innings but weren't used in the playoffs contributed. When all was said and done, everyone in the Dodgers uniform realized the greatest moment of their professional lives, when Hershiser fanned Phillips to end the World Series.

Less than five years later, though, tragedy struck as the Dodgers lost one of the pitchers on their 1988 team because of a boating accident. Three short years after that, they lost one of the former Stuntmen due to another tragic accident. As centerfielder John Shelby reflects now, the deaths of Tim Crews and Mike Sharperson, who died in 1993 and 1996, respectively, were "very unfortunate tragedies that happened to the both of them. Everyone on the team collectively contributed in a big way, including those guys."

Tim Crews, then a minor-league pitcher, was acquired in December of 1986, along with Tim Leary, from Milwaukee for first baseman Greg Brock. The right-hander debuted with the Dodgers in July 1987 and went on to pitch six seasons for Los Angeles, starting four games, saving 15, and winning 11 with a 3.44 ERA. He signed with Cleveland in January 1993, but tragically died on March 23 when a boating accident claimed his life as well as that of Indians pitcher Steve Olin and severely injured Cleveland left-hander Bob Ojeda.

Jay Howell has nothing but good memories about the forgotten reliever. "Tim was my good friend on the team," Howell says now.

> He was just a really unique guy. He was from that north Florida kind of cowboy; he was a northern Florida cowboy. He'd wear the cowboy boots and sometimes he'd even wear a cowboy hat. He loved the western gear. His aura was more like a "bull rider." You could see that even in his walk. There was this walk that he had that I gave him a really hard time about. It was like you were watching—when he walked out to the mound—he was like a cowboy who just got dusted off by a bull. He was a little stiff and he was walking on back. Tim had that kind of walk. I used to ride him, talking about how he was a Dirt Farmer. I used to ride him about it. He didn't really grow crops or anything. He didn't have bulls to ride. He certainly had that aura about him. And he was a self-confident guy. He was self-confident.
>
> He had a good year—he had a few good years in there—and he'd always take the ball. There wasn't a day when he wasn't available to pitch. For the rest of the guys, you kinda admired that and appreciated

that. He wasn't too worried about saving himself when he wasn't fresh. He'd still take the ball. We noticed that. We were best friends. It was a terrible tragedy what happened to him. I really was fond of Tim. He was one of those guys in the bullpen—the other guy down there was [Brian] Holton, another one who was the same way. His stuff wasn't extraordinary. He put up some really good numbers. As far as the makeup that we had in our bullpen, it was solid. We all got along. Generally speaking, we all got along. And that was big. There was a lot of getting together after games. We were always a group. Tim was a really, really unique guy. He was always under the radar.

But the Dodgers acquired left-hander Ricky Horton in August 1988 and left Crews off the postseason rosters. "In fact, it was quite upsetting for him," Howell continues. "He'd pitched really well. We added a left-hander. He didn't cry about it. He showed up. He was there. He suited up. And again, he felt like he should've been active but the Dodgers felt like, 'Hey, we need a lefty. The Mets have some really powerful left-handed hitters and we need to cover ourselves.' He took it like a man."

Tim Crews, known by his teammates as the "Dirt Farmer," was outstanding in the Dodgers' championship season in 1988. *National Baseball Hall of Fame and Museum, Cooperstown, New York*

Howell saw Crews as the ultimate team player, a guy whom he trusted to always have his back. "How did [my] friendship develop with Tim?" Howell asks rhetorically.

Well, when you spend a lot of time down in the bullpen, you get to know people. It's sorta like what they say about playing golf with somebody. You can learn a lot about a person just playing a round of golf. Sitting in the bullpen is no different. When you have a teammate who's hoping for a chance to take a spot and move up, move up in the ranks, go from a long man to a middle guy, for example, and you know what has to happen there. The guy in front has gotta fail, has gotta have a tough game, and get into a funk. When you've been down in the bullpen a long time, you can sense it.

It's one of those human nature things when you have someone who's hoping for failure for someone else that will create an opportunity to get the ball more often. It's not unlike a hitter who is on the team and he goes 3 for 4 with a couple of RBIs and you lose a tight game. And you can see that the guy that's gone 3 for 4 is kind of happy. He's happy with his performance but you've lost the game. For a team, that's kind of a goal. Somebody else went 0 for 4 and yet there's the guy who's gone 3 for 4 with two RBIs and he's happy. And I can tell you that happened a few times on that team and Gibson put an end to that. The music, there was no party after a loss. And I can tell you that Gibson shut that down on a couple of occasions, and I specifically remember that Guerrero incident where he was getting ready to go out with some of his buddies on the Cardinals.

I'm relating what that's like in the bullpen. You go out there and you're going out into the game and you know someone's on your own team that hopes you give it up. That's a clubhouse in danger. That's really not what you're looking for. We didn't have that. We didn't have it. I know how the kind of guy Tim was. Even Jesse Orosco, a guy with the Mets. A great guy. Everybody got along. There wasn't a lot of jealousy or guys who were vying for an opportunity that would require failure on someone's part. You get to know them.

I knew Tim. I knew his makeup. I knew what he was about. And I liked him. We just had a good time ribbing each other, getting on each other. But I always knew he'd have my back. I can say that about everybody who was down there.

CHAPTER FOURTEEN

Mike Sharperson, acquired from Toronto for minor-league pitcher Juan Guzman in September of 1987, was one of the Stuntmen for the 1988 Dodgers. Although he had only 59 regular-season at-bats, Sharperson did have two plate appearances in the NL playoffs, including an eighth-inning bases-loaded walk off Randy Myers in Game 3. He was then left off the World Series roster in favor of Dave Anderson, who'd returned from an injury.

Although Sharperson would go on to represent the Dodgers in the 1992 All-Star Game, the trade is regarded as a lopsided one in favor of the Blue Jays, as Guzman would become one of the AL's best pitchers from 1991 to 1993, winning 40 games over that stretch and helping Toronto to a pair of World Championships. Sharperson, meanwhile, was mostly a platoon player during his eight-year career, playing primarily second base and third base. In his best season, 1990, Sharperson batted .297 in 129 games with 15 stolen bases while setting career highs in games, at-bats (357), hits (106), triples (two), home runs (three), RBIs (36), total bases (133), and stolen bases. In 1992, Sharperson matched his career high in homers and RBIs.

Former Reds outfielder Herm Winningham, a childhood friend of Sharperson's, shares his memories of the Dodgers' All-Star utility man. The two men, born less than two months apart in 1961 in the small town of Orangeburg, South Carolina, both dreamed of playing Major League Baseball while growing up. Both succeeded, with Winningham winning a championship ring of his own in 1990. "Mike and I grew up together," Winningham says today from Orangeburg-Wilkinson High School, where he played high school ball in his youth and where he's currently coaching baseball.

> We grew up in each other's houses. We started playing together at the age of seven or eight—that was when we signed up for the recreational baseball program or the summer program, baseball-wise. And it just took off from there. We never played against each other; we were always on the same team together from Little League, Dixie Youth, high school, American Legion, and college. We played our baseball together. We grew up together in Orangeburg, South Carolina [which as of 2010, had a population of just under 14,000]. He was just a wonderful friend. We pushed each other.

I got to the majors first with the New York Mets in 1984, and Mike was signed by the Toronto Blue Jays [and debuted in the majors in 1987]. When we were in the minor leagues, we never played against each other. Then, we finally got a chance during spring training. I think it was my second big-league spring training, and I believe it was Mike's first. He ended up with the Blue Jays. I think it was in Clearwater, Florida. I was with the Mets. That's when we finally played against each other. It was the first time since we were growing up. We always wanted to outdo each other, and that's how we pushed each other. It was for hometown bragging rights. He came into the game late, and he played shortstop and I was in the outfield. I think I grounded out to him, and I believe he got one at-bat and flew out to somebody. That was it. It was even—we both made outs—but he said, "I got you out!" Because I had hit to ball to him, he had the bragging rights. We just tried to outdo each other throughout our whole careers; we just pushed each other.

Coincidentally, both men played for underdogs that upset the Oakland A's in the World Series. "Mike got a World Series ring with that 1988 Dodger team," Winningham recalls.

I was so proud of him. I said, "Wow!" That year they won the World Series on Kirk Gibson's dramatic home run off of Dennis Eckersley. We got together afterward in the winter time that year, and then after that we went back to work! He lived in Atlanta at the time, and I still lived in Orangeburg, our hometown. But we always conversed with each other. And when he and his wife wanted to come home, they'd stay with my wife and me. It was mutual on both sides. Anyway, I told Mike, "This is great—I gotta get me one of these," meaning a World Series ring. Two years later, I got mine with the Cincinnati Reds. . . . I think his wife has his World Series ring, if I'm not mistaken. I can't tell you for sure, but I think she has it. My own ring is right here in my house. I don't wear it. I mean, I wear it occasionally, but I don't flaunt it or anything. But I do have it.

Of course, Winningham does, from time to time, wear that ring to inspire his high school students. "I mean, I wear it in front of the kids that I coach just to show them what hard work does, what you can accomplish. Show me someone with this much ability, that much desire and that much heart, and they're gonna be successful in anything. Where you lack in ability, those other two will make up for it."

As for their friendly rivalry, it was Sharperson who'd wind up accomplishing more in the majors. While 1992 marked Winningham's final big-league season—when he was with last-place Boston—Sharperson batted .300 that year while starting 72 games (39 at third base and 33 at second) for a Dodgers ball club that uncharacteristically lost 99 games. "Mike got more bragging rights than I did, because he was an All-Star and he was the only Dodger player to make it to the All-Star team that year. I was very proud of him because he worked so hard," adds Winningham.

Other than being a hard worker, Sharperson was also an upbeat and cheerful individual. The one thing that ex-teammates and coaches remember about him was that he was a fantastic team player—and a great person. He never did anything to embarrass his teams. Nobody ever had a bad word to say about him. That was the way Sharperson was raised. "We were taught—I don't care what the day brings—you should put a smile on someone else's face, regardless of what's going on in your life," explains Winningham. "There's someone that's gonna have a worse day than you. We called it being humble, staying even keel, like, 'Hey, I don't care what happens. You just stay steadfast and believe in yourself.' We were just happy-go-lucky. We were from the south. We were raised Southern Baptists. We were gonna have fun. Not that we didn't have trials and tribulations. But we got to the big leagues and we worked very hard to get there. Hey, what else can you do? We were grown men trying to play a little boy's game—and getting paid for it!"

Sharperson left the Dodgers as a free agent after the 1993 season but spent nearly all of 1994–1995 playing Triple-A ball in the Red Sox, Cubs, and Braves organizations before signing a minor-league deal with San Diego in November 1995. Then came the news that shocked the baseball world on Sunday, May 26, 1996. Sharperson, at age 34, was killed early that morning in a one-car crash in Las Vegas. He'd been scheduled to leave Las Vegas—where he'd been playing Triple-A ball—on a flight to Montreal to join the Padres, who were set to open a three-game series against the Expos the following day. According to news reports, Sharperson was driving southbound on Interstate 15 when he apparently realized he missed his turn onto Interstate 215. He tried to make a right turn onto I-215, said a witness, but lost control in the rain and went into a dirt median. He died due to being ejected through the sun roof.

Those who played with and coached Sharperson were devastated. "First of all, I was numb," says Winningham now.

> I heard it from a classmate of mine. He called me at about two or three o'clock in the morning. And I said, "No!" So, I turned on the TV to find out something—I think it might've been ESPN—but I called his sister and I called his mom. But I couldn't get an answer or anything. And I finally saw it on ESPN. I was just numb. A good guy taken too soon. I honestly believe Mike would've been a great coach in the big leagues or a manager somewhere. He had that type of personality. People clung to him. They listened to him. He was a rare breed. He was a student of the game. And he wasn't afraid to tell you or to try and teach you about the game. He'd always help the young guys. Always. Showed them how to be a professional, how to play the game. The game lost a guy that, I think, would've done wonders in the game of baseball. He was taken too soon. But only the Lord knows.

Going back to October 1988, Sharperson's Dodgers had two memorable late-inning walks that led to comebacks against the Mets and Athletics. John Shelby walked ahead of Mike Scioscia's game-tying, ninth-inning NLCS homer. Mike Davis walked ahead of Kirk Gibson's famous World Series homer. As for Sharperson's bases-loaded walk in Game 3 against Mets stopper Randy Myers, it could easily have gone down in Dodgers postseason lore too, had Los Angeles hung on to win. With the score 3–3 in the eighth, Sharperson pinch-hit for Danny Heep and worked the count to 3 and 2 before watching ball four go by, forcing pinch runner Jose Gonzalez in for the tie-breaking run. Alas, the Dodgers gave up five runs in the next half inning and lost, so Sharperson's walk is no longer remembered.

Fittingly, Winningham would also have a key moment in his team's championship run. In Game 4 of the 1990 World Series, the Reds were poised to finish off the sweep against the A's, but Oakland's Dave Stewart nursed a 1–0 lead into the eighth inning. With a runner aboard and nobody out, Winningham got a bunt single off Stewart on an 0-and-2 pitch, and Cincinnati went on to score twice in that inning en route to the sweep. "All game we couldn't get a guy to second base," recalls Winningham.

We couldn't move 'em over for whatever reason. It was one of those times. And I came up, and the bunt sign was on. First pitch, I bunted through. Second one, I took for a strike. I looked down at my coach, Sammy Perlozzo, and he took the bunt sign off. So, I had a chance to hit. So, when I was looking down, I said to myself, "Man, this is how you got to the big leagues. You can bunt. Just go ahead and hunt it." In the corner of my eye, I watched [third baseman] Carney Lansford back up. He was on the grass, and he backed up. Once I saw him back up, I said, "Shoot, I'll put it down." And I just put it down, not expecting to be safe, but just to get the runner over. But I was safe, because Carney was a little too far back. And the rest was history. I scored the winning run. I came home on a sac fly and that was the winning run, and we closed it out.

Having played baseball at Orangeburg, both Sharperson and Winningham were taught the fundamentals of the game. One included bunting, which the two childhood friends could do in the key moment of a game. While Sharperson was a good bunter and Winningham's bunt helped set up the runs needed to clinch the 1990 Series, Winningham acknowledges that the bunt—along with the steal—has all but disappeared in today's game. "Bunting is a lost art. Stealing bases is kind of a lost art," reflects Winningham. "Both are the fundamentals of the game. I tell people, 'Do not watch Major League Baseball because these guys have perfected the art, the habits, the way they do things that you wouldn't teach young kids coming up. You'd watch great colleges, [or] go to the minor leagues and watch minor-league games, because that's where the fundamentals are there or are gonna be there.'"

Winningham does still follow MLB to a certain extent. When asked about the current playoff format—with the play-in game and wild-card round—he acknowledges there are pros and cons to the way the postseason is structured now.

It's a business now. The more games you play, the more money owners get. And players. But I think a one-game playoff isn't fair. In that, maybe the best team had a bad day, let's say, and they lose. I don't think it's fair to them to have a one-game playoff. I think you should do a best two-out-of-three. That's my way of thinking. But like I said, it's a business. And you gotta treat it like a business. It's a little boy's game.

But I mean, it's great to have wild cards. It puts money into the pot. It makes the season go a little bit longer. But just remember the kids now fall apart pretty quick. You don't give them enough time to heal. That's why you have some arm problems. That's why you have a lot of guys on the disabled list all the time. You play winter ball, and then you go home for about a month, and then you've gotta go back again because it's spring-training time. But I think you still need to give your body enough time to recuperate.

With Mike Sharperson gone too soon, Winningham and the Sharperson family do try to keep Mike's memories alive in Orangeburg. For starters, Winningham still stays in touch with the family and frequently interacts with one of Mike's nephews, who's playing baseball in middle school.

[Mike's] sister lives in the same neighborhood that I live in. Mike's nephew—we call him "Little Mike"—has got Mike's talent. Maybe a little more. He'll be in the ninth grade [beginning in August 2017]. It's gonna be fun watching him. It's gonna be fun. "Little Mike" is a catcher. . . . So, yes, we are still in contact. I'm in contact with his sister and his brother Vince. I'd tell "Little Mike" stories about his uncle Mike. I'd see things that he does playing the game. I'd tell him all the time, "You play just like your uncle," or "That's just like your uncle." You know, Mike might not be here, but he *is* here, because we keep him alive.

Finally, Winningham believes kids today can learn from what he and Sharperson accomplished in baseball.

We grew up together as kids, and yes sometimes we did crazy things. But we were always riding bicycles to practice. Or we would always run to practice. We loved the games. We were focused on trying to get to the next level, whatever that was. Our stories would be more of trying to get there. It was about trying to get there no matter what it took, whatever we had to do. We made it possible. Our families love the game of baseball. We were just little kids that had a dream. And our dream came true.

And the older I get, the more precious that time is. And it goes by fast. That time is very precious. It makes me understand what we did, what both of us did. Winning a ring hasn't changed me, but I appreciate it more. When you're playing, when you're in the heat of the battle, you just do it. But now, 28 years later, when you look back, you go, "Wow." And you look at the tapes, the replays or the highlights of the game, and you go, "Man." First thing I think is, "Oh man, I was thin back then!" You really start to appreciate what you did.

CHAPTER FIFTEEN
TALKING RINGS AND WHAT '88 MEANS

I'll have to say many fine things happened to me there [during] the time I was there under the [Peter] O'Malley ownership. Probably the highlight of the 17 years that I was there under his watch was the '88 World Championship team. That's probably the highlight of my time. As a member of the team, I didn't play or anything but I did coach third base. I think I was involved in a lot of things that was going on—because that's what your responsibilities are as a third-base coach. I would say that was the highlight for me my whole time there. Every day was a real wonderful pleasure for me.

—Joey Amalfitano, Dodgers third-base coach

That year, I got sent down and I went to Triple-A and I started playing really good. I never, ever got promoted to the big leagues that year. I feel sad for myself but at the same time I felt happy because that year the Dodgers won the World Series and they beat Oakland. Yes, when I saw the Dodgers on TV celebrating in Oakland, I thought, "I could be there right now." But to me, even though I was in the minor leagues, I felt very good and very satisfied for the organization for winning another World Series.

—Mariano Duncan, two-time world champion

Joey Amalfitano began his major-league playing career in the 1950s. He won a championship ring as a 20-year-old rookie with the 1954 New York Giants—without playing a single game in that year's World Series against Cleveland. Thirty-four years later, he won his second World Series ring as the LA Dodgers' third-base coach. When the

233

Giants won their first-ever title in San Francisco, Amalfitano received his third championship ring.

At the end of the day, as far as Amalfitano is concerned, winning championships is what the game is all about. While he knows he didn't earn that 1954 ring—Amalfitano appeared in only nine regular-season games and went 0 for 5 with four strikeouts—he knows he made a difference coaching third base with the 1988 Dodgers. "The money comes and goes—I hear people go, 'Oh, it's the money'—but no, it's the ring . . . it's the championship [that stays and is the most important]," Amalfitano says with a smile from his Arizona home today. "When you win, you're a champion! Yeah!"

Amalfitano's situation is unique because he began with the Giants as a player, went to the Dodgers as a coach, and returned to the Giant, where his role since 2005 has included roving infield instructor and special assistant in player development. Although he has spent more time with the Giants, his days with the Dodgers still have a special place in his heart.

"Every day was a real wonderful pleasure for me . . . because the Dodgers . . . had such a tradition. Being part of a New York Giants team and then my career as a player, and then as a player in San Francisco, the rivalry of the Dodgers and Giants. . . . That still exists today. They took it west with them when both franchises moved," reflects Amalfitano, who's proud of having World Series rings with both organizations. "I'd always kind of admired the way the Dodgers played the game on the field. And then to be over there, to be a part of that, and having the success of the '88 team, which was a nice group of guys. . . . They all pulled on the same end of the rope. It was a pleasure going to the ballpark every day. It was a fun time for me."

Nearly 30 years have passed, and some of those '88 Dodgers are still excited to talk about that ring. Some still proudly wear that ring today while others have that memento locked up somewhere. Some, sadly, have had it stolen. But everybody has a story about that 1988 ring.

Infielder Tracy Woodson's big-league career lasted for just parts of five seasons, but he's a proud owner of one of those 1988 rings. In the World Series, Woodson went hitless in four pinch-hit at-bats, though in the Dodgers' pivotal 4–3 victory in Game 4, his seventh-inning groundout off Oakland reliever Greg Cadaret scored Alfredo Griffin (when Steve Sax, the runner on first, took off on the pitch to break up a potential double play) to put Los Angeles ahead 4–2. It was the final RBI for Woodson in a Dodgers uniform, but more importantly, the one-run victory also put them on the doorstep of the championship. The following night, Los Angeles won again—thanks in part to homers from unlikely heroes Mickey Hatcher and Mike Davis—to become world champions.

Following his brief two-plus seasons in Los Angeles (1987–1989), Woodson suited up for the St. Louis Cardinals (1992–1993) and a half dozen other teams in minor-league ball—including stops in Vancouver, Canada; his hometown of Richmond, Virginia; Louisville, Kentucky; Rochester, New York; Columbus, Ohio; and Des Moines, Iowa—before retiring. Since then, Woodson has gotten into managing—first in Rookie League ball, Double-A, and Triple-A in the Pirates, Padres, and Marlins organizations before moving into collegiate baseball in 2007—and is now back in his hometown as the head baseball coach of the University of Richmond.

Surely, Woodson, one of the Dodgers' unlikely heroes himself, still has his 1988 ring? "Absolutely. Absolutely," Woodson says with a laugh.

> I got a box full of rings, and that's one of them. I won a ring in Double-A for when I managed in Carolina, I won three Triple-A rings, I won two rings at Valparaiso [University in Indiana] for getting into the NCAA tournament, I got a Marlins ring from [2003] because I was their Double-A manager when they beat the Yankees in [2003]. When I first got to Valparaiso [in 2007], I was wearing it [the Dodgers ring] all the time, using it as a recruiting tool. Charlie Weis was doing that in Notre Dame—and I thought it was a pretty good idea—when he was the football coach there. But I don't really wear it now.

It appears that nearly everywhere he has gone, Woodson has been a winner. And he loves it. Whether it was the three Triple-A championship rings he won as a player—with the 1987 Albuquerque Dukes (Pacific Coast League), the 1995 Louisville Redbirds (American Association), and the 1996 Columbus Clippers (International League)—or the rings he won at Valparaiso, where he guided the Crusaders to back-to-back Horizon League titles in 2012–2013 (ending a 44-year NCAA tournament drought), the former Stuntman simply loves winning. In his only season managing the Southern League's Carolina Mudcats in 2003—the Florida Marlins' Double-A affiliate—the team won the league championship.

And as a 33-year-old on the 1996 Clippers, he was named the New York Yankees' Triple-A MVP on a team that had future big-leaguers Jorge Posada, Ricky Ledee, and Ruben Rivera.

Out of all those titles and accomplishments, though, 1988 stands out the most. "We weren't the best team, period," Woodson recalls of that Dodgers team.

> You look at the players that we had—Hershiser was unbelievable that whole season and Gibson was the quintessential leader—so we had the Cy Young and the MVP. But we just had role players around them. Sax was a good player. Scioscia was a good player. But the Mets [won 100 games]. The A's won over 100 games. Everybody thought that was gonna be your World Series. I think we played very well together. We lost a lot of guys during the season due to injuries, and they always had somebody to plug in. They called them the "Stunt Guys," the "Stuntmen." They'd stick guys in there at certain times [and they'd deliver].

The starting center fielder for the 1988 Dodgers, John Shelby, wasn't a superstar player by any means or even a household name, but he quietly put together a solid season and was one of the few regulars to survive the entire postseason without being injured. When the Dodgers won the '88 World Series, Shelby had his second championship in six years as he, like Rick Dempsey, was also a member of the 1983 Orioles. With neither the Orioles nor Dodgers winning another World Series since then, Shelby (like Dempsey) has the unique distinction of being a member of the last World Championship team from both Baltimore and Los Angeles. "1988 was and will always be a special year," says Shelby from his home in Lexington, Kentucky. "Not only were we the '88 World Series champions but we were also a close-knit team like a family." Although he batted .444 in the 1983 World Series for Baltimore as a rookie, Shelby acknowledges the 1988 ring means more. "I wear my '88 ring every day," he says. "I also have [that] '83 championship ring. Both are special and with great memories, but I love wearing the '88 more."

When asked to compare the 1988 Dodgers to other past champions, Shelby naturally brings up those Orioles, who defeated Philadelphia in five games. As the former center fielder explains, though, Baltimore was expected to win. But not Los Angeles. "The only comparison I have is with that '83 championship team. In '83, we had a really good team and no one doubted that we [would] win the World Series. Other than us, not many people thought that that we had much of a chance against the A's."

Another Dodger who seemed to be a winner everywhere he went was Dempsey, who acknowledges his 1988 ring isn't the most important one in his possession. "I'd been so lucky to have been on so many good and great teams, winning championships at every level, including Triple-A as a manager," Dempsey says proudly.

> I played on three World Series teams, twice on winning teams in 1983 and 1988. I also played in the 1979 series; we lost in the seventh game to Pittsburgh. I don't wear the '88 ring like I wear my '83 ring. I was the Most Valuable Player of the 1983 World Series. I'm back here in Baltimore doing pregame and postgame. So, I live here for half the year. Although it is a very, very special ring, I can't say that I cherish it as much as I do the 1983 World Series because I played for the Orioles for 12 years—and that was just a culmination of a lot of hard work and some great teams I played with there—plus the fact that I was a regular everyday player. I was the MVP of that World Series. So, I have to give that the edge over the other one. I still have it. It's important. But, for me, it's not as important as my '83 World Series ring.

Likewise, fellow Stuntman Danny Heep had won a ring earlier in his career, with the 1986 Mets. Prior to his two seasons in Dodger Blue in 1987–1988, Heep spent four years in New York. Because Heep, like reliever Jesse Orosco, was also a member of the 1986 World Champion Mets that defeated Boston in seven games, a natural question is, which championship means more? Heep's answer, as you'd expect, is obvious. "I kinda grew up with the Mets one," Heep, known during his career as a valuable role player and clutch left-handed pinch hitter, acknowledges.

> When I was first brought over to the Mets [from Houston in a December 1982 trade for pitcher Mike Scott], we lost 90-plus games [in 1983]. Then, four years later, we won 108 regular-season games and 116 [including the postseason]. Everybody on that Mets team got along. We were like a college team, a bunch of friends doing what they liked to do. We were a very close-knit group of guys.
>
> The difference was I don't think anybody really took us [the 1988 Dodgers] seriously in the playoffs. The Mets were still really good in '88 and had a good club—maybe even a little bit better than the '86 team

that we had. But we went in there—and anything can happen, obviously, in the playoffs; we weren't expected to win. We were expected to win it with the Mets. We weren't expected to win it with the Dodgers. We had the best record in baseball with the Mets. We had one of the better offensive lineups in the league. We had one of the better pitching staffs in the league. I mean, we were expected to win. Anything short of that was gonna be kind of a mediocre season.

Us just getting to the World Series in LA was a good season for us! Now, obviously, as professional baseball players, we weren't satisfied with that, but that was a step that nobody expected us to make. And you look at that A's lineup that we beat; they were pretty good! And for us to beat them in five games . . . I mean, we just played well, we got hot, the pitchers pitched well, and we scored just enough runs.

Being on both championship ball clubs meant Heep was on the winning side of two of the most memorable comebacks in World Series history—the Mets' unbelievable rally in Game 6 in New York as well as

Danny Heep, shown here in a Mets uniform, was a winner everywhere he went, being a member of the 1986 Mets, 1988 Dodgers, and division-winning clubs in Houston and Boston. *National Baseball Hall of Fame and Museum, Cooperstown, New York*

the iconic Gibson homer in Los Angeles two years later. When Gibson hit that famous homer, Heep got a view from the Dodgers' dugout. Two years earlier, it was a different story with the Mets down 5–3 with two outs in the 10th inning against Boston. By then, Heep had retreated to manager Davey Johnson's office, where he watched the game with several teammates on the television. When Mookie Wilson's groundball went through Boston first baseman Bill Buckner's legs, the players were all head-butting each other, and Heep knew the Mets were winning Game 7—it had to be destiny. Just like the way it unfolded two years later when Gibson connected off of Eckersley; Oakland never recovered after the stunning Game 1 defeat.

Like fellow Stuntman Tracy Woodson, Heep is now a head coach in college baseball. While Woodson used his 1988 ring as a recruiting tool and proudly wore it every chance he got in the early years of his college coaching career, Heep has never done that. He does still have both the 1986 and 1988 rings; he just doesn't wear them at all. It's not who he is. He simply isn't a guy who likes to flaunt his rings around. "That [1988] ring is in my house; it's next to my Mets '86 ring. I haven't worn either one of them at all. I'm just not a big jewelry guy, and because I'm a baseball coach, I can't walk around with that thing on," Heep explains. "[With] batting practice [and] working around here doing stuff, it'd just get in the way. But really, I just don't like wearing a lot of jewelry; I just don't feel comfortable with it. They're kind of big and clumsy, and plus, the other thing is I didn't want to beat it up. I want to keep it the way it is."

Hitting coach Ben Hines, who began his professional career as a 24-year-old in 1960 as an infielder/catcher in the Baltimore Orioles' minor-league system, also owns multiple rings. He acknowledges the 1988 ring is special but also admits he doesn't wear it much these days. He does keep all of those mementos safe and cherishes each and every one of them. "Not much," Hines says when asked specifically if he still wears the 1988 ring. "I [also] have an NCAA Hall of Fame ring, I have a Boulder [Colorado] Collegians ring from the NBC [National Baseball Congress] tournament [from 1975], and I have a ring for the Triple-A championship in 1987."

Wait a minute—Triple-A championship in 1987? That's correct. As Hines explains, he was sent down to Albuquerque for a season because of Tommy Lasorda. "Al Campanis hired me [after the 1984 season], and so

Tommy put up with me for two years," the former batting coach says to-day. "And then in 1987, Tommy decided he wanted me out of there. So, he made a deal with Al Campanis, and I was sent to Triple-A to be their hitting coach. In Triple-A that year, we won the Pacific Coast League championship and then won the Triple-A World Series."

After that one season in Albuquerque, Hines returned to the Dodgers and resumed his role as the team's hitting coach. So, essentially, he won championships in back-to-back seasons within the Dodgers organization where he played an active role working with the players. Of course, all that fans remember about today is 1988, and they still talk to him about that year. "You get it all the time," Hines acknowledges. "I went through a ball autographing thing about two or three months ago. The lineup of people bringing either a picture or a ball for me to autograph, and half of them would have a question about the World Series that they wanted answered, so I would get into a little discussion about the situation that they would bring up. It was always fun."

Hines never gets tired of the questions. He considers himself fortunate to have the chance to talk about 1988 all these years later, considering the fact that many great players throughout the game's history never even sniffed the Fall Classic. "You just think about it: A lot of guys coached and played for years and years and never got to a World Series. You think about Ernie Banks with Chicago; he never got to the World Series," Hines explains. "I was so fortunate that I had a chance to be on a World Series team, because most people don't get that chance. But the 1988 season was absolutely wonderful. The way they played during the playoffs was just absolutely wonderful. Just a magical season for the Los Angeles Dodgers."

Count Steve Sax—who won rings with the Dodgers in both 1981 and 1988—and Chris Gwynn as two others who don't really wear that ring. Ditto Charlie Blaney, the Dodgers' farm director from 1988 to 1998, who also has a pair of Dodgers championship rings.

These days, Sax is a motivational speaker but he doesn't carry his championship rings around during his speaking engagements. He is proud of both rings, but he's simply not a jewelry guy. "The '88 ring is in my safe," explains Sax.

I'm gonna keep it for posterity, for my kids. I don't wear it. I've never worn it, as a matter of fact. I've never worn the ring—because I don't wear rings. I guess that's why I've never worn it. They're awful big. It's a beautiful ring. I just have never worn it. I sure do like it. My kids are gonna enjoy it. And I'll pass it on to them. Same thing with the 1981 ring. I don't wear rings, but it's beautiful too. It's a very, very traditional type of ring. Both of them are just beautiful rings. I've seen a lot of rings. That '88 ring is as nice as any of the ones I've seen, that's for sure.

When asked if 1988 changed him in any way, Sax doesn't hesitate in saying yes. "Well, it made you realize that you got to a pinnacle that a lot of great players don't get an opportunity to do," he reflects. "[Red Sox Hall of Famer] Ted Williams never got to win a World Series. There's a lot of players that never even get to play in a World Series. I feel fortunate just to be able to play in one, but to win two of them, it's something that kind of separates you. To be part of a team like the 1988 team, it's amazing."

Like Heep and Sax, Gwynn doesn't wear his 1988 ring at all. "I got a World Series ring from that '88 team," Gwynn, a September call-up who had only 11 at-bats, says today. "It's in my house and I don't really wear it. I'm not a big jewelry guy. Quite honestly, I felt like I didn't do much to get the ring. So I felt like I didn't really deserve to wear it. It's funny now that I've gotten older, I am really proud of it, but I'm just not a jewelry guy."

Now the president of the California League, Blaney cherishes his two Dodgers rings but also acknowledges he doesn't wear them now because of his current role with his league. "I very proudly have that [1988] championship ring," Blaney, who in 2010 was inducted into the Albuquerque Baseball and Florida State League Halls of Fame, explains today from his league office in Oxnard, California. "I actually have two World Series rings from my time with the Dodgers: the '81 championship and the '88 championship. I keep them polished and locked up; I don't want to bang them up too much. As league president, I get a championship ring from the Cal League every year, so that's what I wear each year representing the Cal League."

Like Sax, first baseman Franklin Stubbs has passed his ring down. Now a minor-league hitting coach in the Arizona Diamondbacks organization, Stubbs doesn't wear that ring to motivate his players in Single-A Hillsboro (Oregon). But he does appreciate having it. "I don't wear the ring. I actually have it at home, but I already gave it to my oldest son," Stubbs explains. "I do not wear the ring but I do have it. I have a National League pennant championship ring from the Braves when I was in the organization as a coach early in my [coaching] career. I have some other minor-league stuff. But that 1988 ring was my only one in the major leagues."

Sadly, some Dodgers have had their 1988 rings stolen. Mickey Hatcher's ring was stolen in 2009—but his story, like the 1988 season, has a happy ending. His wife surprised him by contacting the Dodgers organization to have an exact replica made up, so he does have a Dodgers ring these days. Naturally, because he still gets asked to do events for both the Dodgers and Angels, his replica 1988 ring and his 2002 Angels World Series ring do come in handy. "I do a little bit of public relations for both the Dodgers and Angels," Hatcher explains about his ties to both organizations. "When I go do something for the Dodgers when they call me up to go speak at a Little League [event or] go do autographs and stuff like that, I always wear my ring because fans always want to either get a picture taken with it or see it. I do that a lot." Adds Hatcher with a laugh: "And then when I do something with the Angels, I wear my Angels ring—so I got both sides covered."

For third-string catcher Gilberto Reyes, who was traded away in the spring of 1989, his major-league career was over within three years. As for that 1988 ring, he no longer has it. It is gone—seemingly just as quickly as his career. "I lost that ring. It was [stolen]," Reyes, who still had rookie status in 1988, says today. "Somebody [broke] into the house and stole everything. If I have the permission from the Dodgers, I'm gonna get it back. When I get enough money, I wanna buy it back. Some day when I can get permission, I'm gonna get [an exact replica made up]."

Ramon Martinez, another rookie in 1988, is a third Dodger who had his ring stolen. Promoted prior to August 31st, Martinez was eligible for the playoff rosters but didn't appear in any postseason games. "So, because I got called up in August, I was able to qualify in case they needed me," Martinez explains when asked if he received a ring. "I got called up before September, so I think probably also the guys who were on the 40-man roster also received a ring, but I don't really know. Because I got called up so early, I qualified to participate in case of an emergency. I could be available to pitch in the World Series in case they needed me."

Martinez played for three other playoff teams later in his career—pitching in the postseason for the 1995–1996 Dodgers and 1999 Red Sox—but never won another championship. "Unfortunately, my ring was [stolen] in the Dominican. So, that's pretty sad," Martinez laments. "But they gave us the ring, and also a small medal with the '88' that I still keep—they gave that to the [players'] wives. That one I still have, and also I still have the small '1988' trophy that we received."

A pair of Dodgers who received rings in 1988 do not wish to talk much about them today. Ross Porter and Jay Howell both still have their rings, but they prefer discussing memories from that year instead of a piece of jewelry.

Porter, a play-by-play voice for the Dodgers for 28 years before being let go by the organization in 2004, acknowledges having that ring still—as well as the 1981 ring—but does not want to bring too much attention to it. Now the play-by-play man for Cal State Northridge Matadors baseball, he calls games from Northridge's Matador Field proudly wearing the 1988 ring on his finger. "I got my second World Series championship ring to go with the 1981 ring. I wear the 1988 ring every day," Porter says.

Instead of speaking further about the rings, Porter prefers reflecting back on the night of Gibson's memorable homer. Porter, of course, was at Dodger Stadium working on the radio side. By the top of the ninth, he'd gone down to the home clubhouse and was waiting for the game to be over. "I had to do the postgame interview on radio," recalls Porter.

> Gibson was seated on a trainer's table shirtless with his game pants on watching a television set above him. Vin Scully said on the telecast to Joe Garagiola, "There's one guy we won't see tonight—Kirk Gibson. He can barely walk." When Gibson heard that, he shouted, "Mitch! Mitch!" and clubhouse attendant Mitch Poole came running. Kirk told Mitch, "Go tell Tommy I can hit." Poole came back in about two minutes and reported to Gibson, "Lasorda says to get dressed, but don't show yourself because he doesn't want [A's manager Tony] La Russa to know you can play."
>
> Number 23 put on his jersey and cap, then went to a batting tee next to the tunnel which went to the dugout. He took about eight swings hitting baseballs into the netting. Then someone called to Gibson from the dugout and told him he could come out. I followed him. The Dodger Stadium crowd went absolutely bonkers when he walked up the dugout

steps to the field. Standing in the corner of the third-base dugout and looking over the right-field bullpen, all I could see were red brake lights of cars leaving the stadium to beat the traffic.

With two outs, Dennis Eckersley had walked Mike Davis, who infrequently drew a walk. Perhaps it was because Eckersley noticed Dave Anderson in the on-deck circle and decided to pitch around Davis, who had some power.

Indeed. Davis, while with Oakland just a year earlier, had clubbed 20 homers (while batting .292) by the All-Star break. But from the second half of 1987 through the end of the 1988 season, he had hit a total of four homers with a .208 average, thanks in part to a hyperextended knee suffered in Oakland that never fully healed and a sprained left ankle suffered during the spring of 1988. Still, Davis was more of a power threat than Anderson, who over a 10-year career would hit just 19 homers with a .242 average.

With Gibson at the plate and behind in the count, Davis stole second base. If he had been thrown out, Kirk Gibson would never have become a hero. Before the game that evening, Dodger advance scout Mel Didier, who had been watching every A's game for several weeks, gave a scouting report on the Oakland team. One of his comments was, "If you are a left-handed hitter and Eckersley ever has a 3–2 count on you, he will throw a backdoor slider." Gibson remembered that when the count on him went to 3 and 2. Sure enough, here came the backdoor slider. Kirk took what looked like a one-handed swing and delivered the home run which has been voted the number 1 moment in Los Angeles sports history. It was Gibson's only at-bat in the 1988 World Series.

Howell also still has his 1988 ring but—like Porter—isn't really interested in talking about it much. "I have that ring. It doesn't fit anymore," Howell says, sounding surprised when asked about it. "I don't wear it. It's funny that you ask that because I actually went to dinner not too long ago—and I wore it on my pinky finger. It's not very often that I wear it, but I still have it of course."

For Howell, that ring is precious but it's not what he wants to talk about. The Dodgers closer prefers, instead, to discuss the players and memories—the events that made the team world champions. Howell points to the NLCS, where he was suspended for Games 4 and 5 for having pine tar on his glove. When he tuned into Game 4 on television in Manhattan, Howell noticed his teammates had his number 50 written on either their helmets or their uniform.

> I got things going toward the end of the year, but it's one thing to get kicked out of a game and have the entire team wear your number on their helmet. That, to me, was . . . that would exemplify a team, if there ever was such a thing.
>
> That was just a significant change at that time, with the idea that we weren't satisfied if we got beat as a team, and that's what Gibson reflected. To me, looking back at Gibson that year, the way he played, it was just all-out all the time. He just wore himself down. The other significant guy was Hershiser. The crazy thing about that was, Hershiser was finishing the year throwing shutout after shutout. . . . So, we had two captains, one on the pitching staff in Hershiser and one in Gibson. Gibson was the leader, no doubt about it. And these other guys, from Hatcher to Belcher to Leary. . . . Belcher was really fantastic. I think Hershiser helped him out a great deal. Leary came out of nowhere [to win 17 games]. And he had a nasty split-finger that he'd been working on—and he made it work. Leary was tremendous. But Hershiser led the way.

Being a World Champion in 1988, acknowledges Woodson, has changed his life in terms of his post-MLB career. It has especially helped him in his current role as a head coach in college baseball. "I'm sure it has. I do get asked a lot about what it was like [to be on that '88 team]," Woodson explains. "People tell me, 'Hey, I remember where I was [when Gibson homered]. I was sitting on my couch with my father-in-law . . .' things like that. It's something that I can use. I use the hell out of it for recruiting. When I go to California to recruit, and they're Dodger fans, I use it like crazy. It's like, 'Geez, you played for the Dodgers? Wow . . .' So I can get in on the kid a little bit easier. It helps with recruiting. So I would say, in that sense, absolutely."

"But with the way I am, I dunno," continues Woodson, referring to the fact that he has always wanted to be a champion, a quality he was born with.

> I don't think it's changed me as a person. I'm the same guy, man. I wanted to win. I took a lot of flak from the players just because if you

watch Gibson's home run, I'm there and you'll always see my back jumping up and down with "Woodson" on it. If you see the final out when
Dempsey caught strike three and everybody's running out for Hershiser,
I jump on top of the pile. Guys started joking with me about it. "Man,
how did you end up on top of the pile?" I wanted to win so freaking bad.
And I loved winning. And I get excited about it. I probably get more
excited than other people. In that sense, I loved it.

Joey Amalfitano would be the anti-Woodson. In professional baseball since 1954, Amalfitano has lasted longer in "the show" than the
Dodgers infielder. When asked if he has seen another championship
team like the 1988 Dodgers—one that pulled together and overcame all
sorts of adversity to win it all—Amalfitano immediately points to the
2010s San Francisco Giants. "I've been fortunate to be with the Giants
now since 1999 with the exception of three years [when] I went back to
the Dodgers [from 2002 to 2004]. I've been with the Giants organization for quite a number of years," says Amalfitano, who is in his sixth
stint with the franchise, this time as a special assistant in player development (since 2005). Previously, he had three different stints as a player in
the organization (1954–1955, 1960–1961, and 1963), and he was also a
major-league coach (1972–1975) and special assistant in player development (1999–2001).

> Those three championships in 2010, 2012, and 2014, I'd have to say not
> being there every day with them, but being in spring training with them
> a few of those years, and watching what goes on when I do go up there
> to watch them play and have access to the clubhouse, they resemble
> some of that—because I think they all like one another, so consequently,
> what happens to you? You get on the same end of the rope, and you pull
> on it. That can pull you through storms, and what I mean by a storm
> is a slump and all that stuff. But I can't say about any other teams be-
> cause I'm not directly connected to them and I'm not with them every
> day. Neither am I with these guys that won those three championships
> every day . . . but I was with them for several days. And just talking to
> some of the players that are on that team that have come through the
> minor-league system of the Giants, [they're] home-grown. They played
> together in the minor leagues. So, they bring that with them. And that's
> kind of important; it really is. For me, it really is.

While he witnessed Giants Hall of Famer Willie Mays's legendary over-the-shoulder catch of Vic Wertz's deep drive to center field at New York's Polo Grounds in the 1954 World Series and has also seen three more Giants' championships in San Francisco, Amalfitano still points to Gibson's famous homer as his number 1 moment. "For me, being in uniform, my most memorable nonplaying day in uniform is Gibson's home run," Amalfitano says. "That's the highlight of my time in the game. I hope there will be something that surpasses that. Well, I'm running out of them." He pauses and laughs for a moment. "You know what I mean? There's more time behind me than in front of me. But I know one thing: I was thrilled to death in Texas when the Giants won in 2010."

When the Giants played against the Rangers in the 2010 World Series, the organization invited Amalfitano to attend each game. And he wore his 1954 New York Giants championship ring for good luck. "I was sitting next to my very close teammate, whom I lost [in February 2016, former Giants third baseman] Jimmy Davenport, and how excited we were that the Giants had finally, in San Francisco, won a World Series," recalls Amalfitano. It was the Giants' first World Championship since 1954, when the club was still in New York.

And then they went on to do it again in 2012 and 2014. I was truly excited and proud that I was a member of that organization. To me, the big thing was the players that we—both Jimmy and I—had worked in the minor leagues. And that's what we do: we're in player development. [Buster] Posey. Brandon Belt. Joe Panik. [Brandon] Crawford. [Pablo] Sandoval. These guys all came through the system. To see them on the field and have the success and the fun that they had, that's the ultimate. They were the champions. Did we have anything to do with it? Well, maybe we said something that registered with them. Yeah, I think we did have something to do with it, to be perfectly honest with you. I think we did. To this day, when I see Crawford or Panik or even Buster, they acknowledge me, and they make me feel like I made a difference. That's important to me. As an individual, that's important to me. You're making a difference in a guy's career. How much? Maybe a little bit, I dunno. But those guys are all successful players, successful, very good players. They show me respect. By their mannerisms, the way they talk to me, they show me respect, and I appreciate that.

As he was in the Giants organization in 1954 and in 2010, Amalfitano has the unique distinction—one he shares with Willie Mays—of being a member of the Giants' last championship team in New York and their first in San Francisco. Not only that, he is a member of the Dodgers' last championship team of the 20th century. Naturally, because he was the Dodgers' third-base coach, 1988 means more to him. In 1954 Amalfitano was a rookie, going hitless in five at-bats. With the 2010s Giants, he wasn't with the team on an everyday basis. "In my first two years with the Giants, I sat on the bench," Amalfitano says. "But in 1988, I was a part of it where I had something to do with it, because I was coaching at third base. That was very, very special to me."

Charlie Blaney, the club's farm director for 11 seasons beginning in 1988, has two World Series rings with the organization. Being with the Dodgers organization for the last two championships, Blaney recognizes that the 1981 and 1988 teams were vastly different even though the titles were won just seven years apart. But one thing does stand out—the Dodgers always gave their players an opportunity to play, and, to this day, still do. "[Other than] a few of the same players—Mike Scioscia and Steve Sax—[they were] two different teams," Blaney reflects. "Fernando [Valenzuela] had just started his career in 1981. After losing the first two games to the Yankees in New York, the big turnaround was the third game of the series where Fernando went out and pitched a [complete-game victory], and the Dodgers swept the next four games and won the series 4–2. That's what stands out from that series. But they were always known for giving their young players an opportunity. They've had a number of Rookies of the Year, and they're still doing it now, so it's a great tradition that has carried on."

He gets no argument from Steve Sax. "One was a very veteran-based team, the '81 team," Sax says today.

> The '88 team was a mixture of different guys. The '81 team was almost like it was coming because they had the battles with the New York Yankees before that [and lost the 1977–1978 Series to the Yankees]. They'd been there recently, kind of like Kansas City [of the mid-2010s] when they knocked on the door, got into the [2014] World Series, and won it the next year. That's kind of what the Dodgers of '81 were. The '88 team was a mishmash of different players. We made trades that year, and that

was a team that was kind of put together through patchwork in different ways. It's a team that Lasorda brought together and it worked out.

Jerry Reuss, a member of the 1981 team, had been released by the Dodgers in April 1987; in 1988, the veteran left-hander pitched for a White Sox team that finished 71–90.

Reuss, when asked if he lamented not being in Los Angeles in 1988, simply shrugs. "No, I don't believe I missed out on anything in 1988," Reuss says today.

> My destiny had me in Chicago with the Sox! [For me, being a part of the 1981 team] was the dream that all players have about playing in the big leagues and playing in the World Series. With Chicago, I was 13–9 for a team that was 19 games under .500, [and it was] one of my most satisfying seasons. [The A's were a] great team, but I wasn't shocked to see [the Dodgers] win. They just outplayed Oakland. I was happy for them. [Although] the players that I was closest with all moved on before I did with the Dodgers, I knew many of the players and was happy that they won the championship. Over the past few years, I've said hello to a few members of the '88 team but I don't keep in touch on a regular basis.

Although Reuss pitched in the postseason for Los Angeles in 1981, 1983, and 1985, he's never tried to compare any of those teams. And certainly not with the '88 Dodgers. "To this day, I've never stopped to compare them. [In respect to the 1981 and 1985 teams specifically], both had a dramatic end to an interesting season," says Reuss. "[After leaving the Dodgers], I was more concerned about my next team. Never evaluated the Dodgers one way or another regarding championship potential. I was happy in Chicago. [Hershiser] in 1988 [had] one of the best seasons a pitcher could ever experience. [Scioscia] was managerial material in the early '80s. No surprise about his managerial success. [As for Tommy Lasorda, he was] the best manager I ever played for." During the 1988 season, Reuss kept tabs on teams that Chicago would be facing; since interleague play didn't exist back then, he didn't pay much attention to the Dodgers or any other NL club. "I followed all teams but was more concerned about the teams I had to face in the American League. I wasn't shocked to see them win. As I said, I was happy for them."

Signed by the Dodgers two months after the 1981 World Series as an amateur free agent at the age of 18, Mariano Duncan debuted in the majors in 1985 and batted .222 in that year's NLCS. By 1987 he'd slumped to .215, and he spent 1988 in Triple-A. Surely, it had to hurt watching the Dodgers celebrate in Oakland that October? "To me, it didn't bother me so much," Duncan says today before pausing for a moment. "Maybe just a little bit," he continues.

"After the Triple-A season, I went back to my country, to the Dominican Republic, and got ready to play winter ball. For some reason, I watched the Dodgers on TV. When the Dodgers celebrated winning the World Series, it bothered me a little bit because at that time I said to myself, 'I could be there right now.' But at the same time, I felt very happy for the organization that they'd won another World Series."

Duncan doesn't have any hard feelings toward Fred Claire for trading him; he insists the move changed his career for the better. "There's no doubt about it," Duncan says now. "For me, it was a dream come true. By being sent down in 1988 and getting traded in 1989, and then in 1990 having the opportunity to go to the postseason and winning the World Series. . . . That was something that I can say I got lucky. But at the same time, my whole career changed [after] that year."

Charlie Blaney is happy that Duncan got a shot to be an everyday player in Cincinnati. "I remember Mariano as a quality, polite, talented player—1988 was my first year as farm director and I had interactions with him. He'd played with the Dodgers for three years prior to 1988, but not that year as he was in Albuquerque."

Interestingly, Reuss never had hard feelings toward the Dodgers even though he was released just a year prior to the championship season. "Never. None," says Reuss without any hesitation. "To this day, I consider Fred Claire a good friend. You might be asking, 'Why? Isn't he the guy who released you?' That's true. But it's what he gave me in the process that's had a huge impact on my life."

Reuss goes on to recount a story about how he was assigned a Dodgers–Braves night game in Atlanta while working as an analyst for ESPN in the early 1990s. The next morning, he upgraded to a first-class seat on the first flight back to Los Angeles. As he was placing his carry-on in the overhead section, Reuss noticed a familiar face in the seat next to his—it was none other than Claire, who was jotting notes on his notepad.

The two men exchanged hellos while Reuss got settled in his seat. As Claire continued writing on his notepad, Reuss decided to break the ice. After all, it could be an awkward five-hour trip—or he could turn it into a trip to remember. "I looked at Fred and said, 'I owe you a huge thank-you!' That got his attention," Reuss recalls with a smile. "He put his pen down, turned to me with a smile on his face, and a perplexed look in his eyes. 'How so?' he asked."

> I told him, "For years after I joined the club, I would introduce myself as Jerry Reuss, pitcher for the Los Angeles Dodgers. After my release, I introduced myself as Jerry Reuss . . . with no qualifier! It dawned on me that I was Jerry Reuss before I ever played a game of baseball, and I'm still Jerry Reuss now that my playing days are over." Fred was still with me as I continued, "In effect, when you gave me my release, you also gave me something that I was missing for years. Fred, you gave me . . . ME!" Fred [smiled and] looked at me and said, "Then I guess it really was a good deal!" We both laughed. . . . It turned out to be the best trip ever from Atlanta to Los Angeles.[1]

WHERE ARE THEY NOW?
Life after 1988

With Scioscia out [for] the final game [against Oakland], we got permission to add Gilberto Reyes to the roster. He arrived just as we were celebrating the World Series victory. He's had many turns in his life—some downward—but [is] now back on track.

—Fred Claire, Dodgers GM

I go to California to recruit quite a few times. I've had to in the few years I've been here [in Virginia] because it's all the way across the damn country! I went last year to a recruiting event. I actually took my wife and my son. They'd never been out there. So, we actually went to two Dodger games. I played in St. Louis also, so when I was at Valparaiso [in Indiana], we'd go once a year on a weekend. I'd get tickets for a weekend series in St. Louis. I still go occasionally—I try to use my contacts—and I take my son.

—Tracy Woodson, Dodgers third baseman

Baseball fans know what's happened to Hershiser and Scioscia after their playing careers. Surely, you know what Gibson's been up to. Perhaps Dempsey too. But what about the Stuntmen? What about the lesser-known players who also played key roles in 1988?

"It's interesting to see where everybody has gone after 1988, because everyone's journey is different," Fred Claire says, reflecting on Gibson's life after baseball. "You have Kirk going from that memorable home run to the end of his career shortly after, and then moving to coaching and announcing, battling Parkinson's, and now back as an announcer."

Gibson, who following his Dodgers stint would play in Kansas City and Pittsburgh before returning to Detroit (where he'd begun his career), became a coach with the Tigers from 2003 to 2005 and the Diamondbacks from 2007 to 2010. The former NL MVP was promoted to interim manager in 2010 in Arizona, and stayed on as the D-Backs' skipper until 2014, winning the NL West and NL Manager of the Year Award in 2011. He also served as a television analyst for Tigers' broadcasts for several seasons. Gibson made headlines again in 2015 when it was announced that he was diagnosed with Parkinson's disease. Two years later, the former Michigan State All-American wide receiver was inducted into the College Football Hall of Fame, joining a star-studded 2017 class that also included NFL stars Marshall Faulk, Matt Leinhart, Peyton Manning, Adrian Peterson, Brian Urlacher, and coach Steve Spurrier.

"And you talk about Orel—what a journey he's had following his pitching career, going from pitcher to pitching coach to announcer," adds Claire about Hershiser. The Bulldog worked for ESPN as a broadcaster following his 18-year pitching career and had a stint with the Texas Rangers as a special assistant to general manager John Hart in 2001. He

It was time for a reunion at Dodger Stadium in 2017 as Orel Hershiser was in uniform for this photo with Fred and Sheryl Claire. *Fred Claire*

served as the Rangers' pitching coach from 2002 to 2005 before returning to ESPN for eight more years. In 2014, Hershiser left ESPN and rejoined the Dodgers as a television analyst for their new regional sports network, SportsNet LA.

Dempsey, meanwhile, has also remained in the game as a broadcaster. Following his playing career, he became a manager in the Dodgers' and Mets' farm systems and then a member of the Dodgers' major-league coaching staff (1999–2000) before rejoining the Orioles as an analyst in 2001. While he served as a coach in Baltimore for five years in the 2000s—coaching first base and third base—he has since gone back to the booth calling Orioles games on Mid-Atlantic Sports Network, where he also appears on *O's Xtra* pre- and postgame shows.

"I haven't talked to very many [ex-Dodger] guys," acknowledges Dempsey.

> I saw Mickey Hatcher. We were fairly close for quite a while, especially when he moved on to coaching with the Angels. Never really got much opportunity to get back together with any of them. I still was making some rounds. I left the Dodgers and went to Milwaukee and then back to Baltimore. Just never ran into those guys very often. But we shared a time in baseball that was as good as any 10 years that I ever spent with anyone else. Fred brought it all together where it was a special time. Just a special time. That's the only way I can describe it.

Dempsey is happy to speak about his post-1988 journey in baseball. After all, he doesn't get a chance to reminisce about it every day. "I hung in there for another two years with the Dodgers, [where] things weren't going so well—they were trying to make changes. I wasn't even playing as much, at that point, as I did in 1988 in the platoon system. So, I left the Dodgers and went to the Milwaukee Brewers as a backup catcher—which was different from a platoon guy—to B. J. Surhoff. I didn't get to play much, but sparingly I did pretty well." By playing for Milwaukee in 1991—where he batted .231 in 61 games—Dempsey became one of only three catchers to play in the majors in four decades, joining Tim McCarver and Carlton Fisk.

> It came time [after] that one year to move on again. I still wanted to play, and I had an opportunity to go back to the Baltimore Orioles, a

team I'd previously spent 11 years with. I talked to the general manager. They were very excited to have me come back to the city where I spent most of my time. I joined the ball club there, made the team out of spring training, but they didn't put me on the 25-man roster until a week or so later. When Chris Hoiles broke his hand [in June], they activated me. But I only started one game all season with nine at-bats, and so, the writing was on the wall. It was time for me to retire and to move on. It was a very, very tough decision after all those years. I know I could've still played. But I was 42 years old and it was just time to get out, and go into Phase 2, which was managing in the minor leagues.

It was the Dodgers who gave him that opportunity in 1993. "The guy that really respected me more than anyone else was Fred Claire, who wanted me to stay in the Dodgers organization and manage in that organization," Dempsey says now. "I had some difficulties trying to connect

Rick Dempsey joined the Brewers for one season in 1991 after leaving the Dodgers, becoming one of three catchers to play in the majors in four different decades. *Milwaukee Brewers*

255

back with the Orioles at that point. So, I took the job with the Dodgers."
Alas, in his rookie year as a manager, Dempsey's Class-A Bakersfield
Dodgers finished 42–94, dead last in the 10-team California League.
"I was a horrible Class-A manager in Bakersfield. Just tried to be Earl
Weaver, who was the manager that I probably respected the most dur-
ing the course of my career. Fred Claire took me off to the side and said,
'Listen, Rick. You've gotta be yourself. You can't be someone else!'"

Remarkably, Dempsey then went from worst to first overnight, albeit
with a different group of players in 1994. "And then he surprised me by
giving me the Triple-A job for the Dodgers right out of Class-A ball in
Bakersfield," Dempsey says of Claire.

> That year I managed in the Pacific Coast League, and we ended up win-
> ning the Pacific Coast League title. Again, Fred Claire showed a lot of
> faith in me. It gave me a lot of confidence that I could adjust to being a
> minor-league manager—and it all worked out.
>
> But later on, when Tommy [Lasorda] was getting to the point where
> he was going to have to step down, things weren't going to work out at
> that point as [far as myself] getting a managing job with the Dodgers. So,
> I was forced to move on, and I did a lot of things. I became an advance
> scout for the Colorado Rockies, and then on to managing in the minor
> leagues for the New York Mets [in 1997–1998]. Eventually, I just moved
> on from there, and I became a [bullpen] coach [in 1999–2000], actually,
> for the Dodgers when Davey Johnson became the manager. I spent a lot
> of good years with the Dodgers. Peter O'Malley was an amazing owner,
> probably one of the best owners ever in baseball. The game really misses
> him. I think everybody in baseball who really was into it realizes that 1988
> was a miraculous season for the Los Angeles Dodgers.

Another member of the 1988 Dodgers currently in the broadcast
booth is pitcher Rick Horton, who in 2018 enters his 15th season as a
television play-by-play announcer and analyst for St. Louis Cardinals
games on Fox Sports Midwest. The left-hander, who went by "Ricky"
during his playing days, once recalled his first broadcast assignment from
1997, when he worked a Cardinals–Braves series. "My first game, [Car-
dinals pitcher] Alan Benes had a no-hitter going into the ninth inning,"
he recalled. "I really felt the pressure of the job." He was probably only
joking about the "pressure" bit, for broadcasting is a job he truly enjoys.

"I get to go on weekend trips, stay at a Ritz-Carlton and watch baseball games and get paid for it," he once said. "What's not to like about that? And then I get to come home and take out the trash and become a normal person again." In addition to his broadcasting duties, Horton is the director of the St. Louis area chapter of the Fellowship of Christian Athletes, a poistion he's held since 1993.[1]

Jay Howell, the Dodgers closer, was a regular on the Braves' postgame show for several years in the 2010s, where he was reunited with Don Sutton, a longtime broadcaster in Atlanta following his own Hall of Fame pitching career. "Don Sutton is a huge fixture with the Braves. [For me being part of their broadcasting team], that was just a few years," says Howell, who also coached baseball at Cal State Northridge from 1998 to 2005 and has been involved in antique furniture dealing.

> I had some fun doing the postgame. It was the end of Chipper Jones's career. They were coming on. They were the Baby Braves and they looked like they were gonna get there, but they just always came up short. I worked a bit for them in the postgame call-in show, stuff like that. It was quite enjoyable. I really enjoyed my time there, and I can't say that I had any keen insight. But they were close; I felt like they were maybe one player away. They had a tough situation where they'd signed a couple of free agents, and they stayed with them. Dan Uggla [at second base] and B. J. Upton out in center field. They were paying them a lot of money, and they were bewitched. Couldn't put it together. And they stayed the course. Stayed with them, and they were only able to get so far. They just couldn't seem to punch through. They seemed to always lose in the first round almost all those years. I was very hopeful for them. They had a lot going for them. But they certainly had the bullpen. They had maybe one of the best bullpens around in the game, and they just couldn't punch their ticket. I do think it is harder now with the format. I think it's a real mental grind, you know, the playoffs.
>
> So I did that a little bit. That was good. I was able to be at the stadium and I would see some of the guys that would come through, the coaches who I'd go in and talk to, old teammates of mine. I would see Gibby and different guys that I'd played with that got into coaching. That was quite enjoyable. I quite enjoyed that. That was great.

Besides Gibson, others have been involved in coaching or managing in the majors. Tim Belcher, for instance, served as the Indians' pitching coach from 2010 to 2011, helping oversee breakout seasons for Cleveland starters Justin Masterson and Josh Tomlin. Scioscia and Alfredo Griffin, meanwhile, were still part of the coaching staff with the Los Angeles Angels as of 2017. Scioscia, who spent several years as a coach in the Dodgers organization following his retirement (including a stint as manager in Triple-A Albuquerque in 1999), was hired to manage the Angels after the 1999 season. Upon his hiring, Scioscia brought in Griffin and Mickey Hatcher as coaches, and as of 2017 Griffin was still the Angels' first-base coach.

While Scioscia has been the Angels' skipper since 2000—winning Manager of the Year awards in 2002 and 2009—he isn't the only Dodger from 1988 involved in managing. Outfielder Mike Marshall and Stuntmen Danny Heep and Tracy Woodson have become head coaches at the collegiate level. Heep is currently the head coach for the University of the Incarnate Word Cardinals baseball team, a private Catholic college in San Antonio, a position he has held since 1998. Marshall, meanwhile, is the associate head baseball coach with the New Mexico Highlands University baseball team, working alongside head coach Shannon Hunt, a former San Francisco Giants scout. Marshall, who has also been heavily involved in recruiting for the program, has held the position since December of 2014.

A native of Richmond, Virginia, Woodson became the head coach of his hometown University of Richmond Spiders baseball team in July 2013. But it was a long road before he wound up back home. He began his coaching journey in 1997 as the hitting coach for the Double-A Carolina Mudcats and then managed for the next seven years (1998–2004) for minor-league clubs in the Pirates, Padres, and Marlins organizations. After taking some time off, Woodson became the head coach at Valparaiso University in Indiana—a position he held from 2007 to 2013—before landing the Richmond job. "After I finished playing, I was a hitting coach in Double-A," says Woodson. "Then I managed for seven years in the minor leagues from rookie ball all the way to Triple-A. Then, I got re-married, had a little girl [in 2004], and since then had a son too [born in 2006]. So, I got out of it. I took a year and a half off. I opened up an indoor facility, and then I coached at Valparaiso for seven years. And now [in 2017], I'm in my fourth year in Richmond."

Woodson adds that he learned a lot from pitching coach Ron Perranoski during mound visits. Whenever Perranoski went to the mound to talk strategy with the pitcher, Woodson would go too. Being involved in those meetings, Woodson acknowledges, has helped his coaching career.

> When I left college, I knew I wanted to stay in sports somehow, and I always figured coaching was probably gonna be it, so I wanted to learn as much about the game as I could. And I tried to use anything that I could for coaching and managing. I always wanted to know what was said. So, if I ever had to go out later in my career to talk to a pitcher, I wanted to know what needed to be said. Some of the stuff was to kind of loosen the guy up, maybe joke around, [while] some of it was about strategy, so I tried to use that as much as I could. So, I tried to go in there every time.

As for Hatcher, he has had a lengthy coaching résumé of his own. Although he is probably best known, as a coach, for his time as the Angels' hitting coach from 2000 to 2012, he did spend six seasons coaching or managing in the Dodgers' minor-league system in the 1990s. For three years he managed for the Dodgers' rookie ball (1996–1997) and Class-A ball (1998) clubs and was a coach in Triple-A Albuquerque for two other seasons (1992 and 1999) before moving on to the Angels.

Hatcher acknowledges that having a World Series ring could have helped guys land coaching jobs after their playing careers—it certainly couldn't hurt to be labeled a champion. "I think it definitely helps, especially guys in baseball, they want to bring people into the organizations that have won, and know what it's like to win," explains Hatcher, who in 1997 guided the Dodgers' rookie-league team in Great Falls (Montana) to a first-place finish and an appearance in the Pioneer League Finals. "Part of coaching is teaching the young players, how important it is for the leadership to get out there on the field and play to win. I could see that getting people a lot of opportunities. Guys that have had the experience and have gone through it—that makes their value even more. I can see that happening with a lot of players. It's a great thing for all these guys to look back on. You know, the Belchers. . . . You look at Orel right now being in broadcasting and what kind of year he had."

Hatcher remained the Angels' hitting coach until May 2012. A month later, he was rehired by the Dodgers as a special assistant to general manager Ned Colletti, a position he held for the rest of that season.

Today, he isn't with either club but is still asked to do public relations for both teams from time to time. "I had an opportunity to be on two World Series teams in California. They happen to be side by side. So, it's worked out great for me," says Hatcher fondly.

> [I'm in touch] more with the Angels. I don't really have any more ties with the Dodgers. The organization has changed so much that I only know a few of the lady secretaries there and a couple of other people. Really, there's not much contact there from the '88 World Series. Ron Cey, [Steve] Yeager, and a bunch of the guys [from the 1981 championship team] that I came up with are still working for them. When I go do something with the Dodgers, I go say hi and talk a little bit. It's long in between—it's like months apart before I get a chance to see them.

"There's a few I've seen," says Woodson of running into teammates from 1988.

> I've talked to Gibson a few times. I've seen Lasorda probably more than anybody. He's actually helped me do some fundraising for my jobs and he made a call in when I was interviewing for the job at Valparaiso. I haven't seen Mickey Hatcher in a while. Same with Scioscia. Tim Leary's probably the one that I've talked to the most just because he was a college pitching coach. He'll send me an email—if he's got a player in California that's looking for a place to play, he'd send me an email so that I could recruit [that player].

There are other ex-Dodgers in various organizations, in roles other than coaching at the big-league level. Ramon Martinez, for instance, is now a special assignment pitching instructor with Baltimore. His role is to concentrate on developing Latin American pitchers throughout the Orioles organization. Chris Gwynn, meanwhile, took on several roles— including being a scout and player personnel director—and is now out of the game after some 15 fun years of being back in it. When he was still in the game, though, Gwynn always enjoyed reminiscing with some of his old teammates such as Martinez, Scioscia, and Belcher.

"[I've been] working with the Baltimore Orioles for the past three years. [Before that], I was with the Dodgers for five years as a coach," says Martinez. "I saw Kirk Gibson in spring training when we were playing in

Lakeland. I said hi to Kirk and we talked. I've also seen Mike Scioscia. I still see some of the guys that played [on the later Dodger teams], such as Lenny Harris, who didn't play on that 1988 team [but arrived in a July 1989 trade that sent Tim Leary to Cincinnati and spent five seasons in Los Angeles]. I've seen Dave Anderson; he works with the Orioles here too [as a minor-league infield coordinator]."

Being in the game for a number of years following his retirement as a player—as a major-league scout and farm director—Gwynn had a chance to come across several ex-Dodgers. "I talk to Mike Scioscia probably at least once a year," Gwynn says fondly.

> I haven't talked to Mickey Hatcher in a while, but I used to see him when I was the farm director with the Mariners. I've seen Mariano Duncan [who was in Triple-A Albuquerque in 1988 but not on the major-league roster]. I saw Ramon Martinez in spring training one year; he was the roving pitching instructor with the Dodgers when I was with the Mariners. I hadn't seen him in years. He's like a brother to me—awesome guy. Tim Leary, I saw him about five or six years ago; he seems to be doing well. I saw Tim Belcher two years ago; he's doing well. That's about it. I don't really see anybody else. I was still involved in baseball for a lot of years—and you see some of the guys you played with on different teams. I literally just got out of baseball this past year.

As Gwynn explains, it was his connections with San Diego that had gotten him back in the game. "After my playing career, I took one year off, and then Kevin Towers—the GM with the Padres—called me and wanted to know if I wanted to get involved in baseball [again]," Gwynn says.

> I ended up scouting [and working in the Padres' scouting department] for [the next] 12 or 13 years. I scouted for four years [as an] area scout in Southern California. [Then] I became a West Coast cross-checker [a regional scouting role that involved ranking the prospects in all of the western United States in order]—and I did that for three years. Then I became a major-league scout. Did that for four years, and then I became the player personnel director with the Padres, and that entailed a lot of flying all over the world, really. Then I got the farm director's job with the Mariners [following the] 2011 [season]. And then, I resigned after

the 2015 season. Now, I do whatever I want. I play golf. I'm having fun. It's been good.

Although 30 years have passed, Gwynn still believes the 1988 team delivers a wonderful message for kids involved in sports. "What I'd say about being on that team—or just watching and experiencing it—is anything's possible," Gwynn explains.

> You need to work hard and be prepared, and you just never know. And the best thing about sports is no matter what people say, you still have to play the game. It was a consummate team. We were playing well. We had just enough hitting, really good starting pitching, and we would defend pretty well. So, it just goes to show that you just never know. You go out and play the game, be prepared, do the things you're supposed to do, and you have a chance. We weren't favored against the Mets. The Oakland A's were saying they wanted to face the Mets because they were "the better team." We ended up playing Oakland and beating them in five. I think we beat the Mets in six [actually, seven]. And just a whole bunch of memories of big plays: Mike Scioscia taking Dwight Gooden deep in New York; Kirk Gibson making a great catch in New York, rainy field, tough conditions. Guys were just prepared and they played well. Especially as a young player, it was very good to see game plans being executed the correct way with that mind-set.

Center fielder John Shelby has quietly had a lengthy career in coaching—with six different major-league organizations—but admits he doesn't follow the game as religiously these days. "Unfortunately, I don't watch MLB today as much as I used to. I run into a few teammates every now and then since there are a few of us still active in the game as coaches or other areas," Shelby says before describing his post-1988 baseball journey. "I played for the Detroit Tigers in 1990 and 1991, and finished my playing career with the Pawtucket Triple-A team in 1992. I managed and coached in the Dodgers' minor-league system from 1993 to 1998, and then joined their major-league staff from 1998 to 2005."

Following the 2005 season, Shelby moved on to the Pirates' major-league coaching staff for two years in 2006–2007. And, like former Oriole and Dodger Dempsey, Shelby also eventually returned to Baltimore, where he was on the Orioles' major-league coaching staff for three seasons from 2008 to 2010. "[After that, I spent the] 2011 to 2015 seasons on the Brewers' major-league staff," Shelby continues, outlining the various stops in his post-playing career. "[Then in] 2016, I was the Rockies' Triple-A hitting coach in Albuquerque, New Mexico. In September of 2016, I was offered—and accepted—the position as the minor-league outfield/base-running coordinator for the Atlanta Braves organization."

Hitting coach Ben Hines retired in the mid-1990s but made a brief comeback in the 2000s, playing a huge role in the Angels organization while also serving as a spring-training adviser for Scioscia. "I was with the Dodgers for 10 years," says Hines now.

> I was there in the fall of '84 after I got fired in Seattle [as the Mariners' hitting coach]. I had about five teams that had a job for me if I wanted it, I think: Milwaukee as their hitting coordinator, Kansas City as their hitting coordinator, and one team—the Tigers—wanted me to manage in Triple-A. There were about five jobs by the time I drove from Seattle and got home. I didn't have a cell phone. By the time I got home, I had about five job offers. The Dodgers offer was the one that was the most exciting because I could take it and be home. So, that was one of the reasons I took that job, because I didn't have to travel away and be located at some place like Des Moines or Rochester. I didn't have to relocate; I could be located in LA, be with my family, and stay at home coaching. Most coaches don't have that. They have to travel to get back home.
>
> [After my stint with the Dodgers] I went down to Houston and was a bench coach and hitting coach for Terry Collins with the Houston Astros. Back in 1987 when I was coaching in Triple-A Albuquerque, Terry was the manager. When he became the manager of Houston, he saved a spot for me on that roster, so starting in '94 I was the hitting coach for the Astros, the year [first baseman Jeff] Bagwell had a great year and was the MVP. But then I resigned after the strike that season and retired.
>
> That was the end of my career—though I did scout later on for the Angels for about five or six years, starting with the year they won [the World Series in 2002]. So, that was my second World Series ring, the one with the Angels. And I was very influential in the signing of Mark Trumbo, who led the major leagues in home runs [in 2016]. I am the main factor for the Angels signing him [after he was drafted in 2004]. Mike Scioscia used to invite me to spring training. I would go down for a week or 10 days every spring, and he always wanted to know what I felt about this or that young kid. He wanted my evaluations on the

young players, whether I thought they were gonna be close to the major leagues. And I did; I told him every spring. I gave him evaluations of the young guys that were making the transition from the minor leagues to the major leagues.

Like Hines, Phil Regan left the Dodgers at the end of the 1993 season. Now with the Mets organization as their assistant minor-league pitching coordinator, Regan fulfilled his goal of throwing batting practice at the age of 80, a feat he accomplished at New York's Citi Field in April 2017 before a Mets–Marlins game. "I'd been going down to winter ball and managing, with the idea that eventually I wanted to manage in the major leagues," recalls Regan.

That was my goal. And I'd done well. I won two championships in the Dominican and one in Venezuela. I told Fred [Claire], "But for me to manage, I needed to get back onto the field." So, in 1994, [Indians general manager] John Hart hired me to be their pitching coach in Cleveland. And so, I did that.

The next year, I was offered the job to manage the Orioles, which was a traumatic year because in 1994, baseball went on strike. They didn't settle that strike until the next spring. We went into spring training and there were no major-league players. Everyone was on strike. Everyone had signed replacement players to have on their teams. But [owner] Peter Angelos in Baltimore would not use replacement players because he'd made his money working with unions and he backed the union on the strike! This was my first year managing. We were in spring training, and everyone else was playing, but all we—me and my staff—were doing was watch our Double-A and Triple-A teams play.

As the start of the 1995 season was approaching, Regan thought the worst was going to happen.

I'm thinking, "This is the first year I'm getting to manage. I'm 57 years old. I've never managed in the United States. This is gonna be my first opportunity. And I'm gonna be 0 for 144—I wasn't gonna win a game because we were gonna forfeit every game that we played!" Then the strike settled, and we had about five days to practice, and 8 or 10 games I think it was [of exhibition games], and then we started the season. All in all, it was a pretty exciting season. I really enjoyed it. The way we started out, we ended up really well—we finished in third place. I guess that wasn't good enough, but it was a tremendous experience!

Regan isn't the only Dodger to be with the organization in at least three different decades. Charlie Blaney, the Dodgers' farm director in 1988, spent more than 30 years with the organization. Now, he's the president of the Class-A California League, a role he's had since 2010. "That [1988] was my first year as the farm director," Blaney recalls from his office in Oxnard, California.

> I'd been, for 13 years prior to that, the managing director of Dodger-
> town, in Vero Beach, Florida, where all of the players lived and trained
> and stayed and worked out during spring training. So, I got to know
> them a little bit during that time. And then, I was fortunate to be named
> the farm director. It was quite thrilling to win the World Series in my
> first year at the major-league level. Fred [Claire] was my immediate
> boss, was a great example and mentor to all of us. My job, though, was
> to oversee the training of the young Dodger players coming up, and to
> organize a staff of about 30 coaches, managers, trainers, that oversaw
> the Dodger farm system. I was not involved in the direct operations of
> the major-league team; our job was to supply players to come up to the
> major-league team.

While Blaney enjoyed his time with the Dodgers—his roles with the organization included being vice president of player development; managing director of Dodgertown; and GM of Dodgers affiliates at the Single-A, Double-A, and Triple-A levels—he realized it was time to move on after Peter O'Malley sold the club. Then, after spending more than a decade away from the game, he'd make a comeback and land the job as California League president. "I was fortunate enough to work for 32 years in the Dodger organization under the ownership of the O'Malley family," Blaney says when asked to recount his journey in baseball.

> The last 11 years I was the farm director, starting in 1988. My last year
> was 1998. After that, I basically retired [and moved to] where I am right
> now, Ventura County, [California]. I'd been a schedule maker, so I did
> a schedule making business until 2010.

That's when the California League, which is a minor league in the state of California, had an opening for the president. I applied, and was fortunate to get that job. So, I'm currently president of the California League, which is an eight-team Class-A league in the state of California all affiliated with the eight western United States major-league organizations—the five in California: the Padres, Dodgers, Angels, Giants, and A's; and then Seattle, Colorado, and Arizona. So, all eight of those western United States major-league teams have farm teams in the state of California, and my job is to oversee that league.

My time with the Dodgers certainly prepared me for this position because [even at that time] the Dodgers had a team in the California League. So, as the farm director of the Dodgers, I knew the league and some of the executives. So, it was great preparation for what I'm currently doing and I'm in my eighth year now [in 2017].

Alejandro Peña, who quietly pitched three shutout innings and was the winning pitcher the night Scioscia homered off Gooden, also worked two scoreless innings in the Kirk Gibson homer game. He was the winning pitcher that night too. Traded to the Mets in December 1989, Peña would join the Braves on August 28, 1991, and go on to record 11 saves down the stretch and three more in the 1991 NLCS against Pittsburgh—including a pair of 1–0 gems by Atlanta left-hander Steve Avery. That September, he teamed with Kent Mercker and Mark Wohlers for a combined no-hitter against San Diego in a 1–0 victory, picking up the save. By 1995, he was no longer a closer. But he still won two games in the 1995 NLDS for the Braves against Colorado, the year Atlanta finally won the World Series. Peña, who now lives in Suwanee, Georgia, served as the pitching coach for the Dominican Summer League Dodgers from 2010 to 2013 before retiring.

Jesse Orosco, whose legacy with the Dodgers is being the player who put the eye black in Gibson's hat, set the all-time record for career appearances with 1,072 in 1999, surpassing Dennis Eckersley. Orosco pitched in the majors for 24 years, played for nine teams (including the Padres, Yankees, and Twins in his final season in 2003), and holds the MLB record for career games pitched with 1,252.

As of 2017, Franklin Stubbs was in the Diamondbacks organization as the hitting coach in Single-A Hillsboro (Oregon). The Stuntman-turned-starting-first-baseman went into coaching almost immediately following his playing career, getting his start in 1997 as the hitting coach for the Atlanta Braves' rookie-league team in Danville (Virginia). He managed that club in 1998 before being named Atlanta's minor-league hitting instructor in 1999. After a 12-year run in the Braves organization—where he also served as a roving hitting instructor and hitting coach—Stubbs returned to the Dodgers organization in 2009 as a coach in Class-A San Bernardino (California). Stubbs wound up serving as either a coach or coordinator for four different minor-league teams in the Dodgers' chain until 2015. "Professionally wise, I went from playing in my last year in Detroit in 1995 to jumping into coaching with the Braves," Stubbs says today when asked to reflect on his post-1988 journey in baseball. "And I've been coaching in the minor leagues [since then]—either as a hitting coach or as a hitting coordinator, [and] I managed one year. So, I've been in this game for 20 years since I retired, just coaching or coordinating."

Franklin Stubbs, now a coach with Single-A Hillsboro (Oregon), takes time out to talk baseball by the visitor's dugout at Vancouver's Nat Bailey Stadium in July 2017. *Author's collection*

It's the belief that he needs to pass on his knowledge to young ball-players trying to make the majors that inspires Stubbs to remain in coaching. "Pretty much I felt like I had to give something back to the game," he explains. "The game had given me so much that I felt like I had to give back. I thought this was something I could give back—the knowledge to young men trying to get to the same goals and reach the same aspirations as I did, to get to the big leagues. I thought this was my way to give back."

Now that it's been some 30 years since 1988, Stubbs appreciates the fact he's had a chance to stay in touch with several of his ex-teammates.

> I always run into guys. You run into Mike Scioscia and Alfredo Griffin with the Angels. I would see Hershiser a lot when I was coaching with the Dodgers; I would always see him. I've run into Tim Leary. Kenny Howell, one of my best buddies and my best man at my wedding, [whom] I always talk to on the phone or text or something. John Shelby. I ran into Mike Davis a couple of times. You're still gonna see those guys. Those guys have special places in my heart—and hopefully we all in theirs—because when you get a chance to do that with 25 guys—or 28 guys, or 30 guys, or whatever it takes to win it—you don't forget those guys.

Meanwhile, Mike Devereaux, a rookie who had 43 at-bats for the 1988 Dodgers, was in the Colorado Rockies organization as of 2017. Devereaux, whose role involved player development, had been the hitting coach with the Rockies' Class-A team in Asheville (North Carolina) from 2012 to 2016. "It is fun. It is difficult at times. It's sad at times," Devereaux said in 2017. "Obviously, there are guys that get released that have their dreams squashed."

Devereaux, though, probably speaks for all of the 1988 Dodgers who are still involved in the game as coaches when he adds the following:

> But it's also refreshing at times when you see guys you've worked with make it to the big leagues, and follow kinda what I've done in the game. That's really why I do this. I've always loved the game of baseball. It's been part of our family ever since I was a child. I got to the big leagues, played in the big leagues, and then I shut it down for a while. And then I got back into the game and I realized how much I missed it. I love the fact that I have the opportunity to develop players, to actually enjoy the game like I have.[2]

EPILOGUE

That team had a "magic" that transcends baseball. Yet, [it] has barely been given near the exposure of how truly great that season was. Or why. And how it still affects fans and the Dodger organization. And just how difficult it is to win a World Series! I live in Santa Monica, California, 15 miles west of Dodger Stadium near the beach. I grew up here, as a Dodger fan. [In 1988] we were a very "close" team, and the "family culture" was bred and fed by Peter O'Malley. He was a very special owner; [he] did things to only improve both the players' experience, and the fan experience—especially starting with the design of Vero Beach and how it gave fans access to players. It was a season and World Series championship that was really one for the ages. A true team. Peter O'Malley's suite number at his office on Figueroa Street in downtown LA is Suite 1988—that's how much that year's team means to him!

—Tim Leary, Dodgers pitcher

The 1988 championship season marked the closing of a success story for the Dodgers in the pre-wild card era. Dodgers fans could look back at their 12-year stretch from 1977 to 1988 under Tommy Lasorda as a period of success, with six division championships, four NL pennants, and a pair of World Series titles—with the 1988 victory one of the most improbable in baseball history. After 1988, the Dodgers never again returned to the World Series until 2017, where they lost to Houston in seven games.

Observers, when asked to look back, say they remember that 1988 team as Gibson's ball club. "I just remember about the whole Kirk Gibson thing in spring training," Bob Nightengale says now. "I forgot who the player was. I don't remember if it was Jesse Orosco or who it was that put the eye black in the cap, and Gibson went crazy. It was almost like it was Gibson's team—he was there to win. He did not have the stats of a Darryl Strawberry, but he won the MVP award just because of what he meant to that franchise. It was such an overachieving team. No one expected them to get past the Mets or the Oakland A's."

Charlie Blaney still looks at 1988 as a magical season in Los Angeles. "Fred [Claire] made some trades in the off-season prior to that [season], getting Kirk Gibson, and Alfredo Griffin, and Jay Howell. Those were three key players to set the team up to win. And everybody came through. Mickey Hatcher. Rick Dempsey. So, it was just one of those magical years that happened. [But] my biggest disappointment in my 11 years in charge of player development was, after winning the World Series in 1988, we never returned to the series."

Yes, the Dodgers contended for a division title in 1991 with high-priced, free-agent slugger Darryl Strawberry on the team but were eliminated on the season's penultimate day by the Giants after a thrilling final-month pennant race with the Atlanta Braves. The 1993 team didn't contend for a pennant but did eliminate the 103-win Giants on the season's final day—payback for the time San Francisco knocked the Dodgers out in 1991.

In 1994, MLB realigned, with the number of divisions in both leagues increasing from two to three—with a Central Division added to each circuit. The number of teams qualifying for the postseason also doubled, from four to eight, with the three division winners from each league reaching the postseason along with one wild-card team from each league. The Dodgers—with a fine pitching staff considered on par with the outstanding Braves rotation (which included Hall-of-Famers-to-be Greg Maddux, Tom Glavine, and John Smoltz)—returned to the postseason in 1995 and 1996 but were swept in the Division Series by Cincinnati and Atlanta, respectively. By then, the only players remaining from 1988 were Ramon Martinez and Chris Gwynn—though the latter had been traded to Kansas City before returning to the Dodgers.

Despite the lack of postseason success, there were great moments involving the Dodgers in the 1990s. Fernando Valenzuela, who went on to pitch for the Angels, Orioles, Phillies, Padres, and Cardinals, had one last great game as a Dodger, tossing a historic 6–0 no-hitter on June 29, 1990, against St. Louis. It marked the first time in major-league history that two no-hitters had been thrown on the same day, as Oakland's Dave Stewart had twirled one in Toronto hours earlier. In 1992, Kevin Gross threw a 2–0 no-hitter against San Francisco in an otherwise forgettable season that saw the Dodgers finish in last place for the first time since 1905. Martinez (1995 versus Florida) and Hideo Nomo (1996 in Colorado) also threw no-hitters. The Dodgers had five consecutive NL Rookies of the Year from 1992 to 1996, with Mike Piazza, the '93 top rookie, going on to capture MVP honors in the '96 All-Star Game played in his hometown of Philadelphia.

From 1989 to 2016, the Dodgers never played in a World Series, much less won one. To Tracy Woodson, it's not that big a surprise because of the additional playoff round introduced in 1994 with the wild card. Under the current format, there's also a play-in game, making it, as Woodson says, "a mental grind" to go through the entire postseason and win the whole thing. To others, though, it is shocking that Los Angeles went 28 years without playing in a World Series.

"I am surprised because—even though the Dodgers had gone through a little bit of turmoil [under the Frank McCourt ownership from 2004 to 2012]—they always played the game right. I'll give you an example," recalls Phil Regan.

> Playing the Dodgers, when they were good and winning, [you really had to prepare for them]. I was rooming with a guy named Jim Hickman [an outfielder-first baseman with the Cubs]. We roomed together for six years. We'd both come from the Dodgers. We were playing in Chicago. I can remember waking up one day and he said, "Phil, we're playing the Dodgers today. They've got all that speed. I'm gonna have to hurry everything we do. I've gotta hurry; I've gotta be in a hurry." But he was thinking about that, and that's the way [the Dodgers] played the game. They always took the extra base. They went into second base hard. They bunted. They scored. They always had good pitching. They were fundamentally sound.

"I am a little bit surprised," adds Franklin Stubbs about the fact the Dodgers never won a pennant from 1989 to 2016. "They've had some good teams. Unfortunately, sometimes in the playoffs it's just a matter of who gets hot. A lot of times they weren't able to finish the race. They've had some good enough teams to actually get there. They just ran into a couple of teams that were pitching well and had hot hitters."

While Stubbs's Dodgers didn't have to deal with an extra playoff round the way that division winners do these days, he points out that they did have to beat two very tough teams to become champions. "I don't know what kind of advantage we had," says Stubbs, responding specifically to the idea that his Dodgers might have had an easier route without the extra wild-card round that teams today have to deal with. "When you gotta go through the Mets and then go through Oakland, I don't know if that was an advantage. But we didn't have to play as many rounds. We only had to play pretty much the one round against the Mets, a very talented, great team at the time. To get through them was hard enough, and then to have to deal with Oakland in the World Series was just as hard. So, I don't know if it was 'easier,' but we didn't have to go through as many rounds as they do today."

"The Dodgers have had some good personnel, and some very, very good players," Joey Amalfitano says, referring to the 2013–2016 Dodgers.

> In fact, the leader of the pack there is the pitcher, [Clayton] Kershaw, who's gonna go into the Hall of Fame. When you start to think of the Hall of Fame, they have a guy over there who's very, very good . . . probably the best left-handed pitcher in the National League, if not in baseball. I am surprised they [haven't] advanced farther in the playoffs. But they sure have been there knocking on the door the last four or five years. It will happen for them because they do have a good team. You know what, though? It's the personnel but there's also a great deal of luck involved, meaning injuries and [other factors]. There's some luck involved. Maybe that luck hasn't swung their way in the playoffs, I don't know. But they do have good teams. They do.

"They made it a little bit easier in the fact that a second-place club could be in the playoffs, get hot, and win the whole thing," Mel Didier said in April of 2017, just months before his passing at the age of 90 that September. "I mean, that's happened. I'm not sure that's the best way. But with baseball and television . . . there's so much money involved, that they're gonna continue to do this. That's what's gonna happen. That's just the way it is."

The Dodgers, despite making Kevin Brown baseball's first $100 million man in 1998 (giving the right-hander a seven-year, $105 million contract), never made it to postseason play during his five-year tenure in Dodger Blue. By the end of the 2003 season, Brown was gone, having been traded to the Yankees. In 2004, the Dodgers, under manager Jim Tracy, won the NL West thanks in part to a franchise-record 53 comeback victories, securing the club's first trip to the postseason in eight years.[1] In the third game of that year's best-of-five Division Series, Jose Lima blanked St. Louis 4–0 on a complete-game five-hitter, ending the Dodgers' eight-game postseason losing streak. The Dodgers still lost the series the following night. Two years later, they won the NL Wild Card under skipper Grady Little, only to be outscored 19–11 in a three-game sweep by the Mets in the Division Series.

Under Hall-of-Famer-to-be Joe Torre—the club's sixth manager since Tommy Lasorda's 1996 retirement—Los Angeles reached the NLCS in back-to-back seasons in 2008–2009 but both times lost to Philadelphia four games to one. With former Yankees standout Don Mattingly managing the club in the 2010s, the Dodgers won three consecutive NL West titles from 2013 to 2015 but advanced no further than the NLCS, losing in six games to St. Louis in the 2013 Championship Series (and not advancing past the Division Series in either 2014 or 2015). Dave Roberts took over as manager in 2016, but the Dodgers fell in six games in that year's NLCS to the eventual world champion Chicago Cubs.

The Dodgers finally returned to the World Series in 2017, winning their first pennant since 1988. By winning an unprecedented 52 of 61 during one stretch, the 2017 Dodgers were 91–36 after 127 games—on pace to tie the single-season mark of 116 victories—before suddenly losing 16 of their next 17 (including a Los Angeles–record 11 straight) and still finishing with baseball's best record at 104–58. On October 15, 2017, Justin Turner clubbed a three-run walk-off homer with two outs in the ninth, giving Los Angeles a 4–1 win over the defending champion Cubs in Game 2 of the NLCS en route to a five-game victory. Turner's blast, just the second walk-off homer in Dodgers postseason history, came on the 29th anniversary of the first one—Gibson's 1988 pinch-hit blast off Eckersley. In the World Series against Houston (which had switched leagues in 2013, moving from the NL Central to the AL West), the Dodgers lost a 13–12 classic in Game 5, as the 101-win Astros rallied from deficits of 4–0 and 7–4 against ace Clayton Kershaw. With George Springer being Houston's Mr. October with five homers (tying a World Series mark originally set by Reggie Jackson against the Dodgers in 1977), the Astros went on to win 5–1 in Game 7, celebrating their first world championship at Dodger Stadium.

Hershiser's record-setting 59-consecutive-scoreless-innings streak, of course, eventually ended. It actually ended in his very first inning of 1989 when Cincinnati's Todd Benzinger stroked a two-out single to score Barry Larkin. In 1989, the Dodgers stumbled to fourth place, never leading the division for a single day and finishing 77–83 for their third losing season in four years. Hershiser, meanwhile, notched a 2.31 ERA and barely lost the ERA crown to San Francisco's Scott Garrelts, who had a 2.28 ERA. But hampered by poor run support—as injuries to Gibson and Mike Marshall slowed the offense—the Bulldog finished just 15–15. Remarkably, Los Angeles went 34 innings without scoring for him in one stretch from mid-August to mid-September. And while he finished with a .500 record, Hershiser did lead the NL in innings pitched for the third consecutive season.

But all of those innings took their toll on Hershiser. Just four starts into the 1990 season, his elbow was done. He underwent Tommy John surgery that April, and didn't return to the mound again until May 1991. After posting three consecutive nonwinning seasons, Hershiser saw a renaissance when he joined Cleveland as a free agent in 1995, winning 45 games in three years with the Indians. He also led a long-suffering Indians franchise, which hadn't finished in first place since 1954, to AL Central titles in each of his three seasons in Cleveland, capturing the 1995 ALCS MVP award along the way. After one-year stops in New York with the Mets and in San Francisco, the Bulldog returned to Los Angeles in 2000 for his final season at age 41. He put up a 13.14 ERA in 10 appearances before his release and retirement in June.

Gibson, who played in a total of only 160 games in 1989–1990, left as a free agent after the 1990 campaign. Even with his subpar 1989–1990 seasons, the iconic World Series homer has cemented his place in Dodgers history. A man with a flair for the dramatic, Gibson, while with Detroit in 1984, had homered twice in the fifth game of that year's World Series against San Diego—a two-run blast to open the scoring and a three-run shot in the eighth off Hall-of-Famer-to-be Goose Gossage—to clinch that championship for the Tigers. The second dinger came with Detroit ahead 5–4, and put a dagger in the Padres' hearts. Of course, the 1988 walk-off shot off Eckersley was his second dramatic World Series homer against a Hall of Fame reliever.

Mel Antonen, who covered both World Series, offers his perspective on the two late-inning dingers. "[The] fact that he was on the trainer's table [in] Game 1, World Series 1988, is even more memorable," says Antonen.

> There was really no drama [in 1984 because] the Tigers were gonna win the World Series, whether they won in five games, six games, or seven games. They were in complete control. But the fact that the Dodgers were the underdogs, Kirk Gibson was on the trainer's table, nobody knew for sure if or when he was gonna play. . . . Vin Scully had said, "Where is Kirk Gibson?" on the national broadcast. Kirk had told his wife to go home because he wasn't gonna play. The story with the batting practice, with the clubhouse guy pitching batting practice thinking it was a waste of time. The drama in the 1988 World Series with the Gibson home run was so much more dramatic than the one against San Diego. The one he hit for the Tigers obviously helped seal the World Series championship, but it didn't come close to the drama that we had in Los Angeles.

Gibson, who had two more productive seasons in Detroit in 1993–1994, reflected on the aftermath of his 1988 homer with broadcaster Dick Schaap on Classic Sports Network shortly after his retirement in 1995. As Gibson told Schaap, the home run was the reward he got for forcing himself to go up to bat against Eckersley, and he didn't regret the physical pain he suffered and the games he missed over the next few seasons.[2]

As it turned out, though, the injuries from the NL playoffs were much more serious than anyone thought. When Gibson's left hamstring was finally surgically repaired in September 1989, doctors found that the ligament connecting the hamstring and knee was torn—with team physician Frank Jobe saying he'd never seen that kind of injury.[3] Unfortunately, Gibson missed the final two-and-a-half months of 1989 and the first two-and-a-half months of the 1990 campaign.

The rejuvenated Gibson would finish his career with Detroit from 1993 to 1995, where he was primarily a DH but also played center field regularly for Sparky Anderson's Tigers. "It took me, really, four years after that. I ended up having surgery the following year on that leg, and it was a major surgery. It took me three, four years, after that to where I really got back to 100 percent," Gibson, who batted .394 in the first six weeks of 1993 and contributed 23 homers in 1994, told Schaap. "But it was all worth it to me. I sold out. You know, I was going for the championship trophy, and I made that decision to do so. And I had to be accountable for the three years that I had to take off after that to basically get 100 percent."[4]

As the years go by, Gibson—who in a 17-year career hit .268 with 260 doubles, 255 homers, and 284 steals—gets to relive his glory every time he returns to Chavez Ravine, especially from 2007 to 2014 when he regularly did so as a member of the coaching staff of the division rival Diamondbacks. "Whenever I come to Dodger Stadium, I immediately look out to right field and the seat where I think the ball landed that I've named Seat 88," Gibson acknowledged in 2013. "It's a good affirmation for me in my life. I remember how hard it was and how lucky I was to have done it. . . . It's evidence that anyone who believes that they can't do it, can. I gave them a reason to believe that they could. Someway, somehow the ball went out of the ballpark and we won the World Series."[5]

In the mid-1990s, the Dodgers turned to Ramon Martinez as their staff ace. While he'd go on to enjoy a solid career, Martinez does regret that he never returned to the World Series. "It was something that I wish to [have been able to] participate [in] after that, [later in my career, to go to] the World Series," says Martinez. "That's the goal of every player: to play in the World Series. We made it to the playoffs a couple of times, but we couldn't get past the first round in either year."

When asked today about his most memorable Dodgers moments after 1988, he didn't hesitate. "The most emotional moment, I think, was when I pitched my no-hitter," says Martinez, who on July 14, 1995, allowed only one Marlins baserunner in his 7–0 gem.

I would say it was the most exciting because I remember it was like, each time you go out there, every inning—once you pass the fifth inning—you start to get that feeling of having butterflies. It's because you know you're pitching a no-hitter. I remember I was perfect going into the seventh inning [actually, the eighth]. I got [Tommy] Gregg—he was a left-handed hitter on the Marlins—on a 3-and-2 count, and I threw my inside fastball. The umpire almost called a strike, but it was kinda close. So, I walked him. But once I walked him, I kinda took the pressure off myself, and that was with two outs, and then I came back and struck out the next guy. That was the only guy who got on base. After that, I had everything in control.

Martinez also points to an 18-strikeout game from 1990, when he pitched a shutout against Tom Glavine and the Braves. The 18 strikeouts tied Sandy Koufax's single-game franchise record. "I didn't even know that [I'd] tied Sandy Koufax's record in strikeouts," Martinez recalls.

> I remember in that game I was just striking people out. LA fans don't get too excited; [as the game was going on] they didn't know [I was close to that record]. But I remember the first 15 guys, I struck out about 12. [Actually, 12 of the first 15 outs came via the strikeout, with one single coming in that stretch.]
>
> So, [in the later innings] the fans then started getting excited, because it was just swing-and-a-miss, swing-and-a-miss. I remember going into the ninth inning, I already had 18. In the ninth inning, I didn't strike out anybody! And then suddenly the fans were expecting it because the National League record was 19 and they wanted to see me break it. I gave it a try—but it was all right. That one was exciting too.

For Chris Gwynn, his most memorable post-1988 moment involving the Dodgers came, ironically, against them when he was with San Diego. "I was traded in 1991 to the Royals, where I played for two years," says Gwynn.

> Being in the other league, everybody wanted to know about the Dodgers. That's where I had come from. There's something about the Dodgers [that intrigues opposing players in both leagues]. A lot of people won't admit it until they actually play for the Dodgers. The Giants and Dodgers [are a huge rivalry]—that natural rivalry obviously comes from New York. There were some great games in the past, and [there] still are. Being on the Padres that one year I was there, I was lucky enough to play with my brother [Hall of Famer Tony Gwynn] for a year and actually get the [division]-winning base hit to beat the Dodgers. That was in '96.

That division winner—an 11th-inning pinch-hit double off Chan Ho Park in the season finale on September 29, 1996—proved to be the final regular-season hit of Gwynn's career.

Because of the wild card, though, Los Angeles advanced to the playoffs anyway. "It was very strange," says Gwynn.

> It was very weird. That year, the Braves were a real juggernaut. They were really good. They had great pitching. And quite honestly, nobody wanted to play them in any kind of series. The loser of our [season-ending] series had to play the Braves [right away in the Division Series]. For us, we had to sweep them to win the division. We wanted to win the division, and it really didn't matter to us who we played. We just wanted to win the division because we thought that was a more positive step. We knew that whoever lost was gonna play the Braves. So, you're gonna be facing Glavine, Maddux, and Smoltz. Good luck with that. I mean, that's the truth.

Gwynn's division-winning double completed a three-game sweep and clinched the 1996 NL West title for San Diego (91–71)—and the wild-card spot for the Dodgers (90–72), who blew a two-and-a-half-game lead with four to go by ending the year with four consecutive losses. While Gwynn's Padres avoided facing Atlanta in the first round of the playoffs, they still got swept 3–0 by the mediocre Cardinals (who'd won the NL Central by six games despite their 88–74 record). The Dodgers, meanwhile, were also broomed, dropping three straight to the 96-win Braves. They never returned to the postseason for the rest of the 20th century.

Tom Candiotti, a knuckleball pitcher with the Dodgers from 1992 to 1997, reflects on the 1996 collapse. "We had some pretty good teams after realignment in 1994, but we just couldn't get it done in the playoffs when we got there. The way it was stacking up that year, if we won our division, we wouldn't have to play the Braves [in the Division Series]. We much rather would've played the Cardinals, the NL Central champion." But the Dodgers, of course, had to face the Braves. "We went three-and-out and that was it. The Braves were really dominant through the mid-1990s. . . . [But] if we'd concentrated on winning that division, and got to play the Cardinals, then we probably would've had a better chance of advancing at least one round. It would've been nice to be able to win one series and then play the Braves in a more meaningful fashion."

Mike Scioscia, a two-time World Series champion as a player with the Dodgers, would go on to win another ring as the manager of the Angels in 2002. *Michael McCormick*

When you ask members of the 1988 Dodgers if we'd ever see another ball club quite like theirs, there are varying opinions. Mike Scioscia, who played on both the 1981 and 1988 championship teams, once opined that 1988 was more satisfying because that club didn't have the talent of the previous one. As Scioscia explained, the '81 team "had a much better ball club" while the '88 club had "much more of a team." It was "much more gratifying to win it when everyone [contributed]," he added.[6] Mickey Hatcher, meanwhile, doesn't think any other world champion in baseball can look back and say how special it was, the way it was special with the 1988 Dodgers. Some, such as Alejandro Peña (1991–1992, 1995) and Jay Howell (1993), were fortunate to play for close-knit Atlanta teams later in their careers.

Howell notes that, for him, the '93 Braves—despite losing to Philadelphia in six games in the NLCS—most closely resemble the '88 Dodgers in terms of chemistry. "The closest thing ever, for me, was getting to experience it with the Braves—when they'd turned it around in 1991— and I came over there in '93," explains Howell, who at age 37 notched a 2.31 ERA in 54 appearances for the 104-win Braves. "That atmosphere over there was the closest thing that I'd seen to that group that we had in LA. But there in LA, we took it all the way. With the Braves we came up a little short. But it was a pretty good crew from the standpoint of character. If I had to compare, in my career, guys with character, I could go with Glavine, Smoltz, Maddux, Fred McGriff, [Mark] Lemke, [Jeff] Blauser, right on down the line. Also Deion Sanders."

Howell also makes a unique comparison between Gibson and the Braves' Sanders, the multisport star outfielder who moonlighted as a defensive back in the NFL throughout his baseball career. "Interesting [is] the correlation between Deion and Gibson with the football background, the two of them," says Howell.

> Both of them worked as hard as anyone I ever saw. I was thinking that when I saw Deion with the Braves, I thought, "Well, he'll probably just kinda go through the motions." But not so. He worked harder than anybody on the team. I noticed it was the same way with Gibson. Same thing, those two.
>
> I played for 14 years, and from a character standpoint, the Dodgers and then that Braves team—those two teams—had that ingredient, the chemistry. I know that with all the metrics they use in baseball, the one that's most difficult to quantify, or to put a number on it, is chemistry. Do you have the right mixture of personalities and do you have the right manager to steer the ship? I don't know that there's any way that you can do that. As a GM, I think you do the best you can. I don't know [how he did it, but] Fred did a helluva job. He was the [*Sporting News* Executive of the Year] for a really good reason. Lasorda was able to make that group work, let that chemistry take care of itself. Tommy let the team kinda administer the style of play, the attitude, the team kind of

concept, the "I'll-pick-you-up" kind of deal. I saw it twice in my career. It's no wonder when I do watch the playoffs now. From the time that I left baseball, the most interesting thing to me as I look at the teams that end up being there, and invariably, what will be talked about is the character, the chemistry on the team; almost 99 percent of the time they'll talk about that. I find it interesting.

Under today's postseason format, the 1988 Dodgers would have had to play an extra round. Had the wild-card format existed then, would the Dodgers have been able to beat teams such as Pittsburgh or Cincinnati in a divisional series? Tim Leary believes so. "As far as our team matching up [against other teams had there been additional playoff rounds], pitching and defense, and timely hitting is the winning formula," says Leary. "With Orel being so dominant in October and the other nine pitchers all having sub-3.00 ERAs, I think we could've matched up with any World Series team just on pitching alone! And we won with Kirk Gibson only having one at-bat. But we had a scrappy team of veteran players who never flinched under pressure! That gave us an edge over the A's, who had young guys [Canseco and McGwire] batting numbers 3 and 4."

As far as Leary is concerned, whoever pitches better has a greater chance in the postseason in any year. "It's impossible to say who [would have won] this or that [had we played against a different team in a different year], but I know that if you don't give up many runs, you're always in the game," Leary adds, when asked specifically if the 1988 Dodgers could have beaten powerhouse teams like the '75 Reds or '98 Yankees. "So, I think we would've been a tough team to beat in any World Series."

Tracy Woodson believes a huge underdog like those 1988 Dodgers can win a World Series today—even though there are big-spending teams now like the 2017 Dodgers (under the ownership of Guggenheim Baseball Management, a group that includes former LA Lakers great Magic Johnson), Tigers, and Yankees with $200 million payrolls while small-market clubs such as Pittsburgh and Cincinnati are fielding teams with payrolls under $93 million. (The Dodgers were MLB's top spending team in 2017; their Opening Day payroll was the highest at $225.6 million. Detroit, at $199.8 million, and the Yankees, at $195.3 million, rounded out the top three.)

"I think at some point, you will," Woodson says of the possibility of another underdog winning a World Series.

The disparity and the money and the salaries for teams like the Yankees and Dodgers, with their $200 million payrolls [is huge]. But you've got some teams now [like Kansas City getting to the World Series in 2014 and 2015]. It's depth. I'm gonna say this about other sports. I talk basketball a lot. You'll never see an underdog in basketball win. [If a team's got] one superstar, they're not winning against three superstars on a team. In baseball, if you could pitch, and you get hot, you can win. College baseball is the same way; I can go in there with a shitty team, and if I pitch and play defense and score a couple of runs, I can win a tournament on a weekend. Baseball is a bit different now that they've added the play-in game and the extra round and all that. Back then, it was the one series—the National League Championship Series—and then you're in the World Series. So, it's a little bit different.

Woodson acknowledges it was easier for a team to win a World Series during his playing days; you just had to win your division and then go through two rounds. That was it. The key, of course, was to win your division.

We clinched a week ahead of time, and we were able to set things up, just like the other teams. But we just played good baseball during the playoffs, period. We didn't make many mistakes. Hershiser pitched [four] different times in the National League Championship Series. He came in relief a night after he pitched, and he got a save. That will not happen in today's game, period. We'd bunt. We'd hit-and-run a little bit. That doesn't happen in today's game either. Now, it's "Let's hit a two-run or three-run homer." So I think that's where everything changed as well.

Howell still does follow MLB today, and he does compare the '88 Dodgers with championship teams over the years since then. He brings up the 2016 Chicago Cubs as an example. "*That* was a team. The main thing there was [manager Joe] Maddon. Of course, they had the GM and they had a lot of guys that can play. They could flat-out play. But they seemed to have a team."

"Even [Jason] Heyward didn't have the kind of numbers he expects out of himself," Howell continues, referring to the Cubs right fielder who'd just signed an eight-year, $184-million contract in the off-season before batting .230 with a career-low seven homers in 2016. "He's the guy who calls the meeting," adds Howell, referring to the players-only meeting Heyward called during a 17-minute rain delay prior to the 10th inning of Game 7 of the World Series to inspire his teammates. "It was refreshing to watch. It reminded me the Cubs were destined. They had quality people. Most definitely the talent. But I think it's more than talent. It takes more than that."

For a team to succeed, it's not just luck but everything else needs to align properly—for example, getting clutch hits, getting good pitching, and cashing in opportunities. These are the ingredients of a championship ball club, as far as Howell is concerned.

> [But] the Cubs, for years, just didn't have it. And I'm not talking about luck. It's more than that. Gibson hitting that home run. Literally, what are the odds? Eckersley doesn't give up many home runs. The odds were incredibly low. You can't give it to luck. It wasn't luck. It was more than luck, for sure. I guess that's part of Gibson's legacy. But this is one of the best closers in the game. I have a lot of respect for the Eck. I mean, this guy did it all. He was the best. This was the best, and that home run, I think was the thing that was like, "It's our time. Somehow, we're gonna do it."

Over time, that home run seems to be what most people remember. Mel Antonen, for instance, confesses that he doesn't remember who else, other than Gibson, was on that team. "It's amazing how when you say the 1988 Dodgers, you think about Kirk Gibson. To me, that makes it historic. That makes it iconic. I don't even remember who was in the Dodgers' rotation that year, right off the top of my head," Antonen says now. When reminded that Hershiser was their ace, he backtracks a little before admitting that most people couldn't name another starter on that ball club. "Orel Hershiser led the team. Who else was there?" asks Antonen rhetorically. "Yeah, obviously everybody remembers Hershiser. But again, the 1988 Dodgers are always going to be defined by Kirk Gibson's home run, and the way they beat the Athletics in the World Series."

But will we see another championship team like these Dodgers? Antonen and Nightengale share their thoughts, and both just happen to name some of the same clubs that have shocked the baseball world over the years. "The 1987 Twins came out of *nowhere* and won the World Series [against the favored Cardinals]. The first two that come to mind are the 1987 Twins—nobody expected *that* to happen—and Cincinnati manhandling Oakland the way they did in 1990," Antonen recalls. "I've covered every World Series from 1980 on. I'd say the Twins in 1987 was a really big surprise. A lot of drama. The Twins in 1991, given that it was the Twins and the Braves, both last-place teams the previous year in 1990."

"We've certainly seen some upsets, for example, in 1990 when the Reds won it—that was a big stunner," says Nightengale. "The Braves and Twins in 1991—both had finished in last place the year before, so both were surprising. We've seen it, but not to that degree, though. [The Dodgers] were so beat up. Gibson had just that one at-bat in the entire [World Series]. That one still stands out as possibly the most unlikely World Series championship team."

Antonen, however, also goes through teams that won the World Series on one swing—in walk-off fashion in the seventh game. "To a certain extent, the Marlins' [championship] in 1997 was pretty dramatic, given how that ended. That was something," says Antonen, referring to Florida's 11th-inning victory over Cleveland. "And then, of course, it's pretty hard to argue with the 2001 Diamondbacks, the way they won that," Antonen continues, citing Luis Gonzalez's World Series–ending blooper over second base off Yankees stopper Mariano Rivera. "I think, though, from pure individual accomplishment, one swing of the bat changing the whole emotion of the series, I think 1997 with [Edgar Renteria] getting the winning hit [off Cleveland's Charles Nagy], and then Luis Gonzalez in 2001 with the Diamondbacks. . . . Those circumstances would probably come close to matching Gibson. But it's pretty hard to compare anything to what Gibson did."

And it's pretty hard to compare anything to what the Los Angeles Dodgers did during the course of the 1988 season, from the spring all the way to the last pitch of the World Series. From the bench players—the Stuntmen—wanting to win spring-training games once they got into the contests to their fiery leader demanding they show up every day to win every game; from a historic scoreless-innings streak by their ace to one of the most dramatic homers in World Series history by their injured leader; from the Stuntmen filling in when the regulars went down to those same players coming up huge in the World Series; from the way the team defeated the Mets to the way it somehow outplayed Oakland. There won't be another World Championship team quite like these 1988 Dodgers.

NOTES

Chapter One

1. Tim Kawakami, "Destiny's Team: 1988 Dodgers Revisited," *Los Angeles Times*, September 15, 1998.

2. Atomjackfuser, "Battle Lines: 1988 World Series Dodgers/Athletics," ESPN Classic video posted on YouTube, October 20, 2013, www.youtube.com/watch?v=r8PLkSYGrIQ.

3. Steve Delsohn, *True Blue: The Dramatic History of the Los Angeles Dodgers, Told by the Men Who Lived It* (New York: HarperCollins, 2001).

4. Interview with the author. Unless otherwise noted, all quoted material comes from phone, email, or in-person interviews conducted by the author.

5. Atomjackfuser, "Battle Lines."

6. Atomjackfuser, "Battle Lines."

7. Arash Markazi, "Gibson in '88: 'It's a Good Story,'" ESPN.com, October 17, 2013, http://www.espn.com/los-angeles/mlb/story/_/id/9821079/25th-anniversary-los-angeles-dodger-kirk-gibson-world-series-home-run.

Chapter Two

1. Sam McManis, "The World Series: Oakland Athletics vs. Los Angeles Dodgers; It's a Title Out of the Blue," *Los Angeles Times*, October 21, 1988.

2. McManis, "The World Series."

3. George Vecsey, "Sports of The Times; Going Straight," *New York Times*, October 16, 1988.

Chapter Three

1. Josh Suchon, *Miracle Men: Hershiser, Gibson, and the Improbable 1988 Dodgers* (Chicago: Triumph Books, 2013), 126.
2. Sam McManis, "Valenzuela Is Baffled by Worst Performance; Dodgers Survive, 6–4," *Los Angeles Times*, June 26, 1988.
3. Jean Marbella, "Superstitions Important to Many Players," *Baltimore Sun*, June 3, 1990.
4. Rob Rains and Keith Schildroth, *St. Louis Cardinals: Where Have You Gone? Vince Coleman, Ernie Broglio, John Tudor, and Other Cardinals Greats* (New York: Skyhorse Publishing, 2013), 80.
5. Sam McManis, "Dodgers Hand Sutton His Walking Papers and Call Up Martinez," *Los Angeles Times*, August 11, 1988.
6. McManis, "Dodgers Hand Sutton His Walking Papers."
7. Bill Plaschke, "Ex-Dodger Mike Marshall Tries to Repair His Reputation," *Los Angeles Times*, July 21, 2013.
8. Plaschke, "Ex-Dodger Mike Marshall Tries to Repair His Reputation."

Chapter Four

1. Bryan Curtis, "The Steroid Hunt," Grantland.com, January 8, 2014, grantland.com/features/mlb-hall-fame-voting-steroid-era/.
2. Ken Burns, "Baseball: The Tenth Inning," YouTube video, www.youtube.com/watch?v=JVTx5397Of4.
3. K. P. Wee, "'Jonesing' for Success." *Vancouver Canadians Professional Baseball Club*, 2016, http://www.milb.com/documents/6/6/2/184807662/2016CsProgram_9yc85oga.pdf.
4. Sam McManis, "After Dodgers Win, 8–5, Rose Predicts They'll Lose in End," *Los Angeles Times*, August 11, 1988.
5. Ross Newhan, "Danny Jackson Pitches Cincinnati Past Dodgers, 5–2," *Los Angeles Times*, September 10, 1988.
6. Mike Penner, "Dodgers Run Out the Reds: Gibson Starts Rally, Hamilton Finishes It, 5–3," *Los Angeles Times*, September 12, 1988.
7. Penner, "Dodgers Run Out the Reds."
8. Corey Stolzenbach, "Corey Stolzenbach Interviews John Tudor 3-4-2016," YouTube video, March 4, 2016, www.youtube.com/watch?v=T_zVeQtK6SM.

Chapter Five

1. Ross Newhan, "Hershiser Earns 20th Victory, Puts Dodgers 5 Up by Beating Reds," *Los Angeles Times*, September 11, 1988.

2. Tim Kawakami, "Destiny's Team: 1988 Dodgers Revisited," *Los Angeles Times*, September 15, 1998.

3. Joe Goddard, "Pain-Free Jackson Set for Opener," *Chicago Sun-Times*, April 8, 1991.

4. Atomjackfuser, "Battle Lines: 1988 World Series Dodgers/Athletics," ESPN Classic video posted on YouTube, October 20, 2013, www.youtube.com/watch?v=r8PLkSYGrIQ.

5. Sam McManis, "The World Series: Oakland Athletics vs. Los Angeles Dodgers; It's a Title Out of the Blue," *Los Angeles Times*, October 21, 1988.

6. Corey Stolzenbach, "Corey Stolzenbach Interviews John Tudor 3-4-2016," YouTube video, March 4, 2016, www.youtube.com/watch?v=T_zVeQtK6SM.

7. Josh Suchon, *Miracle Men: Hershiser, Gibson, and the Improbable 1988 Dodgers* (Chicago: Triumph Books, 2013), 76.

8. Suchon, *Miracle Men*, xi.

Chapter Six

1. Sam McManis, "Guerrero Gets Suspension of 4 Days, Fine," *Los Angeles Times*, May 25, 1988.

2. Joseph Durso, "Mets Play Catch-Up, Yanks Play June Classic, but Both Lose," *New York Times*, June 2, 1988.

3. Gibomber, "1988 NLCS game 1 New York Mets at Los Angeles Dodgers PART 2," YouTube video, https://www.youtube.com/watch?v=iMtV5hOS9O4.

4. David J. Halberstam, "Vin Scully on Life and Lessons from His Rookie Year with the 1950 Dodgers," *Sports Illustrated*, July 17, 2015.

5. Gordon Edes, "National League Championship Series: Dodgers 6, Mets 3," *Los Angeles Times*, October 6, 1988.

6. Josh Suchon, *Miracle Men: Hershiser, Gibson, and the Improbable 1988 Dodgers* (Chicago: Triumph Books, 2013), 196.

7. Steve Delsohn, *True Blue: The Dramatic History of the Los Angeles Dodgers, Told by the Men Who Lived It* (New York: HarperCollins, 2001).

8. Jim Hynes, *Miracle Moments in Montreal Canadiens History: The Turning Points, the Memorable Games, the Incredible Records* (New York: Sports Publishing, 2016), 139.

Chapter Seven

1. John Harper, "The Home Run That All but Ended an Era of Met Dominance," *New York Daily News*, October 5, 2013.

2. Joel Bierig, "Baylor's Gut Feeling of Howell," *Chicago Sun-Times*, October 15, 1988.

3. Arash Markazi, "Gibson in '88: 'It's a Good Story,'" ESPN.com, October 17, 2013, http://www.espn.com/los-angeles/mlb/story/_/id/9821079/25th-anniversary-los-angeles-dodger-kirk-gibson-world-series-home-run.

4. Markazi, "Gibson in '88."

5. Mel Antonen, "'That Was a Cool Feeling': An Oral History of Kirk Gibson's Iconic 1988 Home Run," *SI.com*, October 15, 2013.

Chapter Eight

1. Phil Elderkin, "Series Managers Have Impressive Credentials," *Christian Science Monitor*, October 17, 1988.

2. Atomjackfuser, "Battle Lines: 1988 World Series Dodgers/Athletics," ESPN Classic video posted on YouTube, October 20, 2013, www.youtube.com/watch?v=r8PLkSYGrIQ.

3. Jacob Unruh, "Collected Wisdom of Knuckleballer Charlie Hough," *News-OK.com/The Oklahoman*, August 5, 2017.

4. Elderkin, "Series Managers Have Impressive Credentials."

5. Atomjackfuser, "Battle Lines."

6. "Tony La Russa's Glory Days Recalled by Former A's Stars," *Alameda (CA) Times-Star*, July 27, 2014.

7. Michael Martinez, "The World Series: Evangelist vs. a Calm Analyst; La Russa's Method Is Scholarly," *New York Times*, October 16, 1988.

8. Kevin Neary and Leigh A. Tobin, *Closer: Major League Players Reveal the Inside Pitch on Saving the Game* (Philadelphia: Running Press, 2013), 98.

9. Joel Bierig, "L.A.'s Davis Creates Storm for Athletics," *Chicago Sun-Times*, October 23, 1988.

Chapter Nine

1. Bob Nightengale, "Gibson's Magical HR Resonates 25 Years Later," *USA Today*, October 15, 2013.

2. Atomjackfuser, "Battle Lines: 1988 World Series Dodgers/Athletics," ESPN Classic video posted on YouTube, October 20, 2013, www.youtube.com/watch?v=r8PLkSYGrIQ.

3. Mel Antonen, "'That Was a Cool Feeling': An Oral History of Kirk Gibson's Iconic 1988 Home Run," *SI.com*, October 15, 2013.

4. Antonen, "'That Was a Cool Feeling.'"

5. Dan Shaughnessy, "Term Covers All the Bases," *Boston Globe*, June 24, 2005.

6. Shaughnessy, "Term Covers All the Bases."

7. Antonen, "'That Was a Cool Feeling.'"

8. Nightengale, "Gibson's Magical HR Resonates 25 Years Later."

9. Antonen, "'That Was a Cool Feeling.'"

10. "1988 Dodgers: Where Are They Now?" *Los Angeles Times*, 2013.

11. Antonen, "'That Was a Cool Feeling.'"

12. Antonen, "'That Was a Cool Feeling.'"

13. Mike Lopresti, "Gibson's 1988 Homer Still a World Series Highlight," *USA Today*, October 7, 2008.

14. Peter Gammons, "A Case of Orel Surgery," *Sports Illustrated*, October 31, 1988.

Chapter Ten

1. Steve Wulf, "Destiny's Boys," *Sports Illustrated*, October 31, 1988.

Chapter Eleven

1. Other sources, however, indicate Marshall suffered from a headache that day—including Tommy Lasorda's biography and various newspaper accounts.

2. Tim Kawakami, "Destiny's Team: 1988 Dodgers Revisited," *Los Angeles Times*, September 15, 1998.

3. Jerome Holtzman, "Howell Puts A's on Ropes," *Chicago Tribune*, October 20, 1988.

4. Holtzman, "Howell Puts A's on Ropes."

5. Corey Stolzenbach, "Corey Stolzenbach Interviews John Tudor 3-4-2016," YouTube video, March 4, 2016, www.youtube.com/watch?v=T_zVeQtK6SM.

Chapter Twelve

1. Bill Plaschke and Tommy Lasorda, *I Live for This! Baseball's Last True Believer* (New York: Houghton Mifflin Harcourt, 2007), 161.

2. "Dodgers Honor Fred Claire," MLB.com, June 13, 2017, www.mlb.com/video/dodgers-honor-fred-claire/c-1493576383.

3. Bill Plaschke, "Almost Forgotten, Fred Claire Played a Crucial Role in the Dodgers' Last World Series," *Los Angeles Times*, April 8, 2017.

Chapter Thirteen

1. K. P. Wee, "'Jonesing' for Success," *Vancouver Canadians Professional Baseball Club*, 2016, http://www.milb.com/documents/6/6/2/184807662/2016CsProgram_9yc85oga.pdf.
2. ClassicPhillies TV, "August 1995—Dodgers vs. Phillies @mrodsports," PRISM broadcast from August 24, 1995, posted on YouTube, January 5, 2016, www.youtube.com/watch?v=L7s88XRCJGg&t=27s.
3. ClassicPhillies TV, "August 1995—Dodgers vs. Phillies."
4. Bill Plaschke, "His 1988 World Series 'Minute' Sustains Gilberto Reyes," *Los Angeles Times*, August 4, 2013.
5. "Sports People: Baseball—Reyes Suspended," *New York Times*, February 8, 1992.
6. Tim Korte, "N.M. Marijuana Case Sidetracks Former Major Leaguer," *Albuquerque (New Mexico) Journal/Associated Press*, April 8, 2009.
7. Bill Plaschke, "Brian Holton, the Forgotten Dodger of '88, Struggles to Live in the Present," *Los Angeles Times*, August 12, 2017.
8. Plaschke, "Brian Holton."
9. Plaschke, "Brian Holton."

Chapter Fourteen

1. "Former Athletics, White Sox Infielder and Outfielder Tony Phillips Dies," *Chicago Tribune/Associated Press*, February 19, 2016.

Chapter Fifteen

1. Jerry Reuss, *Bring in the Right-Hander! My Twenty-Two Years in the Major Leagues* (Lincoln: University of Nebraska Press, 2014), 224.

Chapter Sixteen

1. Rob Rains and Keith Schildroth, *St. Louis Cardinals: Where Have You Gone? Vince Coleman, Ernie Broglio, John Tudor, and Other Cardinals Greats* (New York: Skyhorse Publishing, 2013), 69.

2. Jerry Coleman, "Sports with Coleman: Former Oriole Mike Devereaux Talking Camden Yards Memories," CBS Baltimore, March 23, 2017, baltimore. cbslocal.com/2017/03/23/sports-with-coleman-former-oriole-mike-devereaux-talking-camden-yards-memories/.

Epilogue

1. Steve Springer, "Finley's Slam Is the Grand Finale as Dodgers Pull Off a Stunner, 7–3," *Los Angeles Times*, October 3, 2004.

2. Newton Minnow, "MLB Cut to the Chase: 1988, 1973, 1972, 1965, and 1975 Finishes," Classic Sports Network video posted on YouTube, July 31, 2016, www.youtube.com/watch?v=oKgE814FkdU&t=2312s.

3. Richard Justice, "Notebook—Henderson, McGriff, Puckett, Sierra: Who's AL's Most Valuable Player?" *Washington Post*, September 17, 1989.

4. Minnow, "MLB Cut to the Chase."

5. Arash Markazi, "Gibson in '88: 'It's a Good Story,'" ESPN.com, October 17. 2013, http://www.espn.com/los-angeles/mlb/story/_/id/9821079/25th-anniversary-los-angeles-dodger-kirk-gibson-world-series-home-run.

6. Sam McManis, "The World Series: Oakland Athletics vs. Los Angeles Dodgers; It's a Title Out of the Blue," *Los Angeles Times*, October 21, 1988.

BIBLIOGRAPHY

Books

Delsohn, Steve. *True Blue: The Dramatic History of the Los Angeles Dodgers, Told by the Men Who Lived It.* New York: HarperCollins, 2001.

Hynes, Jim. *Miracle Moments in Montreal Canadiens History: The Turning Points, the Memorable Games, the Incredible Records.* New York: Sports Publishing, 2016.

Neary, Kevin, and Leigh A. Tobin. *Closer: Major League Players Reveal the Inside Pitch on Saving the Game.* Philadelphia: Running Press, 2013.

Plaschke, Bill, and Tommy Lasorda. *I Live for This! Baseball's Last True Believer.* New York: Houghton Mifflin Harcourt, 2007.

Rains, Rob. *St. Louis Cardinals: Where Have You Gone? Vince Coleman, Ernie Broglio, John Tudor, and Other Cardinals Greats.* New York: Skyhorse Publishing, 2013.

Reuss, Jerry. *Bring in the Right-Hander! My Twenty-Two Years in the Major Leagues.* Lincoln: University of Nebraska Press, 2014.

Suchon, Josh. *Miracle Men: Hershiser, Gibson, and the Improbable 1988 Dodgers.* Chicago: Triumph Books, 2013.

Wee, K. P. *Tom Candiotti: A Life of Knuckleballs.* Jefferson, NC: McFarland, 2014.

Newspapers/Magazines/Websites

Alameda (California) Times-Star, July 27, 2014.
Albuquerque (New Mexico) Journal, April 8, 2009.

Antonen, Mel. "'That Was a Cool Feeling': An Oral History of Kirk Gibson's Iconic 1988 Home Run." *SI.com*, October 15, 2013.

Baltimore Sun, June 3, 1990.

Boston Globe, June 24, 2005.

Chicago Sun-Times, October 23, 1988; October 3–4, 1989; April 8, 1991.

Chicago Tribune, October 20, 1988; February 19, 2016.

Cincinnati Post, July 15, 1996.

Daily Herald (Arlington Heights, Illinois), January 11, 1989.

"Dodgers Push A's to Edge; Howell Provides Relief as LA Wins 4–3." *NewsOK.com/The Oklahoman*, October 20, 1988.

Elderkin, Phil. "Series Managers Have Impressive Credentials." *Christian Science Monitor*, October 17, 1988.

"First Fred Claire Celebrity Golf Classic Benefiting City of Hope at Oakmont Country Club, Aug. 14." State News Service, May 9, 2017.

Fullam, Peter. "1988 Dodgers World Series Pitcher Tim Leary Talks Baseball in Whittier." *Whittier (California) Daily News*, January 3, 2013.

Gammons, Peter. "A Case of Orel Surgery." *Sports Illustrated*, October 31, 1988.

Halberstam, David J. "Vin Scully on Life and Lessons from His Rookie Year with the 1950 Dodgers." *Sports Illustrated*, July 17, 2015.

Hancock, David. "Steroid-User Canseco Names Names." *60 Minutes*, February 10, 2005, www.cbsnews.com/news/steroid-user-canseco-names-names/.

Hoffarth, Tom. "Orel Hershiser Zeroed in on MLB Record 25 Years Ago." *Inland Valley Daily Bulletin (Ontario, Canada) News Wire*, September 28, 2013.

Los Angeles Daily News, September 16, 2001.

Los Angeles Times, May 25–October 21, 1988; October 2, 1989; September 15, 1998; October 3, 2004; July 21–August 4, 2013; April 8, 2017; August 12, 2017.

Lopresti, Mike. "Gibson's 1988 Homer Still a World Series Highlight." *USA Today*, October 7, 2008.

Lubbock (Texas) Avalanche-Journal, March 21, 1999.

Markazi, Arash. "Gibson in '88: 'It's a Good Story.'" ESPN.com, October 17, 2013. http://www.espn.com/los-angeles/mlb/story/_/id/9821079/25th-anniversary-los-angeles-dodger-kirk-gibson-world-series-home-run.

New York Times, June 2, 1988; October 16, 1988; February 8, 1992.

Nightengale, Bob. "Gibson's Magical HR Resonates 25 Years Later." *USA Today*, October 15, 2013.

Oklahoman (Oklahoma City), August 5, 2017.

Shattuck, Harry. "Game One Heats Up Fast: Baylor's Rap on Howell Stokes LA's Fire." *Houston Chronicle*, October 15, 1988.

Washington Post, September 17, 1989.

Wee, K. P. "'Jonesing' for Success." *Vancouver Canadians Professional Baseball Club*, 2016. http://www.milb.com/documents/6/6/2/184807662/2016CsPr ogram_9yc85oga.pdf.

Wulf, Steve. "Destiny's Boys." *Sports Illustrated*, October 31, 1988.

Video and Audio

Atomjackfuser. "Battle Lines: 1988 World Series, Dodgers/Athletics." YouTube video, October 20, 2013, www.youtube.com/watch?v=r8PLkSYGrIQ. Originally aired on ESPN Classic, 2003.

Burns, Ken. "Baseball: The Tenth Inning." YouTube video, July 14, 2017, www.youtube.com/watch?v=JVTx5397Of4. Originally aired on PBS, September 28, 2010.

CBS Baltimore/baltimore.cbslocal.com, March 23, 2017.

ClassicPhilliesTV. "August 1995—Dodgers vs Phillies." YouTube video, January 5, 2016, www.youtube.com/watch?v=L7s88XRCJGg&t=27s. Originally aired on PRISM, August 24, 1995.

Dodgers.com/MLB.com, June 13, 2017.

Minnow, Newton. "MLB Cut to the Chase: 1988, 1973, 1972, 1965, and 1975 Finishes." YouTube video, July 31, 2016, www.youtube.com/watch?v=oKgE814FkdU&t=2312s.

Stolzenbach, Corey. "Corey Stolzenbach Interviews John Tudor 3-4-2016." YouTube video, March 4, 2016, www.youtube.com/watch?v=T_zVeQtK6SM.

Interviews Conducted by Author (in Chronological Order)

Fred Claire. Email and telephone interviews, April–August 2017.

Tim Leary. Email interviews, April–August 2017.

Joey Amalfitano. Telephone interview, April 28, 2017.

Mel Didier. Telephone interview, April 29, 2017.

Jay Howell. Telephone interviews, April 30, 2017; May 7, 2017; May 11, 2017; June 15, 2017; August 19, 2017.

Charlie Blaney. Telephone interview, May 4, 2017.

Phil Regan. Telephone interview, May 4, 2017.

Ben Hines. Telephone interview, May 4, 2017.

Gilberto Reyes. Telephone interviews, May 5, 2017; May 9, 2017.

Ramon Martinez. Telephone interview, May 8, 2017.

Mickey Hatcher. Telephone interview, May 9, 2017.

BIBLIOGRAPHY

Tracy Woodson. Telephone interviews, May 9, 2017; June 5, 2017.
Chris Gwynn. Telephone interview, May 10, 2017.
Jerry Reuss. Email interview, May 21, 2017. Telephone interview, June 20, 2017.
Danny Heep. Telephone interview, May 22, 2017.
Herm Winningham. Telephone interview, May 23, 2017.
Mariano Duncan. Telephone interview, May 28, 2017.
Ross Porter. Email interview, May 28, 2017.
Rick Dempsey. Telephone interview, June 5, 2017.
Steve Sax. Telephone interview, June 14, 2017.
Bob Ryan. Telephone interview, June 18, 2017.
John Shelby. Email interview, June 24, 2017.
Mel Antonen. Telephone interview, June 26, 2017.
Bob Nightengale. Telephone interview, June 27, 2017.
Franklin Stubbs. Personal interview at Nat Bailey Stadium, Vancouver, Canada, July 17, 2017.

INDEX

Note: Page references for figures are italicized.

ABOUT THE AUTHOR

K. P. Wee, author of *Tom Candiotti: A Life of Knuckleballs* (2014), the biography of the former Major League Baseball knuckleball pitcher, resides in Vancouver, Canada, and has worked in minor league baseball as the statistician of the Vancouver Canadians. He has also filled in as an official scorer and play-by-play broadcaster with the Canadians organization. A sports fanatic, Wee moonlighted as a reporter for amateur hockey, covering major midget hockey in the province of British Columbia for five years during the 2010s.

In addition to *Tom Candiotti*, Wee has also penned other sports-related books, including *The End of the Montreal Jinx: Boston's Short-Lived Glory in the Historic Bruins–Canadiens Rivalry, 1988–1994* and *Don't Blame the Knuckleballer! Baseball Legends, Myths, and Stories.*

Sports isn't the only thing that Wee is fascinated with; he also has a strong passion for teaching. Educated at the University of British Columbia in Vancouver, he has worked as an English instructor and tutor to college-level students for more than 10 years. He began teaching in 2002 and taught for nearly a decade before leaving the industry to pursue further education. He returned to teaching in 2014—authoring two English grammar-related books in the process—and continues to mentor students today.